The Twelfth Man

Keith McKibbin

THE TWELFTH MAN

THE TWELFTH MAN

ACKNOWLEDGMENTS

I would like to extend a sincere thank you to all my family, extended family and friends who have supported me in this venture.

A special thank you to my amazing wife who has inspired me and made me the man I am today. To my daughter Savannah Rain, a million hugs and kisses for all your time spent formatting the book and for tolerating my obsessive editing. To Olivia Mariella and Amelia Dorothy for entertaining themselves while I was supposed to be looking after them and to Zoe Jane for all your words of encouragement and for giving me a well needed boost.

To my wonderful parents and siblings for always believing in me. To my dad, the Maths teacher who endured endless nights with me, his mathematically challenged son, studying for the Eleven Plus and who continues to challenge my general knowledge when he comes to visit. To the awesome Dorothy McKibbin, my rock who held my hand and has yet to let it go. I am so grateful to have had such fantastic role models growing up.

To my friends who have travelled this journey with me, I look forward to our next chapter.

To my Dad

CHAPTER ONE

On my first day of primary school a neighbour had his legs blown off in a booby trap car explosion. Just above the knees. Like Long John Silver, except the both of them. His name was Archie Daly and he lived over the back hedge and around the corner, three houses up on the left. He kept budgies and little yellow finches in his back quad. We used to look in at them through the fence, our faces pressed between the slats. Quite often it had been drizzling and the smell of damp wood and sawdust was delicious. I liked the way they chirped.

"Can budgies talk like parrots?"

"Don't be stupid!"

"Mummy says they can."

"So why are you asking me?"

"Just they don't know so many words."

"Bet they know more than you."

"No they don't."

It was in all the papers and on the News at Six. There was a big overhead shot of the rooftops and I almost jumped off the couch when I spotted our television aerial. It was hard to miss. Higher up on the chimney and jutting out at a funny angle. Mum had been at Dad for weeks to improve the picture.

"Snow in Coronation Street in August?"

"You're very funny, Del. Are you going to sort it or do I have to get the man?"

So up he went, all elbows and ankles, a big block of concrete at the bottom because he didn't trust anyone to hold it steady. He told Pete to go inside but he didn't seem to mind me squinting up at him. I remember giggling when - even though he was clearly miles out of his comfort zone - he pretended to take a pee with a look of sheer contentment on his face and accompanying *ooohs* and *aaahs*. But he couldn't sort it. He had almost fallen on the third attempt to fix it to the chimney and he said there wasn't going to be a fourth.

"If the Eskimos can live in it then so can Hilda fucking Ogden!"

I didn't know what he meant but it was fun to watch her growling at him.

The neighbour they interviewed seemed rather pleased to be on the telly. I imagined him taking the evening off work to make sure he didn't miss himself. In 1974, only the very rich had video recorders and the rest of us were at the mercy of the television gods. Sometimes you had to wait a whole year to shiver at the child catcher in *Chitty Chitty Bang Bang* or watch Goldfinger get sucked out of the aeroplane window. Shaken, not stirred. The man they spoke to had a really prominent Adam's apple, like he had swallowed a snooker ball. He said it sounded like a garage door coming down off its hinges and you could see, by the twitch of a smile, that he was pleased with what he had said before he remembered where he was and looked grim again.

I was sure I had heard a noise like that when I was spooning in my Rice Krispies. Fancy. Somewhere in between the snap, crackle and pop, a man was losing his legs. Then again, it might just have been a garage door. I hadn't been paying that much attention to my surroundings; I had worries of my own. The detail that appealed to me, which didn't emerge until later, was that he had neglected to check under the car for the first time ever because the ground was wet and he hadn't wanted to get his new trousers muddy.

"Don't think I've ever spoken to him but I know him to see," Dad said, over his sausage and chips. "Big chap – Ford Granada. It's a wonder nobody saw anything."

"Mrs Templeton thinks it was a courting couple."

"Eh?"

"You know - pretending."

Dad gave a little nod. "Aye, right enough, I bet that's how they did it: the darkness of the evening, cuddling up together, and then planting it real fast. It doesn't take long to attach it if you know what you're doing and clearly they did," his knife hovered over his plate, "pay-out will be huge."

"Jesus, Del, it wouldn't pay you – it's the man's legs!"

"Alright, I'm only saying. Christ, you'd think I'd done it." He glowered at her and stabbed his sausage with such ferocity you could clearly hear the scrape of steel on enamel. "At least he'll not have to worry about money."

"Dear God."

He ignored her and turned his attention to me. "How did it go today, son?"

My look of misery was all the answer he needed and with a snort he returned to his meal. Okay, was what he was looking for or something similar. Something that would reassure him and not require any further effort on his part. Unkind. The poor man had to drive into Belfast each day, work his shift at the Corporation Street D.H.S.S, then fight the traffic home. He wanted peace and the paper. Anything else was my mother's domain.

"Kevin, found it quite a long day," Mum offered. "He'll be fine tomorrow – the first day is always the worst."

"You would think that wouldn't you?" this from Pete, my brother. He was four years older than me, had already experienced everything that awaited me and only lived to enlighten. "Actually, the second and third days are worse. You come home from day one in a bit of a daze and after a while you tell yourself that it's all been a bad dream – the screaming kids, the horrible teachers –but then the next day you realise that it was all real and you have it all to do again. The worst thing is-"

"Pete?"

"Yes, Dad?"

"Shut your hole."

"Yes, Dad."

Of course, he was incapable of shutting it for very long. He caught up with me later, just as Tom Baker was offering a jelly baby to a green blubbery thing who clearly had designs on the Tardis. Dad had secured the toilet and Mum was up to her elbows in soapy dishes.

"Did you see Mr Palmer?"

"No."

"Don't ignore me, Rubber."

"Don't call me that. I didn't see him. He's upstairs and I'm downstairs."

On screen, Tom Baker had managed to trip the blubbery thing up with his scarf and was making a dash for the door. He flashed his perfect teeth and said something smart and funny but I didn't catch it because Pete was right in my ear.

"I know he's upstairs, you dozy little turd; he's also the deputy head in charge of the school – he can go wherever he likes, top or bottom. Watch out for him, that's all I'm telling you."

"Be quiet, you're spoiling this! I never spoil your shows."

"It's not even on now – it's just a daft clip."

He stood in front of the telly, hands on hips, obscuring the screen with his little fat belly. "I'm only looking out for you, Kevin. Mind you, he's not the worst. Mr Flynn's the one to watch out for."

Mr Flynn was the headmaster.

"You've told me already." I gestured wildly for him to get out of the way. "Why can't you just leave me be?"

He stepped aside but kept talking. He was having too much fun now. "Aye, old Flynn will soon sort you out. The slipper. Friend of mine got six of the best for not doing his maths homework (he knew maths was my Achilles heel) just about sliced the bum off him. Cross ma heart. Blisters the size of pancakes. On his bare bum."

"What are you talking about, Pete?" Dad was standing in the doorway. He hadn't gone to the toilet after all. He was just letting it bake. He did that sometimes, so he could enjoy it more. "This friend of yours showed you his bare bum? Really? I'm starting to worry about you."

Pete knew he was up against it now.

"Dad, I was only trying to tell him about Mr Palmer and the way he pulls ears."

"What?" he grimaced and froze the expression on his face to make me laugh.

"He does it all the time, Dad. One of my friend's brother's

5

gave him cheek and he twisted his ear out of his socket."

"What a load of crap."

"Del, watch your language!" Mum from the kitchen. She had missed Pete's turd but caught Dad's crap.

"Honest, Dad, it's true-"

Dad silenced him with a raised hand. "Kev, don't listen to him. If Palmer so much as whispers in your ear I'll charge up there and – remember what Foreman did to Frazier?" he pantomimed a slow motion uppercut underneath his chin and staggered onto the sofa. It was his way of apologising for the grunt at dinner. That was probably why he'd postponed the toilet. To make amends. He was great, my dad.

"Well, what about me?" Pete was seething.

"What about you?"

"Mr Palmer twisted my ears last year and you did nothing!"

He acted surprised. "Is that what happened to your lugs? I thought you were pretending to be Big Ears from the Noddy stories."

Pete flew off the couch and ran to the kitchen to find Mum but I knew her well enough to know that she would never challenge Dad over something like this. I watched him out of the corner of my eye as he carefully filled in his "Spot the ball" coupon. He was something of a local celebrity. The Quiz King, the papers called him. He had won dozens of pub quizzes, in a team or by himself, and knew just about all there was to know about boxing, horse racing, athletics and general knowledge. He'd brought home hampers, vouchers, vintage champagne, whisky – and a romantic weekend in Glasgow for him and Mum. He'd been on the radio too, many times; but his greatest moment was when he made it into the final stages of a huge international quiz competition in Belfast. Hundreds of contestants from all over the United Kingdom and there was Derek McBride flying the Ulster flag! It was on the telly and everything. On the night it was aired, people from all over the province phoned up the house to congratulate him. Mum had bought a notebook for the side of the phone to take down their names. No one asked her to do it, she just knew. Before, when someone phoned, you just had to remember the message or tell them to phone back. Seventeen people called that night – nine of them complete strangers. Mum answered the phone each time but then insisted that he speak to them all. The best one was a wee old woman from Londonderry who'd looked up his name in the phone book and told her he'd done the country proud. We could hear him on the phone thanking her and doing his little embarrassed cough. When he came back into the room his face looked serious and you could see the muscles on each side of his jaw working. No one was sure what to say; but then he nodded sternly at each of us and we knew never to mention it again.

He had finished his guess work now and was filling in his name and address. Long elegant fingers, a sprout of fine black hairs underneath each knuckle. Neat, clipped fingernails. Never greasy, he was lost under the bonnet, but occasionally ink stained. You could tell a lot about people by studying their hands. My grandmother's gnarled, arthritic hands were difficult to ignore – especially when she constantly drew attention to them.

"Kevin, could you do a little job for your old granny?"

Here it came.

"What is it, Granny?"

"Just a few wee needles and threads. I'd do it myself but ..." and she'd hold up her banana hands, just in case you thought she was being lazy. "I've laid them out on the sideboard – you're such a good boy."

And by Christ, there they were. Sometimes as many as a dozen. Teensy little needles with holes in the top no bigger than full stops. You had to lick the thread, double it up, and then – Aww, missed the bastard again! Eyes all squinty, tongue hanging out the corner, little fat sausage fingers. And all the while she would be at my shoulder, coaxing and encouraging. "Oh, I'm such a nuisance; it's just as well you've got such nimble fingers, Kevin. Would you like – oh, you nearly had it that time, would you like a nice cup of tea and a choccy bick?"

But it was my mum's hands I remember most. The hands that did the housework, pulled a hundred pints on Friday and Saturday night at the *Angler's Prize* pub. Soft white hands that could solve any problem and conquer the world. That morning, as we walked up the steep hill towards the school, I had clung to hers like a man off the Titanic.

From a very early age we were all taught about the Titanic. The greatest ship that ever was. Built in Belfast by a proud Protestant workforce. Not so much as a scratch on her when she left Harland and Wolff for Southampton. Sank by an Englishman who didn't notice an enormous iceberg right in front of him.

"Kevin, you're going to stop my circulation."

"What?"

"You're squeezing so hard my fingers are turning black."

"Sorry."

But I didn't let go. In fact, I gripped tighter and gave a little yelp as I saw the gigantic pre-war building leering down at me. Oh, God. I'd been here before, of course, half frozen and bored stupid, at Pete the sneak's parent's nights and a couple of jumble sales but I hadn't registered much. All I could remember was charging down the polished corridors pretending to be Evel Kinevel. I was just starting to hero worship him and had recently seen the famous footage of his Caesar's Palace jump – that incredible rag doll tumble that seemed to go on forever. He broke almost every bone in his body. It was just the coolest thing ever. For a while I tried to incorporate his tumble into the way I ran, but it was hard to do – more of a stumble than a tumble - and looked a bit foolish without a motorbike and helmet.

But the memory felt strange and detached now. There would be no running down the corridors today; no one would think it was clever or cool, they would just see a daft little kid with a funny lip.

I didn't want to go. I began to drag my heels and Mum pulled me the way you would pull a dog that paused too long at an interesting smell. The famous bottom lip was starting to quiver and I chewed down on it, hyper aware of my under bite. I imagined it growing bigger in line with my increasing anxiety. It felt like a fat slug glued onto my mouth.

"Mummy ...do I really have to go?"

I looked imploringly up at her. She seemed to be getting taller even as I was shrinking.

"Mummy..."

"Please don't, Kevin. We've been over this. You have to go – but you are going to absolutely love it. You are going to *adore* it!"

There was no way back then. It was forward and up. No reverse, and that terrified the life out of me. I wanted the hill to never end. And if that wasn't possible, I wanted God to press rewind when we got to the top, start at the bottom again and just keeping walking up, up, up in an endless loop.

As we approached the doors I could feel my heart jack hammering in my chest. Other parents were there with their sons or daughters and the thing that struck me was just how jolly and unconcerned they all seemed. Smiles and giggles; waves and annoying little dances. In desperation I looked around for a kindred spirit - some other glum little loner – but there was no one. Was I the only miserable five year old in the whole of Ulster?

"Try not to be nervous, Kevin; once you settle in you'll love it."

As she said it I could feel her try to withdraw her hand but I was wise to it and clamped on like the cockles we tried to scrape off the rocks at Millisle caravan site.

"At least let me wipe your hand. You're sweating. Imagine that? A wee boy sweating on a cold September morning. If you don't let me wipe your hands you won't be able to draw me a nice picture when you get to class." She managed to pull her hand free and produced a half packet of tissues from her pocket. Then, something she never did, she thrust both of her hands deep into her coat pockets.

There was only one thing for it. I wrapped my arms around her left leg and hung there like a Koala bear.

"Oh, for God's sake, Kevin!" She pulled me off with some

difficulty whilst managing a strained *what are they like* smile at one of the other mothers, then she thrust out her hand and gave me a look I had never seen before. There was mule tired weariness in it but also a resentment that shocked me.

The class was bulging. All the five year olds in the world were here and they'd brought a parent with them. Some had brought two. It was an assault on the senses. First the noise, dear God, the noise. Everyone jabbering away, handshakes and phony little introductions as if the kids were adults in miniature. Snatches of nervous dialogue: "This brings me back, so it does…" "Do you remember these wee tables, how big they looked?" "Is that your wee one? God's sake, it's only yesterday I seen you wheeling her down the town. Sure, it's powerful, isn't it?" Mostly mums but a few awkward looking dads as well – desperate to offload and away, back to the safety of dad related stuff. The smell of plasticine, cloying perfumes and the wax on the floor. And body smells as well. Farts and armpits. When you're at child level you get to smell everything. Mum was making conversation with some man so that she didn't have to talk to me. I think she knew him from the pub but I wasn't listening and I didn't care.

"Pete, his big brother, is in Primary four so he'll be able to look after him – you know, show him the ropes and what have you."

Yeah, like that was going to happen.

"Stephanie has been looking forward all summer," the man said, gesturing a shy, pigtailed creature at his side. "Look at the drawings on the wall! Aren't they good?"

Admittedly, they weren't bad. Goldilocks and her three chums featured prominently. You could tell who it was because of the blonde shock of hair and the three chairs – although the grizzlies were mostly represented by brown splodges. On the far wall was the unmistakeable work of an adult: vine leaves that spread up onto the very ceiling. And on the ceiling, there was Jack - dangling from the light, just out of reach of the giant's huge disembodied hand.

"Who drew Jack, Mummy?"

"He's brilliant, isn't he? The children would have helped Mrs Jenkins to paint him."

And so to Mrs Jenkins.

I had been aware of her throughout, weaving her way across the room, shaking hands and raising her eyebrows in recognition of parents – some of whom she had evidently taught. Eventually, it was our turn.

"Of course, Peter McBride's brother. Do you like maths as well?"

"Kevin's more into drawing and reading," Mum said. She seemed suddenly to be just as nervous as I was and I wondered, for a moment forgetting my own woes, if she had hated her school as much as I was going to hate mine.

"I look forward to seeing some of your pictures," Mrs Jenkins smiled down on me. She had thin lips and a large hooked nose. She looked like a little bird of prey and I had her sussed out in that instant. This was all for the sake of the parents. When they left her smile would leave with them. Then she would swoop down for a feed.

"Mummy, please can I go home with you? I won't be a bother. You can teach me numbers and letters at home..."

"Oh, look at the sandpit, Kev!"

There was by now a slight tone of desperation but I had to admit, as she all but dragged me over to the sandpit, that it was pretty impressive. It was occupied by a small boy who was defiantly holding his crotch lest he should succumb to his desperate need for the toilet and have to sacrifice his spot. My eyes shone. The sandpit was full of TONKA toys. I dropped to my knees and reached eagerly for the nearest JCB. TONKA toys claimed to be indestructible. Pete and myself, in one of our rare brotherly moments, had acquired one from a local jumble sale and spent a fantastic day dropping it from the upstairs, hurling it at the outside wall, bashing it as hard as we could with Dad's old hockey stick. Barely a dent.

"Mummy, if I'm good will you buy me a Tonka?"

She didn't answer.

Something was wrong here. I squeezed her hand. She was positioned behind me in such a way that it was impossible to view the sandpit and her at the same time. The ring on her hand felt oddly bigger and her knuckles didn't feel right. I twirled around to face her ... and was met with the buck toothed smile of, I later discovered, the sixty-two year old dinner lady, Mrs Galloway.

The bitch had switched hands!

I was flabbergasted. Too stunned even to cry – at least not quite yet. How could any mother stoop to such depths? I looked to the door then through the grimy windows into the distance. The streets were virtually deserted. Red, white and blue, left over from the marching season, fluttered half-heartedly from the lampposts, but no sign of Doreen McBride.

"She was really fast," a tiny voice from the sandpit. "I seen her grab that woman - then she flewed out the door."

I nodded. I was dimly aware that the rest of the parents, triggered by an unspoken signal, were now leaving and my anxieties were closing in on me. It was all Pete's fault. Him and his stupid stories. Well, maybe not quite all his fault. I'd always been a nervous, twittery little boy; Granny had been the first to comment on it.

"Little boy full of woe. Jesus, Doreen, you should've put anti- depressants in his formula. He looks like he's got half the world on his shoulders. Come over here, Kevin, come over and listen to your old granny. We'll all be the same in a hundred years – remember that son."

I was only three. I asked Dad what she meant.

"Means we'll all be dead, rotting in the ground." Dad wasn't very religious and he didn't much care for my grandmother; she was always catching him off-guard and asking him to do little odd jobs around the house even though she knew he was handless.

"Derek (she always called him Derek) could you hang that picture for me?"

"Yes, Lizzie."

"I'd do it myself only my arthritis."

"No problem. Do you have a nail?"

"No."

"A screw?"

"Yes!"

"Something to hammer the screw in?"

"No."

The boy in the sandpit took a deep breath. "My name's Jimmy Hood. I'm four and three quarters. My birthday is on October fifteenth. I live at number 2, Christine Lane with my mum and dad. I had a dog called Shona. She had seven pups two summers ago. I wanted to keep just one but my dad said no. He gave them all away. Then Shona was killed on the road. A lorry ran over her – or maybe a tractor. They squashed her. "

"I live down Christine Lane," I said amazed. "Number 16."

"I've never seen you." Clumsily, perhaps aping a gesture of his father's, he thrust out his hand – the same hand that had been clamped to his groin all the while. Mistake. The sudden, blessed relief proved to be too much for his bladder and the floodgates opened.

What a glorious sight!

First the huge dark blot in his denim shorts, then the warm gush of it as it cascaded down his leg, soaking his socks and sandals, before puddling in the sand.

Mrs Jenkins smiled grimly, hands perched on bony hips. I later found out that this was her thirty-sixth year of teaching and her thirty-third in this very room. She spoke to no one in particular. "Could somebody fetch the trousers please? And so it begins...again."

CHAPTER TWO

Jimmy's embarrassment raised barely an eyebrow from the beleaguered adults as they mopped him up and provided him with the trousers of shame – an ancient elasticated monstrosity that had stood guard over the urine battlefront since before we both were born. Sand was the perfect sponge. If it could withstand bullets it could handle a little pee. A quick bit of raking and it was as good as new.

I had found my first proper friend. Mrs Jenkins sat us together and handed out some paper and paints, then we set about drawing our fantasies.

"What are you painting?"

"Guess."

Oh God. I concentrated and tried to decipher the purple and grey enigma that Jimmy had painstakingly painted. It looked like a man who had fallen off a tall building and was desperately trying to fly.

Superman?

No, that wasn't it. He was being pursued by a gigantic grey oblong with what looked like wings – that was it, wings.

"You're jumping out of a plane. I'm right, am't a? You're about to pull your parachute – wow, that's brilliant!"

Jimmy frowned pityingly at me. "I am swimming under water ...about to find a pirate ship wreck."

"Is that not your parachute?"

"My oxygen tanks."

"Is that not your aeroplane?"

"That's a whale chasing me."

"Oh."

Yet he seemed pleased at being able to explain his masterpiece. "Yours easy. It's a house."

I nodded. "But what kind of house?"

"A big purple one."

"It's not meant to be purple. It's meant to be black but she didn't have black. Purple was the closest."

"A black house? I dunno. A house that's been burnt in a fire. A house that's been bombed."

"No. Try again."

"I can't think." He was getting irritated now, desperate to get back to his own work.

"A haunted house."

"Oh?"

It was enough to hold him for just a moment longer.

"It is *The House on Haunted Hill* starring Vincent Price. Have you seen it?"

"No."

"Oh," this was a disappointing development. "You don't like horror movies?

"My dad doesn't let me watch them."

"But you would watch them if you could?"

"Maybe. Yes. I suppose."

And that was enough to satisfy me. In fact, at that moment, I don't think I had ever been happier in my life. Elbow to elbow with this new little boy, painting our crap fridge pictures. Utterly miserable half an hour ago and now so elated that I could feel the hairs on the back of my neck prickle to attention. I sneaked a glance at Mrs Jenkins at the front of the class. She was carefully writing in a big book. What were the chances of her just letting us paint and chat for the rest of the day? We could let this one dry and then begin another one.

She did not, of course, and by the end of the morning I had forgotten the magic and the promise of painting with Jimmy and was remembering only the misery of Mum's departure and the certain grief and horror of tomorrow. That was the way it always seemed to be for me. A glint of glorious sunshine and then the clouds descended again. And the clouds were always what I remembered at night. Never the sunshine.

"But what about, Jimmy Hood, Kevin? He's a lovely wee friend. You've told me how much you like him."

I would be in bed, unable to sleep. Shell shocked at the

thought of school the next day. The pillow wet with tears and
Pete gloating in the next room.

"We can have Jimmy round at the weekend. Wouldn't that
be nice? Something to look forward to?"

I would nod, bite my lip in the dark and anticipate every
miserable and frightening possibility that would befall me the
following day. This time it would be me wetting myself, or my
trousers and pants would fall down in the corridor and everyone
would see my thing.

And Pete was always keen to be helpful.

"Don't worry, Kev, Mr Palmer only pulled that one boy's
ear off and they were able to reattach it at the hospital. It looks a
bit wonky right enough but I think he can still hear with it. You've
nothing to worry about as long as you can remember your times
tables."

"Times tables?" I would always buy into it; I couldn't help
it, I was only five. "What are times tables?"

"You don't know? ... Mrs Jenkins hasn't taught you your
times tables? Is it possible she told the class when you were at the
toilet or that day you were off with ear ache?"

Heart pumping. Bowels freezing. The world about to end.

"Don't panic. I can help you. It's actually really simple.
Unless you are thick and you definitely are not thick. I'll start with
the easy ones. Just listen and you'll soon catch on:

"Nine ones are nine

Nine twos are eighteen

Nine threes are twenty-one."

His words were a blur.

"Nine fours are thirty-six

Nine fives are forty-five

Nine sixes are fifty-four."

A little spit flew.

"Nine sevens are sixty-three

Nine eights are seventy-two

Nine nines are eighty-one."

He was getting redder.

But he was happy.
"Nine tens are ninety
Nine elevens are ninety-nine
Nine twelves are one hundred and eight!
Easy, yes?
Now you try!"
And so on.

Mum and Dad really approved of Jimmy Hood. His mother was a teaching assistant at the local nursery school and his dad was some sort of accountant. Dad knew him from the Lion's Club and I overheard him talking about him.

"Never cracks a smile, Dor. Miserable. Couple of times, because of the boys, I've tried to engage him, but nothing. Mind you, it must be miserable counting other people's money all day long."

Jimmy was the prize. We had him over for his tea and he tried out his jokes on them both. He loved jokes.

"What's a ghost's favourite food, Mr McBride?"

"Go on."

"Ice cream. You get it? I scream!"

"Good yin, Jimmy."

"Did you hear about the man who bought a paper shop, Mrs McBride?"

"Go on."

"It blew away. Do you get it? Paper shop? - blew away?"

Pete would try to catch their eyes so they could see him shake his head and snort derisively but they weren't up for it. My parents had a touch of class about them sometimes. And Pete never had any of his friends over.

My first attempt at a friendship hadn't worked out so well. It was in a ball pool the year before and I had accidentally knocked over a little boy at the bottom of the slide. To be fair to him, he wasn't one of those hateful little brats that ran up the wrong way, merely he had happened to be walking by as I flew down.

He went flying head first into the balls.

"Sorry, Sorry, Sorry."

I could feel my own tears prickling as I searched the room desperately for Mum. This was a dangerous situation. Mothers were very protective of their young and the trick was to punish the perpetrator stealthily without causing a major scene. And so, in the rough and tumble of toddlerhood, it wasn't uncommon to have a strange woman – her back turned away from other adults but facing you – to glare ferociously and unblinkingly whilst saying in the sweetest possible tone: "Jordan, don't cry, this nice wee boy didn't mean it; it was an accident. Don't be silly, Jordan, there's a good boy." And you could read her mind too, that was the thing. She glared so hard that her thoughts came out and entered your head. *You ever so much as look at my little boy again and I will kill you! Do you understand, Rubber Lip? Nod if you do!* "Ach, Jordan, the wee boy's all upset! It was a wee accident. These things happen."

And so, not able to see Mum, I braced myself as the boy's mother descended, swooping him up in her arms. "John, John, settle yourself – it was a wee accident." She kissed him, soothed him, and then turned to me. "Don't worry, wee man, he's not hurt just a bit startled. What's your name?"

"Kevin."

"That's a nice name. This is John and I'm Mrs Watkins." Unbelievably, she offered her hand. It was the first time that an adult had ever shaken my hand. Instinctively, I knew she wasn't going to cause me hurt and I shook it dazedly, still befuddled at the complete lack of bitterness.

"Hello, hello, what's happening?"

Mum on the scene. Toilet probably. I watched her drink in the situation. A little boy being soothed, a strange woman shaking her son's hand.

"Kevin, be careful! There are other people here as well you know."

John's mother stood and offered her hand to Mum. I clocked a big ring and those lovely painted nails. "It was a complete accident. It'll teach John not to walk in front of the slide."

I watched Mum's shoulders relax, her face soften. Before I knew it they had retreated to the table and were ordering tea and a Kit Kat. I looked at John and John looked at me. I wasn't that interested in him, to be honest. I knew his type. He was one of those kids who always had snot either running or about to run over his top lip and into his mouth. There was nothing subtle about him. Everything would be done at frantic pace until he burned out in the evening. I would have to keep pace with him during the day and then his parents could relax in the evening when he was flat out. They would have their feet up on the couch and I would have blisters on mine from chasing after him. But they were feeding each other Kit Kat so there was nothing else for it.

We played.

He didn't talk much, this new friend, and any information as to his interests had to be virtually squeezed out of him.

"Do you like Tonka Trucks?"

A shake of the head.

"Do you like Steve Austin?"

"Who's that?"

"The Six Million Dollar Man."

Another shake of the head.

Jesus. He was hard work.

The prospect of future play dates loomed threateningly. This strange little boy with his amazingly friendly mum.

But then, a little ticking time bomb.

"You want to hear a secret?"

We had seen them buttoning their coats and knew that our time in the ball pool was (mercifully) nearly up.

"What?"

He moved closer, cupped a hand to my ear and, to my amazement, managed a husky whisper. "My name's not John – it's Sean!"

"Oh?" I couldn't think of anything less interesting. "Why do you call yourself John, then?"

He screwed up his face, trying to recall a scrap of dialogue he had committed to memory. The amazing thing was that he actually looked and sounded just like her when he said, "It's easier that way: new town, new name. Just easier. Okay?"

The significance of this was completely lost on me and I only remembered it later on at tea time when Mum was telling Dad about the lovely woman she had met and her wee boy who I had, apparently, taken quite a shine to. I watched the smile melt off her face and Dad try not to smirk. All at once the talk at the table ceased and even Pete knew to keep his mouth shut.

Mum was boiling. The veins in her forehead were popping. They only came out when she was seriously annoyed. The last time had been when Dad spilt his Guinness over the new carpet whilst watching football. It wasn't so much the spill – "How many times do you want me to say sorry, Doreen? Will I tattoo it on my arse?" – it was the fact that he had waited till half time before soaking it up and that he had used (this was the clincher) the Queen Elizabeth hand towel that was only meant to be used for the special visitor dishes.

Dad couldn't help himself.

"Was it a four fingered Kit Kat, Doreen – or just a two fingered one?"

She spent an hour and a quarter on the phone to Granny. It wasn't exactly what you would call a two way conversation; Mum would pause for breath every so often allowing Granny to coo "I know, I know," in that soothing way of hers.

"Nobody can say I'm not nice, Mummy. Remember Monica from the street? I gave her my doll and invited her to the party – remember? And then there's Jackie from work. I make sure she gets her fair share of shifts. Look at the Meekins! How can anyone say anything about me when I've got Catholic babysitters? Your children are your most precious whatyamacallit – and I have Catholic babysitters! It's just the sneakiness of it, Mummy, that's the thing that really gets me – the sneakiness."

I knew I wouldn't see John/Sean again and I was quite relieved.

Jimmy's dream was to be a comedian like Laurel and Hardy or Norman Wisdom. He would practise the routines he saw on the television and had all but perfected Ollie's tie twiddle and Stan's tearful scratching of his head. He didn't seem to appreciate that it didn't quite work the same when he did it. Any pocket or birthday money was spent on joke books which he would memorise and, during the adverts or at break time at school, he would bombard me and anyone else with his latest funnies.

He was gracious too. It wasn't all about him and what he liked; because of me he grew to love Evel Kineval. We were too young to anticipate the Snake River Jump – his chute deployed prematurely and he could so easily have drowned – but then he announced something unbelievable for May of 1975.

"Read it again, Dad!" I had decapitated my boiled egg but suddenly I had no interest whatsoever in the runny yellow yolk or the dippy soldiers.

Dad grinned. "Evel Kineval, famous American stunt rider has accepted an offer to perform a jump at Wembley stadium on May 26th of this year. The bike rider, famed for wearing an American stars and stripes jump suit, will be attempting to jump fourteen London buses ..."

I pushed aside my egg; I would never eat again. And then, a wondrous thought. "Can we go, Dad? Can we go to Wembley?"

I saw his face drop and I hated myself even though I was only five. I had ruined the moment. A cheap paper, the pleasure of bringing joy with very little outlay, and yet I had immediately asked for the impossible.

Mum lanced the boil. "Don't be silly, Kevin. We're in Northern Ireland, Wembley is in London. We wouldn't be able to afford to go over there just to see someone jump over some buses."

Mum didn't get Evel Kineval. She didn't get a lot of the things I liked. Once, Jimmy had been over and we had all been watching Laurel and Hardy struggling to carry a piano up a tall flight of steps. Jimmy was roaring and so was Dad, even Pete was smiling. Mum stared hard at the television and asked: "What was it with those two? Was it just that one was fat and the other was thin?"

"It's a waste of Wembley, if you ask me," Pete piped up. He was annoyed because the focus was on something I liked. "Wembley Stadium should be kept for football and boxing, music concerts and stuff like that. It's not meant to be used by stupid, daft Americans and their silly wee bikes."

"I hardly think a Harley Davison can be described as a "silly wee bike." Dad grinned and winked at me, he had recuperated like a top boxer. "How's this for an idea, Kevvie Boy? We'll invite Jimmy over that Saturday, make a big night of it with popcorn and Coke?"

"Invite his dad over too?" Mum suggested.

Dad's smile flickered but held firm. "I'm not sure he'll want to come, but I'm fine by that. Maybe Sean's mammy would like to come over for a coffee as well?"

That did for her.

I was dancing.

Dad was beaming.

I was too elated to notice Pete slipping from the table.

"Can I go and tell Jimmy?"

"Aw, Kevin, it's Saturday morning and you've hardly touched your breakfast."

"Please, Mum!" Suddenly I was desperate. I wanted to see Jimmy's face. The success of Evel Kineval's Wembley jump all hinged on me getting to Jimmy before his dad did. Would they have a similar breakfast set up in the Hood household? Something told me they would not; but the Wembley jump was probably going to be the talk of the television and Jimmy, like myself, was always glued to the set.

"Alright then. Brush your teeth and wash your face before you go."

I was off like a rocket. Down the corridor. Bathroom. Teeth. Face. Out the door. Chubby little legs pumping as hard as they could. Round the corner. Up the path. Panting. Panting. And there, at the door, three of them: Mrs Hood (sleepy) Jimmy (in pyjamas) and ...Pete (smiling)

"Well, my goodness me, this is a real family affair this morning. All the excitement. Pete's told us all about it. I'm sure Jimmy would love to come – wouldn't you Jimmy?"

Jimmy nodded. He looked a little confused at the presence of Pete who had never graced his doorstep before. But he wasn't a deep thinker. In a moment the incongruity of the situation would dissolve and he would completely forget it. And that was the worst part of it. I wanted him to share my rage and detestation for the grinning monster beside me who was so pleased with himself that he was literally hopping from foot to foot.

I suddenly felt incredibly foolish. Purple in the face and panting like a dog; all excited because some guy on a bike was going to jump over some buses.

"Why did you do it, Pete? That was my thing to tell - he's my friend, not yours." I was trudging back to the house in his wake and I wanted to impress upon him that what he had done was as cruel as cruel could be, probably the nastiness thing that had ever been witnessed in the history of the world. But I couldn't find the words, so instead I said, "I hate you, Pete. You're a great big steaming pile of fucking deenge!"

He rounded on me and grabbed me by the collar. I could see his mind racing. He couldn't tell them about the fuck because they would know what he had been up to at Jimmy's, nor could he beat me up because that was the ultimate sin in our house. He couldn't even throw the fuck or the deenge back at me because I had used it first. Mum hated us spitting so that's what he did now just to show how much I had annoyed him.

"You spat! I'm telling."

CHAPTER THREE

Despite Pete's best efforts to suck the joy out of it, the anticipation of the Wembley jump steadily grew and helped to take my mind off school. The papers and news were full of it when the great man and his entourage arrived and Jimmy and I could think of nothing else.

"Do you think he'll make it, Kev?"

"Course he will."

But we couldn't be sure. That was the magic. There was always the risk. That was the excitement. And yet, suppose something terrible did happen? Just suppose he clipped one of the end buses and his bike burst into flames? What would happen if Evel Kineval died at Wembley Stadium? What would the President say? How could you possibly play football there again?

We are in injury time and there's still no score – but wait now, Georgie Best has the ball and the crowd are going wild; he's charging up the field, a one man army, dodging the defenders like the ball is glued to his foot. He's close to the penalty area now - passed the very spot where Evel Kineval was burnt alive – GOAL!!!

To kill time until jump day we created our own ramp at the bottom of the hill that led to the rugby club. We angled a plank of plywood up on some old bricks and carefully placed our toy cars in a row on the other side. Alas, we only had two red buses; the rest consisted of the much abused Tonka Trucks, an old and battered fire truck, Starsky's red Torino with the white stripe and James Bond's Aston Martin – although the little Chinese guy had long since been permanently ejected.

It was awesome.

Up at the top of the hill.

Quick scout round for traffic.

Never anything at that time of the day apart from the occasional work lorry.

This was the best bit.

Pause.

Deep breath.

Pause again.

Thumbs up.

And away!

Pumping as hard as you could on the pedals to build momentum.

Faster! Faster! Faster!

The ramp approaching.

Here we go! Here we go!

It hit the ramp and soared into the air -

The crowd screaming and cheering –

-and then landed, with a thudding crunch, a metre beyond.

Magic.

But very hard on the balls.

Over and over again.

Two wee boys on three wheeler trikes jumping over miniature cars. We must have looked daft but we didn't care. Chopper bikes would have been perfect – the ones with the motor bike handlebars – but we were far too wee and they were far too expensive. The best bit, apart from the jump itself, was being interviewed by the media afterwards. Jimmy, if it was his turn, would hold a piece of wood to my mouth and ask me how I felt the jump had gone. We put on American accents for this, although we both sounded more Elvis than Evel.

"How did you think it went, Mr Kineval?"

"Son, if you've come all this way to see me, you can call me Evel."

"How do you think it went, Evel?"

"Didn't think I was gonna make it, son – almost lost control of her right at the end."

"Any injuries?"

"Might've broke my arse again!"

"Yanks don't say arse – they say ass."

"Might have broke my ass again. Think the bike might be stuck up ma bum."

And we'd dissolve into fits of giggles.

*

The real Evel Kineval was no different. He too liked to savour the moment. The actual jump itself would only last for seconds, it was the build-up that mattered. Ninety thousand people held their breaths in Wembley. We were part of the millions glued to the screen as he raced down the ramp then slowed to a halt at the very top.

Teasing us.

Taunting us.

Flirting with his public.

The poor British broadcaster didn't quite know what to say. "He's changing his bike now. Obviously, not happy with the way the other one was performing. Remember, it is vitally important that he hits the ramp at between 85 and 90 mph; if he doesn't manage this – well, let's not even think about that."

I sat with Jimmy on our big leather sofa. We had a huge bowl of popcorn each but had stopped eating because we were so nervous; Dad sat opposite with his Guinness and crisps. Even Mum was in on the act. Usually, it was only Telly Savallas who could bring her in from the kitchen.

"I think this is it!"

He was revving the engine.

….rem, rem, rem, rem, rem, rem, rem, rem, rem, rem, rem

He was on the top of the world looking down on us all.

He was about to jump the Atlantic from America to Britain.

I could feel Jimmy tensing beside me and I reached for his hand and squeezed tight.

Heart pumping.

Goosebumps.

"Here he goes!"

And just then, as sometimes happens in life, the clock stopped.

I was the only person in the world who could move.

I watched as the bike took off and froze in the air. I saw the wide eyed expression of excitement on Jimmy's face – all silly jokes forgotten – and felt an enormous pride. I had created this experience for him, it was because of my friendship that he was here and had fallen under the Kineval spell. Dad's Guinness moustache grin; he had earned this moment of pleasure – all the traffic, the bills, the stress – this, and little moments like it, were what made it all worthwhile. Mum pleased that we were all happy and not for the moment bickering.

And then he landed.

For a moment it looked like the perfect set down. Just for a moment.

"Oh, dear God!"

The bike seemed to crumple under him. It wasn't anywhere near as spectacular as the Caesar's Palace fall – nothing could top that – but it did look incredibly painful. Fatal even.

"Nobody touch him!"

"Stand well back!"

"Let his own people get to him!"

Dad polished off his Guinness and let loose a colossal belch.

"Derek!"

"Pardon me."

I glared at him. For a second, just a second, I hated him and wanted him to die.

"Is he dead?" suddenly Pete was in the room. He had been watching on his black'n'white portable, not wanting to be part of the occasion.

"He's fine. Look. You can see his legs move."

Slowly, ever so slowly, the great man was helped to his feet. The cameras wobbled a bit and then zoomed in. British cameras weren't used to such overwhelming drama and charisma. They recorded cricket and the queen's speeches - things like that. They didn't know how to deal with Evel Kineval.

"Ladies and gentlemen of this wonderful country, I've got to tell you that you are the last people in the world who will ever see me jump because I will never ever jump again. I'm through."

They wanted to put him on a stretcher but he waved them

away.
> "I came in here walking; I went out walking."
> Jimmy and I were lost for words.
> Never again?
> The world would never be the same.
> "I'm glad." Pete said.

CHAPTER FOUR

All these things were but a distraction.

I hated school.

I fucking loathed it.

Sometimes, on Friday evenings and especially when I was playing with Jimmy, I could push it to the back of my mind and almost forget about it. But I knew it was always there, waiting for me to relax and let my guard down, waiting for me to start enjoying life. Sunday nights it ruled supreme. Even the pleasure of a hot soapy bath was marred by the thought of the clock ticking towards bedtime, a troubled sleep, then the misery of Monday morning. A Friday or Saturday bath would have been a better idea, the opportunity to luxuriate with a trouble free mind, but that would have messed up Mum's schedule.

I'm sure it wasn't only me. There were probably lots of us; but if there were, their masks were far more convincing. My misery was apparent for all to see. And that could make you a target.

Jimmy was a comfort but we didn't do everything together and there were days when he was off sick. His granny didn't keep well and sometimes it was easier for his mother to keep him off to help out.

"How do you help out, Jimmy?"

"Make the tea sometimes."

I was impressed. "She lets you boil the kettle?"

"Sometimes."

"What else?"

"Just talk to her, really. She's a bit mental. She talks to my grandad even though he's dead and she forgets things all the time. Last time she said to me, "Oh hello, wee Jimmy, lovely to see you, thanks for coming."

"What's wrong with that?"

"It was my house and I'd just been to the toilet."

Teachers could still hit children but I don't think that's

what scared me.

I hated to be shouted at.

I hated to get things wrong.

But most of all: I hated to look a fool.

Good at writing; poor at numbers.

There was a girl in our class who shouldn't have been there. She was huge and she was old. There'd been some sort of administration mix up with her birth certificate and, in all the melee, the mistake wasn't noticed until late October. Mrs Jenkins addressed her one morning after break.

"Jessica, you know you are moving class? I just need to check a couple of things first – okay?"

Big Jess nodded, loving the attention.

Mrs Jenkins made her recite the alphabet. I could do that. She asked her a few other questions I can't remember and then, finally, chalked on the blackboard the strangest thing I had ever seen. It was huge, and wobbly, and strangely circular.

88

I felt my bowels loosen. I honestly thought I was going to soil myself. Whatever it was, it couldn't have been more than four inches high and yet it seemed to take up the whole of the blackboard. Bloated, horrible looking thing. I stole at glance at Jimmy and his open mouth caused a wave of relief to wash over me.

Temporarily.

The clock had stopped again and that was just fine because I was going to take a deep breath and turn my head around. If only a few of the others seemed to know what it was I could live with that. As long as the majority were as perplexed as I was. But if they were all nodding knowingly and mouthing the answer then I knew what I would do. I would kill myself. I would

go home, have my dinner, watch a little television - then jump out
of my bedroom window.

But Big Jess did not give me the chance to check.

"Is it eighty-eight, Mrs Jenkins?"

"Well done, Jessica Bruce, you are good to go."

I kept my head down, face flushed, and tried to interpret
the noise. Was that a knowing buzz? Were they all of them,
except Jimmy, privy to knowledge that had been for some
unfathomable reason withheld from me? And Jimmy wouldn't
care. Just to add to the mix. I might ask him outside how he had
felt and what he thought of the situation and, if he even
remembered it, he would shrug and wonder what the big deal
was.

I hated school.

CHAPTER FIVE

Dad bought a caravan in Millisle so that we could enjoy the glorious summer of 1976.

God, it was hot. Mum was a little slow with the sun lotion but you couldn't really blame her. The Ulster sun usually lived behind a grey blanket of cloud and only came out to play on the first week of September when school started back. But not this summer. My skin peeled like an onion. Mum put some soothing stuff on my back and I had to sleep on my stomach, which was fine; but always, *always* during the night I would roll over and scream myself awake. That was the only bad part. The rest of the summer was magic.

The caravan was really just a big long tin hut. Pete and I had a bunk each on either side of the top end; Mum and Dad had a cool double bed that folded up like the one in *You Only Live Twice*, with Sean Connery. The kitchenette had a table that could be converted into another bed although Jimmy's mum never let him come because she had heard stories about the nearby borstal.

No mod. cons. in 1976. You kept your luke warm milk in a bucket of water and you had to use communal toilets which required a key at night and were the meeting and loitering point of scary Belfast teenagers who had little else to do but smoke and spit and scowl at chubby little seven year olds with under bites. If you got caught short during the night there was a wee bucket in the closet and it wasn't unusual for it to be three quarters full of amber piss come morning.

No electric or running water either but we didn't care. There were water taps aplenty throughout the camp and Dad had a spare car battery connected to the portable television.

"We can get two hours a day, Kevvy boy, and when it runs out – simple, we just stick it back in the car and charge it up again. Magic!" He glanced over at my mother, winked and whispered, "*Bloody* magic."

It was bloody magic too. At night, when the whole of Ulster was fast asleep, me and my dad watched the horror double bills. Flickering black and white classics: Karloff, Lugosi, Lon Chaney Jr. Later on, they would jump forward a few decades and offer you Cushing, Lee and (my favourite) the wonderfully camp Vincent Price.

Snuggled up in my sleeping bag. A bag of Maltesers and a glass bottle of Pepsi. I'd glance across at the darkened, flickering figure of Dad. Tall and lean, his legs stretched, relaxed, savouring his Guinness.

He wasn't even that fussed on horror movies.

Karloff staggering across the barren landscape with poor Colin Clive under him arm; Lugosi welcoming Renfield (Jonathon Harker in the book, Universal took a few liberties with Mr Stoker) into his castle before remarking, in his wonderful Hungarian accent: "Leesen to them, the cheeldren of the night! What mewseek they make!"

Doubly delicious: Pete was scared of them. The big woofter. He pretended not to be, of course, and during the daylight hours he would scoff at them and try to run down the battery by watching shows he didn't really want to watch. It was him who put it in Mum's head that the horror movies were inappropriate and she held a family meeting to discuss the things we watched on the television. Why, for example, did we never watch any educational programmes like nature documentaries? And so, we all sat down to endure one and watched a pride of lions pounce upon and disembowel a zebra. They pulled all of its legs off too and the thing was still alive at the end, its tongue lolling out of its mouth. That night we all slept together in the same bed and Mum never mentioned the horror movies again.

The beaches were thronged. Grannies and grandads, mums and dads, girls in bikinis with their diddies jiggling about. You could see jelly fish in the water sometimes and taste the salt when you dived under. Pete and I got along okay in the sunshine. We both had masks and snorkels but there wasn't much to see in three feet of water and neither of us could swim then. The snorkels had a lovely rubbery taste, the same smell you got when you snuggled close to your hot water bottle during the winter.

Mr Mackie, from the caravan next door, came over to talk to Dad. He wasn't as tall but he was really stocky; sometimes in the morning you could see him lifting weights just for the fun of it. I had noticed the strange lettering on his forearms – U.D.A – and asked Dad about it one morning over breakfast.

"Tattoos are private son. I wouldn't ask anyone about them."

"I know. That's why I'm asking you."

Mum was hovering.

"It stands for Ulster Defence Association."

"What's that mean?"

I could feel Mum's eyes but didn't know why.

"It means that Mr Mackie supports the U.D.A or more likely is a member."

"Like a club?"

"Yeah."

"So what do they do in their club?"

He pushed aside his miniature chess set and thought for a moment. "The U.D.A look after people like us. They make sure that we're safe and that nobody causes us any harm."

"Like the I.R.A?"

"Yes."

"Do you like Mr Mackie?"

"He's okay – yes, I like him."

"Do you think he'll be at the parades next Saturday?"

This time he smiled. "Mr Mackie won't just be at the parades. He'll be in them." He looked up at Mum. "He wanted to know yesterday why I didn't march. Very friendly, no hassle, just was interested."

"What did you say?"

"I told him that I'd just bought the boys brand new flags."

"Good for you. Did that do for him?"

Dad gave her his lopsided grin. "He asked me what school I'd gone to."

"He didn't."

"He did."

"What did you tell him?"

"I told him I was an old Instonian and he went away a happy man."

"Did he go to the same school as you, Dad?"

Before he could answer Mum swooped. "Right, young man, go get that kite Granny bought you. Look at the wind. We'll see if she flies."

I was dancing. It was meant to be clothes washing this morning. The kite was scheduled for this afternoon. She'd messed up and I wasn't going to correct her. I ran the length of the caravan and retrieved it from under the bunk.

"What are you doing?"

"Mum's doing the kites this morning. She's forgotten the clothes – are you coming?"

"Nah, I'll just read my book. Actually, I might have to remind her about the clothes. I need my trunks washed."

"Aw, Pete, please don't – remember the fun we had yesterday."

"Go on then."

I thundered down the length of the caravan, loving the tinny racket my feet made, clutching Superman tightly. Pretty soon he would be soaring ninety feet in the sky and the beauty of it was that from the ground you wouldn't see the plastic. It would look like the actual Superman in the air!

*

If you have only ever seen a Twelfth of July orange parade on the television you haven't really lived it. It doesn't matter how high you have the volume, it's not the same. You can have the ornaments dancing on the mantelpiece and you still won't get it all. You need to drown in it. All of your senses are required to get the true value of it: the buzz of camaraderie; a thousand little union jacks clutched in chubby, ice-cream hands; sea-gulls squawking greedily above salty chips; orange everywhere; red, white and blue. Above all else, the anticipation – oh, the anticipation.

Shush, Shush, Listen.

And everyone would hush.

It was coming.

It was in the air.

And then the sweetness of a flute band as the marching feet grew nearer.

Louder….

Louder….

Louder….

A massive cheer as they strode into view, banners aloft. Dozens upon dozens of spruce Protestant men with lips pursed and trousers perfectly creased. Marching and blowing. Flawless music, and the guy at the front, twirling and somersaulting the stick fifty feet in the air and somehow always managing to catch it.

"How can they march and blow, Daddy? Don't they get tired?"

"They practise all year."

"Do they march all the way from Belfast? That's miles away. Don't they get blisters?"

"No, no. They don't march it all. They get the bus down part of it, march and play some, then the bus picks them up again. I think they only really march through towns. There wouldn't be much point marching and playing down the motorway with no-one to cheer them."

Shush, Shush, Listen.

The magic was that the music never completely dissipated. It grew fainter but always loitered, waiting to pass the baton on to the next band. Thus, with the flute music still in the air you could began to hear the accordions and a roar would emerge as they rounded the corner, all sash and splendour, squeezing the life out of their instruments.

Throughout it all, the steady march of bowler hats and orange sashes. Scary looking men. They took their marching seriously: arms swinging just so, faces set. Sometimes if you met their eye you could squeeze a half smile or even a wink or wave; but mostly all you got was a stern pomposity. Some young ones, sons and grandsons, but most seemed to be balding and middle-aged and they made me think of Captain Mainwaring at the end credits of *Dad's Army* – when he's marching across the battle field taking himself all serious when John Le Mesurier and Clive Dunn are just wanting home for their tea.

"Why do they all look so cross, Dad?"

"Don't know. Maybe they need the toilet."

My God. I hadn't thought of that. How awful to be dying for a deenge and having to walk for miles.

"Do they have toilets on the buses?"

"Not sure, maybe those chemical ones. I don't think so."

"So where do they go?"

"Behind a tree, I suppose."

The thought kept me awake. I just couldn't imagine these sober suited, serious sashes with their braces undone behind a bush. Would they keep their bowler hats on?

Shush, Shush, Listen.

The big guns in the distance … growing ever closer.

Rat a tat tat, rat a tat tat – BOOM BA BOOM BA BOOM BA BOOM - rat a tat tat, rat a tat tat …

The drums! The almighty drums!

Louder …

Louder…

Louder …

You could almost imagine the ground shaking.

Hold your breath.

Heart thumping.

Run! Hide! Here they are by Christ!

Dad hoisted me onto his shoulders so that I could get a better view. I dripped some of my choc ice down his neck but he didn't seem to mind; it was really hot and sweaty and he would be changing his shirt later anyway.

Boy, could they play those things. Normal sized ones at the front, blurring the sticks in perfect precision, always resetting underneath the nose. Then bigger ones in the middle, thumping out their support, covering their little brothers backs. And right at the back, the conquering master, the God of all the drums and all the land – the mighty Lambeg.

They were awesome.

Long after they passed you could still feel the blood thumping in your ears. When you went home, back to the caravan or wherever, it was the Lambeg you were thinking of; and when you were about to fall asleep it was the noise it made that lulled you to your rest. And in your dreams it grew bigger and bigger, dwarfing first the drummer, then the street, and finally a drum that only a folk giant might play – its thunder heard and felt around the world. The Lambeg ruled supreme.

The crowd roared at the appearance of King Billy aloft his white charger.

"Who is he again?"

"King Billy. He won the battle of the Boyne."

"Oh."

The power of those drums and that music. The black polished shoes. The way it got under your skin and into your head. You could feel your own sandalled feet itching to join in. They were fun and colourful and noisy. Everything a child could ask for and I longed to join them. Give me shoes and I would march; give me a drum and I would beat it; give me a pretty orange sash and I would wear it with pride.

CHAPTER SIX

Pete and I had tacitly agreed a truce. The summer was nearly over and we wanted to squeeze as much out of the weather without wasting energy hating each other. On holiday he tended to be at his best, less of a pain. He was more tolerant of my existence and even seemed to have more patience when it came to the business of my endless questions.

"Pete, 'member that *Columbo* episode?"

"The one with Spock out of Star Trek?"

"No," although that was a good yin. "The one where the man 'lectrocutes the other man by dropping the TV into the bath?

"Yeah. What about it?"

Pause here. Ordinarily, these were the type of questions that seemed to agitate him.

"If God dropped a TV into the sea, would all the fish be 'lectrocuted?"

He considered it.

"No, only the ones close by. If you dropped a TV into the deep end of the swimming pool and you were in the shallow end, you'd probably be okay."

"Only the fish nearby?"

"Yes."

"What about electric eels? Would they still be killed – or would it make them stronger?"

"Jesus."

We were about to play hide and seek on the beach. It was early evening and the sands were emptying fast; sun weary bathers towelling the sand from between their toes and traipsing back to their caravans, hauling wind breakers, beach balls and various inflatables.

School was looming. Primary five. But it was still far enough away for me to smother it under a blanket. It was a sin to even think about it when the sun, albeit dying now, was on your back and the salty sea breeze was washing over you.

"Right, this is what we'll do," Pete said, tapping his watch and indicating mine. "We'll synchronise our watches and then I'll give you exactly two minutes to find a hiding place. After that, I have another five to find you and if I haven't by then you win and can come out – okay?"

I watched him try to synchronise (a word he clearly liked) the digital watches Dad had bought us and felt strangely sorry for this big brother who had never quite known what to do with his little rubber lipped sibling. I knew he didn't really hate me; perhaps deep down he even loved me a little. Would he be sad and sorry if I was to die suddenly? Definitely, yes. Was that the same as love? I could see that he was enjoying my company by the way he was shaking his head at my questions and pretending to be annoyed. Not nasty or smirky. Almost in a proud way, like he was pleased to be my big brother. In the summertime I was pleased to be his little brother. Several days before he had been snorkelling and I had seen two teenagers nudging each other and making fun of him. Pete hadn't seen them but I had caught his attention and got him to stop so that their fun would end. Then I prayed that the jelly fish stung their things and that Jaws bit their legs off and they bled to death.

"Bugger! It's not working."

"You could use the stop watch."

A flash of annoyance. He hadn't thought of that.

"Remember, you showed me how to work it when we first got them?"

He nodded, found them, pressed down simultaneously.

"You've two minutes from now. Go!"

He turned his back and I raced down the beach. It was practically all ours now. I was in my sandals because of the sharp shells and seaweed and my feet sank into the moist sand as they sought for purchase. Where to hide? The beach was vast but there were only so many places that could conceal a small boy and two minutes was limiting.

45, 46, 47, 48 ….

There were huge algae covered boulders to my right, but

that was a bit obvious and the tide was coming in which would mean the sand might swallow my sandals permanently.

The tall tufts of grass to my left? It would mean having to lie absolutely flat like a sniper and it would be very difficult to see Pete's approach. Half the fun of hide and seek was holding your breath as your pursuer grew nearer, urging them to seek you elsewhere. Also, there might be broken glass and dog shit.

1-15, 1-16, 1-17, 1-18 ....

The dunes further down. Half cliff, half dune. There were three of them: a big one, a little one and a medium sized one - known locally as the three bears. If I was fast, I might just be able to make the big one, climb up part of it and conceal myself amongst the grass and rocks.

1-27, 1-28, 1-29, 1-30...

I was enjoying this. I could only hope that he was playing it fair and hadn't yet begun the pursuit.

Panting.

Purple with exertion.

I began to climb, grasping tufts as grass, oblivious to the scratches on my knees. This was brilliant. If I could just make it to the top...

1-57, 1-58, 1-59, 2-00 – my watch started the tinny beep familiar to early digitals. I silenced it, hugged the dusty rock like a limpet, stole a glance down the beach. Pete had awoken from his slumber and was galvanised, looking north, south, east and west. After a moment, he made a decision and began to stride purposefully out towards the boulders. Good. That would buy me an extra thirty seconds or so to make it to the top where there was plenty of space to lie down in some comfort. I hoisted myself up, over the final little bulge and lay down in the sandy grass.

It was a good vantage point; a cracking hiding place. It would have been an obvious spot but for the fact that Pete wasn't quite aware of how fast I was. I was heavy but I could shift when I wanted to.

I peered over the edge and saw that he had found disappointment behind the boulder.

Just play the silent waiting game. Some of the most satisfying children's games involved doing very little.

Out of the corner of my eye, I sensed movement and automatically froze.

I was alone atop this dune, but beneath me and to the left there was a teenage couple on Mummy Bear's dune. They were snuggled together like spoons in a drawer and it dawned on me, with a flush of hot guilty excitement, that they were kissing and feeling each other. The boy was a skinny red head I'd never seen before, but the girl I did know; I was sure I had seen her hanging round the toilets at the campsite.

I kept my head down, confident that they couldn't see me up here but afraid that they might hear me and then I would suffer the direst of consequences: spying on a couple, even by accident, was mucky and dirty.

"Mrs McBride, your little boy – the fat one with the funny lip – was spying on me and my girlfriend yesterday. Dirty, mucky little bugger. What are you going to do about it? If you don't do something really mean to him I'm gonna burn down your caravan and slash your tyres. Lovely weather we've been having, don't you think?"

Stealthily, I crept back; it was a brilliant hiding place but nothing was worth getting into this kind of trouble for. And yet... and yet ... something strange was happening to me. I could feel my thing, as it sometimes did, getting hard, except this time the sensation was much more painful and urgent.

I strained to hear their voices but all I got was whispered murmurings, instantly lost on the sea breeze.

Movement behind me! I turned round just as Pete was about to yell his victory in my ear. Frantically, I jammed a finger to my lips and gestured, half dragged him to the ground.

"Wha ...?"

"Shush ... down there."

Ginger had his hand up Blondie's jumper and was pressing his lips onto hers. He was groaning audibly and the noise made us both bristle uncomfortably. Clearly visible was the girl's tanned midriff and the pink rim of her knickers. Oh dear God. I could feel my hot breath on my hands and a furtive glance to the left showed that Pete was in the same state of nervous excitement.

Then all hell broke loose.

"You dirty fuckin' Fenyan!"

All of a sudden there were three more of them on top of the dune. I recognised two of them immediately, Roger and Jack Beattie, the other one I had seen but didn't know.

"What do you want?" Ginger tried for a bold tone but the fear and confusion were all too apparent – confusion because Blondie had immediately deserted him and was now at the side of Beattie.

"Are you okay? He didn't hurt you?"

"What the fuck are you talking about? Of course I didn't hurt her! Tell him, Mandy."

"You better shut your hole." This from the other one, the one I didn't recognise; clearly, he was desperate for a line in the movie.

"Can you make it down by yourself?" Roger gazed into Mandy's eyes and I suddenly recalled where I had seen her before. She was on his arm the night of the big bonfire. "I don't want you to see this – it's not going to be pretty."

Ginger made a bolt for it then but it's next to impossible to be fast down a sand dune and the other two had him in a head lock even as Blondie made her way carefully down the mound. From our position all we could see was the back of her head, her eyes glued down for foot and hand holds.

"Hope she breaks her neck," Pete whispered into my ear.

I half turned but he silenced me with gritted teeth and a shake of his jaw.

"Alright, lads, you can take your hands off him now – let him breathe."

Ginger took a step back but not too far; there was barely room for all four of them and I thought suddenly of the three man tent Dad had bought the year before. All four of us, in a fit of wild family camaraderie, had spent one night in it. For the first hour it had been fun – cosy, even – then claustrophobia had set in and you started to imagine that you were running out of oxygen. Dad had brought it back to the shop the next day.

"You tried to rape my girlfriend."

Ginger surprised himself with a laugh.

"You think rape is a funny thing? Are you laughing, Jack? Phillip?

They took a step towards him.

"Do you think I carried her up here against her will?" there was a note of hysteria in his voice. "For fuck's sake, lads, come on! I didn't know she was your girlfriend – I'm sorry." He took a step back and glanced down at the rocks and beach below. If he jumped he wouldn't die but he would likely break his legs and slice himself open. Steve Austin could jump it had he been here -

Christ! How did he manage to jump that?

Why, don't you know who that is? That's Steve Austin, the Six Million Dollar Man.

Blimey!

Look! That's him swimming out to sea at fifty miles an hour. He's gone to kill Jaws!

Won't his bionics go all rusty in the water?

No, no, they're all rubberized and waterproofed.

But Steve Austin was in America. This was here and now. And it was real.

"Please don't call the police." Ginger pleaded, and, poor bastard, even I recognised that tactic.

"Don't worry," Beattie spat. "We won't." He nodded to his companions and they began to rummage in the backpack Phillip was wearing. As they fumbled, my eyes flicked over to Ginger who was clearly again contemplating the risks of the jump. The problem was, if he was to stand a chance of clearing the little ring of jaggy rocks, he would need a run before the leap and they were not going to allow for that.

"There! What do you think of that?"

The look of fear on Ginger's face was exactly what they had hoped for and I registered the expressions of excited glee as my own heart leapt into my mouth. Jesus. Dad had a thing about fireworks. We were allowed to go to organised shows but to even think about buying a firework for the garden or Huey's field was utterly taboo. Even sparklers were frowned upon because, apparently, at their hottest they were the same temperature as volcanic lava – or some such shit.

The thing Roger Beattie held aloft was not a sparkler. It had stripes and a little red cone shaped head and looked a little like a stick of dynamite, except I knew it wasn't that. It was a rocket left over from the July bonfire celebrations. A nod to his brother produced a box of swan matches and, with deliberate and excruciating slowness, Jack began to scratch a red headed match across the sandpaper.

"Jesus Christ, lads, come on! What do you want me to do?"

I could barely breathe. If I so much as sneezed they could turn that thing on me. Burn the face right off me. I'd be like those poor men in Dad's First World War book – the ones they didn't give the parachutes to.

The fuse suddenly caught. It all happened so quickly. There was the suggestion of a spark and then the thing in Beattie's hands just took off. There was a whistling, whooshing sound and it flew out to sea – missing Ginger's left ear by half a foot.

Jesus Holy Christ!

"Wow! That was a bit close - let's try again!"

More fumbling in the back pack, but this time the theatre was completely unnecessary. I don't even know if they had any more fireworks. It didn't matter. They had him now and they knew it.

"Oh, Jesus Christ, please no!" he was on his knees, hands clasped together. "Please don't! Please don't! What do you want me to do? Anything. Anything."

I felt for him, really I did. Yet, if I'm honest, there was a small feeling of disgust as well.

Beattie grinned broadly at his pals. This had clearly gone pretty much how they had hoped and I sensed then that the whole thing had been planned and practised with military precision. The situation; the time of day; there was nobody around to hear anything. The firework – sure, but errant fireworks were a regular occurrence at this time of year, easily explained away.

"Strip!"

The command took me completely by surprise; it was, without doubt, the last thing I was expecting to hear. But Ginger complied immediately. Off came the trainers, the socks, the trousers and the T-shirt; only at the underpants did he pause.

"Come on, lads..."

"Pass me another one, Jack, this fucker's wasted enough of our time."

"Wait! Wait." He pulled them off, cupped his hands over his thing, took in great gulps of sea air.

"Hands behind your back, please."

He meekly obeyed. He looked to have no energy left; even the tears had stopped. His thing looked tiny, sad, and it had an odd fuzzy look which, for some odd reason, was just as terrifying as anything that had gone before.

"Now, we're nearly done. Just one last thing." Beattie leered at his mates. "A little bit of a sing song, if you're up for it? Do you know *The Sash*?

A tiny shake of the head.

"Don't worry. Phil here is a beautiful singer – on you go, Phil."

Phil really wasn't that great. But he started up and Ginger mumbled along, gazing over their shoulders at the incoming tide.

Just one chorus.

And they seemed happy.

And it was over.

*

I almost slipped on the seaweed as we left the beach and walked up the grassy lane that led to the caravan site. I had goose pimples all over my arms and longed for the warmth of the gas fire and the normality of Mum's frowns and Dad's smirks. I glanced up at Pete and knew he didn't want to talk – but I couldn't stop myself.

"At least they didn't take his clothes, Pete; that shows they're not all bad - yeah?"

"Be quiet."

For a while I was. I needed to think too. Up ahead were the caravan lights; we would be home in less than five minutes.

"They could have taken a photograph, Pete – that would've been far worse."

"Just shut up, will you."

"One of those ones like Mr Mackie's – a Polaroid, you don't need to go to the chemists."

"Would you shut up, Kevin."

"I'm telling, Pete."

"No, you're not."

"Yes I am, and you can't stop me. I'm telling Mum and Dad!"

He grabbed me fiercely by the shoulders.

"You know nothing! Nothing. We tell and they might come for us – and not just us, maybe Mum and Dad as well."

"Dad would kick their arse. So would Mum."

"They're nothing, Kevin – just daft teenagers. There's hundreds more in this camp – men just as big as Dad."

That got me thinking.

"And they don't bother with silly little fireworks; they have proper guns and bullets."

"But, Pete, what they did to that boy was wrong."

He was silent and I knew he was thinking hard, trying to come up with some sort of solution or reason that would bring this conversation to a permanent conclusion. Finally, yards from our caravan, he turned to me. It was dusk by now but I could see in the lines of his forehead the middle-aged man he would become.

"We don't know the whole story, Kevin. That boy was a Catholic, right?"

I nodded. That much I had grasped.

"He probably supports the I.R.A. Maybe his family are in the I.R.A. You know the things that they do? Beattie comes from Belfast. He might have had family killed by the I.R.A for all we know. Maybe, that boy deserved to be scared – and anyway, they let him go; that's more than the I.R.A usually do."

I bought into some of it. It was easier that way. Suddenly, I was unbelievably tired. I wanted my tea, I wanted my sleeping bag, I wanted to watch the Belfast ferry ablaze with lights crossing before I fell asleep; but most of all, I wanted my brother back – the sarky, sneery version who always knew the right insult at the perfect time.

A cool, refreshing breeze travelled up from the sea and I felt myself shiver; it was a roasting summer but the nights could be chilly. In a moment my teeth might start to chatter. Little boy in shorts, scuffs on his knees, daft brown sandals with the buckled straps curling up at the ends. Pete had ploughed on and was almost at the caravan steps. I could see through the curtain the gas lit figure of Dad, hunched over his miniature chess set. Chess was another passion for him. If you showed the slightest interest in what he was doing he would bombard you with chess moves from bygone world championships. Russians whose names you could barely get your tongue around. All of a sudden I wanted to be beside him, to smell him, have him wink at me – this lanky thirty-six year old who was always glad to see me. I ran the last few steps.

"Sure, there's the man himself!" he winked and pointed to his chess board: tiny white pieces locked in strategic battle with black. "This is the famous Bobby Fischer game against Spassky – the one where he used Alekhine's Defence instead of the Sicilian!"

*

The following morning, invigorated and refreshed, I asked Mum what rape meant.

"Oh, dear God. Where did you hear that word, Kevin?"

"I read it in one of your magazines at home."

Dad twitched a smile and Mum glared at him.

"Rape, Kevin, is a horrible thing that some awful men do to

women – it's like, kissing and hugging them, when they don't want to."

"Oh." I thought about the skinny blonde girl and the way she had leapt across to be at Beattie's side. She hadn't looked upset at all. I wondered how she was feeling this morning. Did she know what had happened after she left? They must surely have boasted about it. The part about the firework was too good not to talk about. Would she feel guilty? Maybe she was annoyed that she hadn't been able to stay for the main event. Just how poisonous was she? I thought about it as I ate my cornflakes. Then I forgot all about her. It was a bright, sunny morning and there were kites, and buckets and spades, and the promise of amusements. I was seven.

CHAPTER SEVEN

Tommy "Rip" Turnbull joined our school in Primary five. He was short and stocky and came with a reputation of having been the best fighter in his last school. In fact, it had been a fight that had led to his expulsion, something to do with pencils with little pink rubbers on the end. Apparently, according to Rip, he had been play fighting with an older boy, pretending that the pencils were switch blades.

"I was all over him – jabbing him here, jabbing him there – then he gets fuckin' smart and switches to the pointy end – look!" He pulled up his shirt and if you looked closely you could see several tiny puncture wounds.

"What did you do?" Jimmy asked; he loved greeting new kids, especially ones like Rip Turnbull.

"Gave him a good old Glasgow kiss. Do you know what that is?"

None of us did.

Rip gestured for us to follow him to the bicycle shed. He brought his face close to the covering, as if he was looking for a weak spot, then - with a swift cock fighting gesture that caught us all off guard - head-butted it. The whole shed shuddered and two of the group burst into applause.

It was crazy; but pretty impressive.

"He didn't know either - until I fuckin' showed him."

Stanley Brownlie, the fattest boy in the school, wasn't completely convinced. He waited until Rip was a safe distance away then whispered to me. "He came from a little country school."

"So what?"

"They're bloody tiny. You have Primary ones at one table, twos at the next, threes at the next, and so on. There's probably only two big classes and fifty kids in the whole school."

For what it was worth, it was probably true. In any case, I didn't really want to argue with him. He wasn't what I would call a friend but he was a useful fellow to hang around with. When we went swimming, I always timed it so that I would be walking out to the benches beside him. His big diddies jiggled like jelly on a plate and he didn't even bother, perhaps because he couldn't, to suck in his gut. I looked like a stick beside him. One time, we had been standing together in the playground and the High School boys had been yelling down to us.

"Hey, Brownlie, sorry to hear about your mum!"

Stanley's mother - a similar size to him and his dad was no Stan Laurel - had just lost a leg to diabetes.

"Em, thanks."

"That's a real shame," another boy called down and he sounded as sincere as the first. "Tell her all the best from us."

"Right, a will."

"That's a tragedy," echoed another one. "Poor woman."

Brownlie looked anxiously at me. This level of concern from above was unheard of. I could see that it had completely flummoxed him. Then he glanced to the far left of the small group and his shoulders slumped forward. Several boys, their cheeks puffed out to simulate obesity, were hopping madly around in circles, goaded by the sniggering of a dozen or more seniors.

Nice.

But at least they left me and my lip alone.

Jimmy sought me out at lunch time.

"What about Rip?"

"What about him?"

But I knew what was coming.

"I was thinking of asking him back to the den."

I felt a sudden overwhelming possessiveness. He barely knew this new boy and now he was about to get the royal invite back to our special place. "Jimmy, it's your den, you can invite whoever the hell you like. You don't need to ask me."

"Aw, don't be like that, it's as much yours as it is mine. I just thought it would be nice to welcome him."

Jimmy wasn't the brightest but he was pretty shrewd. He had sussed that a muscle like Rip Turnbull, even if he was mostly mouth, was better on your side than someone else's.

Jimmy's granny had died and it was the best thing that had ever happened to us. It was sad and all that but what we gained was beyond our wildest imaginings: her Granny flat.

Not quite.

The flat, in Jimmy's sizeable back garden, had been under construction when her heart gave out and Mr Hood commanded the builders to down tools. But then the dilemma was that he had gone to the trouble and expense to gain planning permission all for nothing. Not to mention the work that was already done. A money wasting bitch right to the last furlong.

Jimmy plucked up the courage to ask for ownership. It was probably the bravest thing he had ever done given his father's temper but I helped form his argument: the flat would mean that we never bothered him again, he could watch his horses and do his paperwork without the slightest noise to distract him. To sweeten the deal, I'd told Jimmy to suggest that the flat would serve as several birthdays and Christmases combined and I promised him that anything I got from my own parents would be shared.

And incredibly, Mr Hood had consented. Our argument was a good one but I think he was also relieved that at least the bloody thing was going to be used for something.

The flat, our den, was awesome. There was one big room and a little kitchenette with running water and a mini fridge; on the other side was a plumbed toilet, so we were completely self-sufficient. It didn't having heating or carpets but it did have wiring so we were able to watch his granny's old colour television. We acquired an old sofa and two comfy chairs and – almost unbelievably - a perfectly serviceable 6x3 pool table that some neighbour was throwing out.

And now there was Tommy.

"It's a pretty cool hang out," Rip conceded, plonking himself down on my easy chair. "What do you do here?"

"Just hang out." Jimmy thought for a moment. "We talk about stuff, sometimes do homework, watch television–"

"Oh, yeah?" strangely, that seemed to excite him. "Where's your T.V?"

"There." I had been about to hang a poster when he arrived and had draped it over the set. "What's your favourite show?"

This straightforward question seemed to throw him. "... *Charlie's Angels* is good."

Jimmy and I grinned at each other. "Look!" I held up the poster so he could see. "Bought this in Woolworth's yesterday."

It was the famous poster of the three original angels: Farrah Fawcett and the other two.

"Jesus," Rip said. "She's got a great set of tits on her."

We were all in agreement then. He helped us to blue tack it to the wall and stood back to admire the effect. Rocky Balboa to the left, the angels in the centre, Starsky and Hutch to their right. Everyone happy.

"Do you know why there are so many red Ford Capris in Ulster?" Rip asked.

Actually, I did. "It's because you can't buy Starsky's Ford Torino. It's a limited edition – hardly any of them were made."

"Well done," Rip said.

"Kev's a real expert when it comes to television and movies. Ask him another one, Rip; go on, ask him a really hard one."

"Okay. Let me think. What do you call the big tall actor who plays Dracula?"

"That depends. If it's black'n'white, Bela Lugosi – colour and it's Christopher Lee."

"Yeah, him. What are the two things that Christopher Lee is most scared of?"

"Easy. Crucifix and silver bullet."

"Silver bullet - isn't that a werewolf?"

"Yes," I said indignantly. "But vampires hate them as well."

We were interrupted by Jimmy, pointing out that it was nearly time for Mr Austin to kick start his bionics. Rip sat beside me on the sofa as Jimmy tweaked with the aerial – it wasn't connected to the roof but the reception was pretty good anyway.

Lee Majors was who I wanted to be. He had bionics, he was handsome AND he was married to Farrah Fawcett. It was a particularly enjoyable episode. Steve fell in love with Jamie Somers who had been almost fatally injured in a parachute accident. He convinced Oscar to save her using bionics but her body rejected them and she died on the operating table.

"Don't worry. Don't worry." I was determined that this unexpected tragedy wouldn't put a dampener on the evening. American television was a bastard for that: it hooked you in and just when you felt like you could reach out and touch a character it snubbed them out. *Little House on the Prairie* was known for it; we all fell in love with blonde, blue eyed Mary and then she went blind and we had to come to terms with the disappointment. "She's not really dead."

"What do you mean?" Jimmy looked to be not a million miles away from tears and Rip, tough guy though he might be, was very quiet.

"My dad showed me an article in a magazine. They're going to make a Six Million Dollar Woman show. That's her. They can't make the show if she's dead. I'll bet you, next week, she'll be brought back to life."

"Like a vampire?" Rip suggested.

"Well, no, not really – yeah, a little, I suppose. I don't know, we'll have to wait and see."

"Clever."

"Yeah."

Rip had to go shortly afterwards to catch his bus. We watched him from the window: hands in pockets, elbows jutting out; he had quite a swagger for a nine year old.

"You like him, Kev?"

"He's okay, yeah."

"I knew you would. It's okay if he comes back?"

"Jim, it's your place, you don't need to ask me."

"But it's okay, yeah?"

"Yes. Jimmy, did you tell him I was into horror movies?"

"I think I did – why?"

"Nothing. Just wondering."

Rip became a regular and, despite my reservations, I grew to really like him. He wasn't two faced, like a lot of the class, what you saw was pretty much what you got. We learnt that his parents were older; they had a little bit of a farm and dealt mostly in pigs. That didn't surprise me, to be honest, since Rip himself sometimes carried the unmistakeable tang of pig shite on his clothes. They were quite religious and, incredibly, did not possess a television.

"No fucking telly?"

We looked at him as if he had cancer.

"So what?" Rip felt the need to defend his freakish parents. "Lots of people don't have a telly. Well, not lots - but some."

"Who?"

"Older people."

I was still reeling. How could you live without a television?

"What do you do nights?"

"Here with you, mostly."

"Yeah, but when you're not here – when you're home?"

Rip shrugged. "We listen to the wireless sometimes – I mean, the radio."

We burst out laughing.

"You homos are right cheeky bastards!"

That was probably why he liked the den so much, because of the television. We didn't just watch telly, of course; we mucked about in the streets, kicked balls about in the fields. None of us were really into football, though, which was unusual. Other boys lived and breathed it. Georgie Best was like a God to most of my school friends. Personally, I wouldn't have crossed the road to say hello to him. No offence. Just not my thing. We watched T.V and we chatted about this, that and the next thing: school, teachers, girls... The topic of girls was irresistible but often best avoided, given that none of us knew what we were talking about. The reality was that girls scared the hell out of us. They were strange, alien creatures; but creatures that smelt so delicious and could make you blush like a fucking beetroot just by glancing in your direction.

"Have you seen Stephanie Gillespie's sister?" Jimmy asked.

"She doesn't have one."

"Aye, she does - she's sixteen. She goes to the Academy."

"What's her name?"

"Joanna." He nodded sagely. He clearly had classified information and was going to milk it. "Do you know what her nickname is?"

We did not.

Jimmy held his hands a foot and a half in front of his chest. "Juggs Gillespie! Her diddies are ginormous!"

"Have you seen her?"

"No, but I've heard about her."

"Who from?"

"Different people."

"Who, Jimmy?"

"I'm not sure – can't remember."

Neither of us were convinced. This mythical, big breasted sister of the lovely Stephanie. Somehow it took the shine off her a little. How could you worship her when you knew she had a big hour glass of a sister strutting around at home, lording it over her?

"Jimmy, why did you tell us that?"

He huffed and puffed, it hadn't gone the way he wanted it to. "I was just trying to point out that if she's got big honkers then hopefully, one day – if we're lucky, Stephanie will have them too."

"How come we've never seen her?" Rip persisted. "I've seen Stephanie in the town before and she's always been with her mum or with friends – never with a sister with gigantic tits."

"I don't think she lives with her. It might be her half-sister. I don't know. I wish I hadn't fuckin' told you now."

"Are you sure, Jimmy, you didn't just dream it?"

"Fuck you, Turnbull!"

"Fuck you, Hood!"

There was an immediate, ominous silence.

It was a delicate situation. Jimmy loved laughter but hated to be laughed at; Rip's temper could easily be triggered by the invitation to fuck himself. The usually relaxed atmosphere of the den was suddenly filled with tension. Strange that could happen so quickly sometimes. You could become weirdly defensive over something that didn't even matter. I could see Rip was simmering. All it would take was one more bump. Jimmy was picking at his nails and looking utterly miserable.

"Here's a joke for you, lads. An Englishman, a Scotsman and an Irishman were on-"

"You're jokes are crap," Rip said.

Jimmy said nothing but there was a tiny nod of the head.

"What about you, Jimmy Cagney? Tell us one of your stories – go on."

He looked up from his nails. Sighed. Shook his head.

"Go on, Jimmy boy."

He took a deep breath.

"Alright, then. My dad told me this, he swears it's true. When he was at school he had a friend called Mervyn and they had this miserable oul bitch of a teacher called Miss Gillen. She was really old – at least thirty – always had her hair up and wore these big long dresses that covered every inch of skin from her chin to her ankles. They had another friend called Ivan who was a little bit ….simple, I suppose."

"A retard?"

This from Rip. Some progress.

"Not exactly. But he would've been on the bottom table -"

I held my breath and registered the flash of paralysed fear in Jimmy's eyes. Rip was on the bottom table.

"- Of course, he didn't have the street smart skills like the rest of the table and he was a crap fighter."

Good boy, good boy.

"Sounds like a dick," Rip said.

"Yeah, but a harmless dick. Anyway, Ivan loved Miss Gillen. He was always dreaming about her and he made the mistake of telling my dad and Mervyn."

"What age were they?" I asked, but I was trying to keep my contribution to a minimum.

"Secondary school. About fifteen. Anyway, one morning, my dad and his pal were walking to school when they saw an incredible sight." Jimmy's monotone had disappeared, he was coming to life again. "There was the bold Miss Gillen, except she looked totally different. She had her hair down around her shoulders and she wasn't wearing the horrible drippy dress and the daft goggle glasses."

"How did she see?"

"Contact lenses. She had a bit of lipstick on as well but, best of all, the blouse she was wearing had the top two buttons undone and you could see the top of her diddies – you know her..." he turned to me, "...what's it called?"

"Cleavage?"

"Yeah, that's right."

Rip leant forward. "It wasn't her, was it? It was her identical twin sister."

"No. It was her alright. My dad thinks what happened was that she probably met someone – like, her first boyfriend - and he completely changed her. Made her come out of her shell, you know like a butterfly out of its..." he looked earnestly to Rip, "what's it called?"

"Koo Koon." Rip said, with a little half grin.

You're a bloody genius, Jimmy Hood. Rip had answered the same question in class the week before and been on a high for days.

"Well, Dad and Mervyn could hardly believe their eyes. And then they had an idea. This would be perfect to play some sort of trick on Ivan. So, they had a little think about it. Miss Gillen taught them geography and guess what they had first period that day? She would be going straight to the staffroom and then to class so hardly anybody – except other teachers – would see her new look. So they ran to the classroom and there was poor Ivan, already at his desk, with his pencils all sharpened and ready to go."

"What did they say to him?"

"They started to act strange and talk gobbledegook."

"Gobble what?"

"You know, crazy talk that made no sense."

"You're making no sense."

"My dad started.

"Alright, Ivan," he says. "If an elephant and a kangaroo played table tennis which one do you think would win? Would they even be able to hold the bat?"

"Huh?" says big Ivan.

Then it was Mervyn's turn.

"Did you hear about John Wayne, Ivan? He's coming over here. He's gonna take over as the new headmaster. What do you think of that? Anyone gives him lip and he'll blow their head off!"

"You're making fun of me?"

"No, no, Ivan," my dad put a hand on his shoulder. "You're just having one of your dreams, son, don't worry. In fact, enjoy it, have a little fun – look! Here comes your girlfriend down the corridor. And look what she's done for you!"

And the poor bastard looked.

And his eyes widened and his mouth dropped open.

Miss Gillen looked like a movie star.

What a beauty! What a dream!

It had to be. There was just no other possibility.

He could do whatever he wanted.

Why?

Because before he got into trouble he would wake himself up.

"What happened then, Jimmy?" Rip's tongue was practically hanging out. "Did he try to kiss her?"

Jimmy took a long drag from my Coke can, enjoying the moment.

"Worse, lads. They were having too much fun to notice how excited big Ivan had become. My dad said, "Why don't you go up and give her a kiss Ivan? Remember, it's only a dream, nothing bad can happen. So Ivan howls like a dog, throws back the table, and runs towards Miss Gillen. But it's only then that they notice he's pulled down his zipper and his dick's sticking up like a barber's pole! Poor Miss Gillen screams like a banshee and points down at his thing then she runs down the corridor with Ivan chasing after her, his Charlie wobbling up and down like a yo-yo!"

I almost fell off the couch.

Rip, too cool to laugh out loud, had managed to restrain himself to a pink faced chuckle, "You are a lying bastard, Hood."

"It's true – I swear to ya!"

CHAPTER EIGHT

We were the three musketeers. Laughing and joking; chatting; watching the telly. We each had our area of expertise. Jimmy was definitely the joker of the pack. I was the movie expert who could tell you anything you wanted to know about old horror films (Boris Karloff's real name was William Henry Pratt) that you might want to know. For his part, Rip brought a little bit of politics into the den.

We had been watching Farrah Fawcett Majors and her two friends slow motion Kung Fu their way out of an awkward situation involving arms running and kidnapping. They were jiggling their diddies for no particular reason and Charlie was congratulating them.

Rip shook his head in disbelief.

"That would never work here."

"What wouldn't?"

"*Charlie's Angels*. It's okay for America 'cause there's hardly any crime over there – but over here? No chance. All their Kung Fu and tits? They'd be fucked."

"They wouldn't come here anyway," Jimmy mused. "It never rains where they are - look at their sun tans. It never stops raining here. You can't fight crime in the rain. The cameras would get all wet."

Rip held his hand up for silence and looked hard at us. "Lads, seriously, have you any idea at all how bad the situation is? What we're up against?"

"What do you mean?"

"I'm gonna trust you here. My big cousin Jack says that if we are not on our guard ... the I.R.A could take over the whole country."

It was hard to swallow.

"How would he know?"

Rip smiled secretively. "How would he know? Jack is in the U.D.A – do you know what that stands for?"

"Of course. Ulster Defence Association."

"Good. Jack is so high up that he was in charge of the petrol during the 1974 strike. That's a fact. If you needed petrol for your car, you had to go and ask our Jack for it. How does he know these things? Because it's his business to know – that's how! He looks after people like you and me and our parents and everybody else. He's also a part-time member of the R.U.C."

"Why did you wink just then?"

"What?"

"When you said that, you winked."

Rip shook his head in annoyance. "Not every Catholic is in the I.R.A – thank God, but nearly all of them support the I.R.A."

"Rip, I don't know if that's true."

"Believe me, Kev, I know these things. My family are more involved in the Troubles than yours are. Catholics want a united Ireland and that's what the I.R.A are murdering people for. Am I right? Catholics hate the British. Listen to this, during the Second World War, Catholics in Belfast used to open up their curtains at night time so that the German bombers knew where to bomb?"

"I didn't know that."

"That's a fact."

"Rip, what's the difference between the U.V.F and the U.D.A?" Jimmy wanted to know.

"The U.V.F stands for Ulster Volunteer Force," he was buzzing now. "It was started by a man called Gutsy Spence."

"But what's the difference? Do people not volunteer for the U.V.F as well?"

"Aye."

"So, why isn't it all called the same thing?"

Rip shrugged, clearly annoyed. "The important thing is that you need to know how dangerous Catholics are. Even the nice ones might seem to be friendly and harmless, but they're always listening to people's business and conversation – then reporting back."

"But we don't really know any Catholics to talk to. They all have their own schools and we have ours. We don't live together;

they've got their part of town and we've got ours."

"But we share the same buses and shops, don't we? It's not like in America, where the whites eat in different places than the blacks; we share nearly everything with the Catholics."

For some reason, despite my hatred of confrontation, I felt the need to argue. It was probably because I considered myself to be more intelligent than Rip and didn't enjoy being lectured at. "Rip, my dad deals with Catholics at his work and he says they're really nice. No difference between them and us, just a different religion."

"No fucking difference, Kevin? Catholics are in the minority now but how much longer do you think that will last?"

I knew now why he was annoying me so much. *In the minority.* He was just rhyming off shite that he had heard at home. Any idiot could do that.

"How many are in your family, Kevin?"

"You know damn well."

"Four. And three in Jimmy's and three in mines. Four kids in three Protestant families. How many kids do you think are in the average Catholic family?"

How much of this was from the mouth of Cousin Jack? How much from his parents, the pig farmers?

"Catholics have more kids – so what?"

"So what? All of those kids will one day have a vote and we'll be fucked. We'll be part of a united Ireland. The Protestants will be in the minority and they'll drown us in a bucket. That's why we have to stamp on them now while we still can!"

I said nothing. I was annoyed at his knowledge and my lack of. I hated watching the news – it bored me stupid - and mine was not a family that spoke much about the Troubles. Oddly, despite being slap bang in the middle of it, it didn't seem to really affect us all that much. We just seemed to accept the situation and get on with it. Of course, there were constant road checks and the occasional bombing, but largely we saw little action. Certainly, it would have been different had we lived closer to Belfast. Dad worked in the city and brought home stories of burnt out cars and flattened landscapes where once had stood buildings. There again, Dad did recount the story of his experience with a young British soldier off the Falls road where he had found himself in the early 1970's. He had taken a wrong turn as a result of a road closure and was told at a road block to get out of his "facking car." The story, when I first heard it, contrasted his friendliness with the curt, cockney swagger of the officer. Over the years, little bits had been added to it, including a shove in the back when Dad had been too slow producing his licence. It was best heard over the card table after he'd had a few drinks.

"Arrogant wee bastard! Nineteen if he was a day. Fuck me."

"Didn't you tell him you were a Proddy, Del-Boy?"

"Didn't get the chance."

This was the best bit, when he did the accent, it was like the Artful Dodger from Oliver Twist.

"'Oime not your Fackin' mate – mate! Turn arand! 'ands on the roof !'

And he shoves me – the prick – acting all hard in front of his mates."

"Why didn't you smack him one, Del?"

"You joking? His two little Action Man bum chums have their sights latched onto me. Trigger happy bastards. If that's the way they treat the Catholics all the time it's no wonder they're well pissed off. Pricks."

"I bet the Waltons were Catholics." Jimmy said thoughtfully. He counted them off on his fingers. "John-boy, Mary Ellen, Jason, Jim-Bob, Erin, Elizabeth – six."

"Six is small for a Catholic family." Rip grinned over at me. He knew he had annoyed me and he wanted to make amends. "Our Jack told me about this Catholic woman he heard tell about. She had a three bedroomed council house and they were all crammed in like sardines."

"Catholics do like fish," said Jimmy.

"She had her first kid at seventeen and her last at forty-seven. Thirty years of plopping them out like fuckin' tadpoles! Ran out of saints. How many do you think she had, Kev?"

I hated maths. Thirty multiplied by twelve, divided by nine, allowing for a little rest in between – oh, fuck it, "I don't know – tell me."

"Fourteen! Four – fucking – teen!"

"Is she still living?" Jimmy wanted to know. "We could get her on *Record Breakers*. Norris McWhirter could count all the children and Roy Castle could sing a song about it." He adopted a Louis Armstrong pose with fingers poised over imaginary trumpet keys.

"How many children can you seeeeeeeee?
Pomp-pa-pomp-pa-pomp-pa –pomp-pomp!
Fourteen Fenians up her faneeeeeee!
Pomp-pa-pomp-pa-pomp-pa –pomp-pomp!"

Rip burst out laughing. He never laughed out loud; he was letting himself go to prove there were no hard feelings between us. He meant well, did Rip. I began to feel a bit shameful for giving him such a hard time.

*

Exactly a week later, I asked Dad if Rip was right about the possibility of war. Eighteen soldiers had been killed by the IRA in Warrenpoint and, later that day, they had killed Lord Mountbatten, his grandson and another boy, in an explosion off the coast of Sligo. It was big news. Huge.

"You're not in danger, son, of course not." His face was ashen as he stared at the television, clutching Mum's hand. "Why did you ask that, Kevin?"

"Something Tommy said."

"What did he say?"

I told him and he shook his head in disgust. "That's what's wrong with this country, Doreen. Daft wee lads being spoon fed this tripe. Kevin, what happened today was horrible and wrong. The people that did that deserve to be hanged; but they're just a tiny drop in the ocean. You understand? Most people here just want to live their lives peacefully. Okay?"

"Yes, Dad."

"Belfast will be jumping tomorrow, Doreen. I worry about the car. I'm always too late for the car park. Maybe, I should just get the bus tomorrow – what do you think?"

She nodded, snuggled closer to him, and stayed that way long after my bedtime, with the dishes still grimy in the sink and all thought of my bath forgotten. She just held him, running her hands through his receding hair. It was a strange sight, as if she was his mother and not his wife. It made me feel funny but it was kind of nice too. Finally, she pulled herself away from him and signalled to me and Pete that it was time for teeth and bed. I watched as Dad pulled himself up from the couch. I had never thought of him as old until tonight but now he looked sluggish and unbelievably fatigued, like a once great boxer called upon for one final round and having nothing left to give. He caught me looking at him and mustered a lacklustre smile.

"Did I ever tell you about the time I came off my bike?"

I shook my head sleepily although he had mentioned it before.

"A bit younger than you, seven or eight. My dad gave me ten minutes head start when we were coming back from his sister's house. I must have been doing forty miles an hour when I blew a puncture. Jesus. I took it all on the knees – sliced the skin off myself; screaming like a banshee – I've never known the like of it. It was as if someone had poured petrol all over my legs and tossed me a match. I thought the pain would never go – thought I was gonna die of it – but eventually it did, a little anyway, and I sat by the roadside, sobbing my heart out, looking at my busted bike and praying for my dad to hurry up. A car pulls up – a green Austin 10 – and this man gets out, I've never seen him before in my life, and he looks down at me and his face is all full of concern and he says, "What happened, son? Did you come off your bike?" He answered his own question which was just as well because I'm still snivelling with snot running down my nose. In between the snivels and the sniffs I tell him about my dad coming soon and he does the weirdest thing: he goes back to his car, says something to the passenger, and the next thing you know the Austin 10 is pulling away and yer man is sitting beside me on the grass verge. A big grown man, sitting on the wet grass. And he starts talking to me about everything – the weather, the cricket, Robert Newton and Errol Flynn – and I know he's doing it to kill time and to take my mind off my bloody knees. And every now and then he smiles at me – and you know what, Kevin? It's the kindest, warmest smile you ever could imagine; and this is a stranger – I've never met him before in my life."

"What did your dad say to him?"

"He thanked him. Shook his hand. Gave him a lift to wherever the Austin 10 had gone."

"What was his name, Dad?"

"I don't know, son. I don't think he ever said. And the funny thing is, I never saw him again; but I reckon I must have thought about him at least a thousand times. That little act of kindness. The way he smiled at me. Here is something I know for a fact, Kevin. The world is full of people like that man. For every horrible person, there are a hundred kind and decent souls who will do you a good deed if they can. You don't always hear much about them because they're really quiet and humble; but they're out there and they always will be. You understand?"

I nodded, and without even thinking, ran over and gave him a hug. He smelt of *Old Spice* and I kept it going for as long as I could. He was always warm and welcoming, but a hug from him was a rare thing unless I initiated it myself and there never seemed to be a right time. Now felt right. Perfect. And I relished it.

CHAPTER NINE

Even at our lowly level, the events in Warrenpoint and the death of Mountbatten were keenly felt. The streets around the school were strangely deserted; the atmosphere in the classroom hushed, teachers whispering in corridors and shaking their heads in stunned disbelief.

"I've finished my book, Mrs Allan." Wendy Williams had her hand up. "What should I do now?"

Mrs Allan was all about reading. Her enthusiasm knew no boundaries. Usually, and Wendy knew this well, it would be: *Oh, well done, Wendy Williams – you are a champion reader! Look to the front class. Remind me again, please, what's the very best way of enhancing your vocabulary?*

Class: By being a good reader, Mrs Allan!

Correct, class. And who has one of the best vocabularies that has ever been seen in Primary six?

Class: Wendy Williams, Mrs Allan!

Correct again, class. Wendy, tell us something about your book...

But today Mrs Allan couldn't care less about reading or vocabulary or creepy Wendy Williams. She just looked up at her, mildly irritated, and said: "Find another book from the back, Wendy."

Good at reading books, Wendy was shit at reading people. "I've read them all, Mrs Allan."

"Then draw a picture, Wendy!"

"A picture? What of?"

"WHATEVER YOU LIKE, DEAR! WHATEVER YOU DAMN WELL LIKE!"

It was awful what happened to those poor soldiers; but seeing Mrs Allan brutalize Wendy Williams just for finishing her reader was flipping fantastic.

Mrs Allan would not have known the soldiers but maybe she was imagining how awful it would be to lose a son in those circumstances. Did she have children? Were you more sympathetic when a young person died if you had children of your own? I remembered how Dad had looked last night and thought you probably were.

Rip caught up with me and Jimmy at lunch-time. He looked very serious but also very smug. "Well, lads? Anybody doubt what I said now?"

There was no reasonable answer to that and he had the grace to be silent for a moment. The playground was buzzing again by now: skipping ropes, chases, various football matches. Children are very resilient and have short term memories. They all knew that something bad had happened but, once acknowledged, there was little else for them to do but get back to their everyday activities. The only grim faces on the playground now were the three retired women who helped patrol during lunch, making sure there were no silly disputes.

"Look at them," Rip shook his head in dismay. "The youth of today. How quick they are to forget."

Me and Jimmy pissed ourselves. It felt amazing; the first proper laugh since the massacre.

"What?"

"The youth of today? It's like something my granddad's granddad would say."

"I'm glad you find it funny, lads. This is a very serious situation. Mountbatten, by Christ; never thought they would go that far."

"Had you heard of him before last night, Rip?" I asked, careful to keep a straight face.

"Course I bloody had. He was the emperor of India. The fucking queen's cousin! They don't get much higher than Lord Louis."

Eighteen soldiers and the queen's cousin. No matter what way you tried to digest the information, it was still mind boggling. The thing I couldn't quite grasp was the idea of excess. Why the hell did they have to blow up the old man as well? After Warrenpoint, couldn't they just have gone home, put their feet up and been content? It was like telling someone that they had cancer and then, just for spite, telling them they had an ingrowing toe nail as well.

"I don't like to panic you lads, but I honestly think our country might now be under attack. I know that sounds a bit heavy but this really was a major strike. This wasn't a daft wee bomb under a car or some poor bastard getting knee-capped. This is huge, lads – and that's a fact!"

The bell rang and we began to move towards the lines.

"I've got a few ideas," Rip said, tapping the end of his nose as his line began to inch forward. "I'll miss the den tonight, stuff to do, but tomorrow I might try to bring a special person – if that's okay?"

"It's not Jack, is it?"

"God, no. Our Jack's far too busy to come farting along to our wee den. It's someone else I think you'll find interesting..."

*

It was after six and we were on the edge of the sofa trying to look cool. I'd had a bath and splashed some of Dad's Old Spice on my face; Jimmy too looked spruced up and party ready.

"Do you think he's bringing a girl, Kev?"

"No."

But of course, the thought had occurred to me – a split second after he had proposed bringing someone.

"What if it's Stephanie Gillespie?"

I felt a strange sensation in my testicles. My stomach churned and the blood seemed to race through my veins just that little bit quicker. God could not be as cruel as that. People might be dying all around me but he would never allow that to happen.

"What if he's got his arm around her?" Jimmy persisted. "What if she's all giggly and says something like, "Oh, Rippy, that feels so nice. Later on, if I'm good, will you give my diddies a little squeezy?"

I punched him in the arm and we were all set for a rug wrestle when the door of the den burst open and in walked Rip and his guest.

"Grab a seat, Sam. Lads, sorry I'm a wee bit late, had a bit of business to attend to and a bit of shopping," he held up a Woolworths bag, exchanged a knowing look with Sam, and sat down beside his guest. "Sam's a friend of the family – a real solid guy. I've asked him here tonight to help us make sense of this."

We nodded. There was nothing else for it. All eyes were on Sam who, naturally, took his time. This was his moment. He was about fourteen, and those four years might just as well have been twenty-four. There was a little aura about him even before he opened his mouth. He had experience under his belt. Wherever he had been and whatever he had done, we had not.

"Alright, lads. Rip tells me you're okay so that's good enough for me." He leant towards us and so did Rip. "I'm going to tell you a few things and they're to go no further than these four walls – understand?"

"Do you want us to take a blood oath?" Jimmy asked and even Rip cringed.

"No mate, if your blood's gonna be spilled it'll not be by me."

Rip's chest swelled at that and he nodded fiercely at us. His friend was a fucking poet to boot. Christ, we were really getting our money's worth this evening.

"I am a member of the U.Y.M. Do you know what that stands for? – not you, Rip."

We both shook our heads.

"Ulster Young Militants. It's the youth wing of the U.D.A. We're the life's blood of the U.D.A. Rip's cousin Jack – I know you've heard of him – him and his pals wouldn't be able to do what they do if we didn't do what we did."

"What do you do?"

He lent back on the sofa, and so did Rip. "We scare the fuck out of the Fenians. We terrorise the terrorists."

"Did I tell ya?" Rip beamed. "Huh? Did I tell ya?"

"What sort of things do you do?" Jimmy asked.

Sam gave a little cough and massaged his throat with his fingers - in an instant, Rip reached into his bag and cracked him

71

open a can of Coke. "Thanks, Rip." He took a long slug, belched, offered the can around. "These three Taigs, thought they were fuckin' hard men, smashed all the windies in old Mrs McDowell's house. Well, me and a few of my mates found out where they lived and we gave their names to the big boys but they said, "Naw, lads, you deal with it – go on yerself!"

"What did you do?" said Jimmy again.

Sam smiled at the memory. "We went round to their house, killed their dog –"

"You killed their dog?" I was appalled. I thought of Snowy at home and how I would feel if someone so much as looked at her the wrong way. I'd put their eyes out. "Why the fuck did you kill their dog?"

Rip glared at me and Sam visibly stiffened. I knew what I'd done to the atmosphere but I was damned if I was going to apologise.

"Kevin, you need to harden yourself," Rip advised. "These are tough times – they kill our soldiers and Kings of India, we kill their dogs."

Sam took a few breaths and softened a little. "I'm sorry, I should've explained. We didn't kill it just for badness. We had to kill it because it was a mean fucker. You see, they kept it as a weapon not a pet. They half-starved the poor thing and then it attacked anything that moved. It was better off dead. I shouldn't even have mentioned it."

"Sorry, Sam," Rip gave me the eyes again. "Go on with your story and we'll try our *best* not to interrupt again."

"Thanks, Rip. Me and my mates surrounded their house. We'd brought two big fucking Lambeg drums with us and we started to hammer the fuck out of them. Christ, what a racket! We could see their windies rattling in the frames and they're looking out. At first they're glowering at us trying to be all hard – but then you could see the fear in their eyes. Fuckin' brilliant, lads. They were shittin' themselves."

"Didn't they call the police?" Jimmy asked.

I thought Rip would be pissed but far from it, he was

delighted with the question, he had heard the story before.

"Aye, they called the police; but it didn't do them any good," Sam winked.

Rip winked.

Everybody was winking.

"It seemed the police were too busy that night to come out. Shame. They must have phoned their pals too but – big surprise – they didn't show up either."

"So what happened?"

"The crowd got bigger and the drums got louder. Finally, I told the lads to stop and I knocked on the door, all polite like. No answer. So I stuck my mouth to the letter box and I yells in: "Whataboutyee, lads? Listen, we'll leave you in peace right now and we won't bother you again, it's real simple. All you have to do is come out and throw bricks through your own windies – the way you broke old Mrs McDowells. Okay?"

"Why didn't you do it yourself?"

"Are you joking? That would be breaking the law."

Rip roared at that and slapped a hand off his knee.

"Did they do it, Sam?" Jimmy was wide eyed. "Did they break their own windows - windies?"

"They did lads, they did. Next morning every single windie in that shitty wee house was smashed."

"And that's a fact!" Rip added.

CHAPTER TEN

I would like to kill the person who invented the Eleven Plus.
It must have been a man.
A woman could never be so cruel.
I would like to kill him slowly by cutting him into eleven pieces
and showing him each piece before the final cut.
That would be nice.

CHAPTER ELEVEN

Pete was well established at the Academy by the time I started Primary six and it was the greatest place that the world had ever known. It had its own tennis courts, rugby fields, all weather hockey ground and even its own swimming-pool. The female teachers were all young and glamorous and the male teachers were more like mates; they treated you like young adults and it felt more like a college than a secondary school.

Places in the school were keenly sought. To secure his, Pete had passed the Eleven Plus examination in Primary seven and it was this formidable test that I would now have to practise for. The preparation began in earnest now, with verbal reasoning tests every Monday afternoon with Mrs McBurney.

Mrs McBurney was one of those teachers you never saw outside of class. You never saw her shopping for groceries; you never saw her out with her husband; you never even saw her at church. This was simply because, outside of the classroom, she did not exist. When the door closed behind you, her arms would drop to her sides and her head would slump forward like the robot in *Lost In Space.* Then, as preprogrammed, she would propel herself to the walk in cupboard where she would remain, recharging, until the next week. Every fibre of her mechanical being was focussed on verbal reasoning strategies and she had little time for anyone who did not share her joy in such glorious word play.

"When I was a young girl I taught myself to recite the alphabet backwards." Her chins wobbled a little as she gazed into the middle distance, remembering her girlhood. "Don't ask me why I did it, I just did. I suppose it was just for the challenge of it."

"Can you still do it, Mrs McBurney?"

"Go on, do it!"

Arse kissers. Still, I was glad of any distraction. Anything at all that would bite into that hideously long fifty minutes.

Deep breath.

"ZYXWVUTSRQPONMLKJIHGFEDCBA!"

Round of applause.

Mrs McBurney was beaming.

Julie Truesdale even managed "That's brilliant," under her breath, but loud enough for the old girl to hear. No surprise that Truesdale was a whizz at the verbal reasoning. I can see her now – the bitch – with her stupid fucking plaits. "My hair's never, ever been cut and it never will be – just like Rapunzel. Tee, hee." I used to dream of creeping up behind her with a pair of sharp garden sheers and slicing them off.

And I found out a terrible truth in Mrs McBurney's class.

What others found easy, I found difficult.

What others found quite hard, I found impossible.

Or is that just a fancy way of saying I was stupid and they were clever?

Maybe.

But I don't think so.

I was on the second highest table and there were boys on the table below who got better marks than me on every single verbal reasoning test we did. So was it just my nerves that crippled me? If you took away the anxiety of failure would that of helped? Perhaps. But thinking that did not help me. Everyone was in the same shark infested water. The difference was that they were swimming safely towards shore and the big fluffy bathing towel; I was sinking fast and the Great White was licking his lips beneath me.

The actual test itself was split into two fifty minute papers: language and a warped kind of arithmetic. The language questions I could manage:

Fill in the blanks in the following sentences with suitable words. There is no need to write the sentences out. Simply put the number of the sentence and after it write the word which you think is correct.

> (1) *Finger is to hand as _____ is to foot.*
> (2) *Den is to fox as _____ is to bees.*
> (3) *Ounce is to weight as inch is to _____.*
> (4) *Umpire is to tennis as _____ is to football.*

(5)   Construction is exactly opposite in meaning to de___.
(6)   Dw ___ is exactly opposite in meaning to giant.
(7)   Beauty is exactly opposite in meaning to _____.
(8)   So _____ is exactly opposite in meaning to joy.

I enjoyed writing essays so this kind of question was reasonably straightforward although still reaching towards a level of sophistication that was new to me. As well as these there were punctuation and grammar questions, other gaps to be filled, strange words that you never used to be sought and inserted.

It was the mathematical questions that did for me. I just couldn't do them. *I just could not fucking do them!* I've heard people since – motivational arseholes – say that nothing is impossible if you put your mind to it. Man taught himself to fly, conquered Everest, walked on the moon. True. But they were the elite. I knew that I would never dance on the moon or stand astride the summit of Everest. And there were parts of the Eleven Plus examination that– even with all the practise and teaching in the world – I would *never, ever* be able to do. That was the terrifying thought.

It began easy, of course, they always did, to sucker you in:
Write in figures the sum of ninety-five and four hundred and eleven.

Fine.

But then:
A train leaves London at 11.30 am and arrives at Bristol at 1.30pm, after stopping from 12.10pm to 12.20 pm at Reading, which is 36 miles from London. It travelled both parts of the journey at the same rate. Find the distance from London to Bristol.

Jesus, God.

I hope the train crashes and they all fucking die.
Mary is 12 years old and her father is 42. Answer these questions:
(a) How old was Mary's father when he was 4 times as old as Mary?
(b) In how many years' time will her father be 3 times as old as Mary?

(c) How old will Mary be when her father is 10 times as old as Mary was 6 years ago?

I didn't even know where to begin. When, where, how or why?

A library has 2,672 "A" books and 5,172 "B" books. During the year in "A" section 514 new books are bought, 398 are moved to "B" section, and 23 are lost. In "B" section, 297 are sent to salvage or lost. How many are there in each section at the end of the year?

Mrs McBurney would demonstrate one or two on the board – she may as well have employed her ability to talk backwards – then she would make a little zip gesture on her lips and indicate that it was time for us to try the examples. I hated that little gesture almost as much as I hated her. It meant it was time for the torture to begin.

Tick Tock.

I can see myself now: the slippery pencil gripped betwixt my sweaty sausage fingers; the discomfort of my belt digging into the flab at my waist; the near proximity of the radiant Stephanie Gillespie and, above all else, my complete and utter inability to work out how many marbles Albert has lost if he has the same amount as the three other boys at the start of the game but now has five less than George, seven more than Dan and nine more than stupid fucking Charles who has been left with thirty-three.

The majority of the rest of them *did* find it easier - that was the real kick in the stomach. If the lights in your house suddenly go out you run to the window to check the street. If all the lights are out you rejoice that it's not just you; you couldn't care less that some poor bastard's life support machine has just packed in and he's even now gasping his last breaths. If they had all been clearly stuck I would have felt better; but they weren't, they simply *weren't*.

Stephanie would give the top of her pencil a delicious little nibble as she pondered the problem then, a tiny nod, and she was away, scribbling down the answer and moving onto the next.

Big Stanley Brownlie did look slightly more perplexed, but even he seemed to make steady progress, scratching away in his jotter with strangely delicate pencil skills that belied his huge girth. Size was no handicap here. His arse might well take up two seats – one for each buttock – but he could still work out how many tins of sardines were in the third case if the total was 789 tins and the first case contained 260 tins, two and a half times more than the second case.

But the worst part, the very worst part, was this:

Jimmy Hood could do them.

My best friend.

He could do them and I couldn't.

He was better than me.

I would glance over at him, I had time to spare, and he would look up and wink. Wink, for God's sake. And it wasn't a smart-ass "I can and you can't" sort of wink – it was the same friendly "How's it going, Kevin?" wink he had given me so many times before.

If Jimmy Hood has winked at Kevin McBride 547 times over the last five years, how many more times, allowing for leap years and full moons, can he wink at him before Kevin sticks the sharp end of his pencil into his eye?

"I just find them quite easy," Jimmy was unapologetic in the den. "Maybe, it's because Dad's good with numbers – you know, at work. They don't really bother me."

It bothered me plenty.

"Do you practise with your dad?

He shook his head like I knew he would. It had been a stupid question. I was just desperate for some answers. The world was round and the sun was orange; and Jimmy Hood was not meant to be cleverer than me – at anything.

"I don't know why you two are so bothered about the Eleven Plus," Rip chipped in. "I know your brother goes there, Kev, but the Academy's for poofters. Snobby little faggots who wank each other off."

Rip had opted not to sit the Eleven Plus which was allowed; in fact, it was positively encouraged as it reduced the numbers and ensured that the High School had sufficient bodies to maintain its role.

"I can't wait to go to the High School."

"Aren't you scared of First Year Friday?"

He gave a contemptuous little snort. "Nobody's gonna be putting my head down any toilet. If there's any shit to be eaten, Rip Turnbull will be dishing it out."

Big, brave words; but I'd seen even a tough guy like Rip – who claimed to have all kinds of connections up top – quivering in the playground when the big boys from above yelled down upon us. The huge grey building, twice the size of our primary, was perched on top of the hill, surrounded by a six foot tall fence. During our break and lunch time you could hear the noises of them from above – the callous laughter, the shouts, the scuffles; and the language, dear God, the language. Down below, we were "bloodies" and "shits" and the occasional "fuck;" from above we heard "Cocksucker," "Cunt," "Fenian bastard," and every mother insult you could imagine. Scary shit. They were a different breed. Even the small, skinny ones were gigantic. You would see them striding effortless up the hill in their coal black uniforms, bags slung carelessly over their shoulders, jostling each other. Sometimes, you would see the better looking boys holding hands with girls. *Holding hands.* There was an almost visible aura around them; an unnatural maturity, a vicious, sadistic knowingness.

Sometimes, when they had nothing better to do, they would stand at the perimeter fence and shout down to us.

"Hey, Dick Face! Yeah, you! Tell your ma' I want my money back – she's given me the clap!"

"Yo, homo! Is that your boyfriend? You fucking better say yes or I'll kick your cunt in!"

I was usually safe enough, especially in the company of Fatty Brownlie, but occasionally my jaw made me a target.

"Hey, Rubber lip! White nigger! Do you want a banana?"

The trick was to look scared (which wasn't that hard) and laugh at the expense of yourself and others – even if they were your friends. The High School boys were hyper aware of anyone trying to salvage a little dignity by ignoring their comments or displaying loyalty:

"Hey, you little faggot! Are you fucking deaf? Didn't you hear me call your ma a whore? What are you going to do about it? That's right – nothing! Don't you ever blank me again you little prick!"

It didn't happen often, but often enough for you to fear even glancing in an upwards direction. I can remember seeing a boy I recognised up there and marvelling at the transformation. Darren Crawford. He was three years older than us and he had been the unofficial king of Primary. In his last year at the school, he had been captain of the football team; ball under his arm, breaking up fights, always leading the line back into the school. The teachers loved and respected him too and would quite happily have headed off to the pub and left Mr Crawford in charge. He had gone up to the High School and when I next saw him he was standing to the left of a large group of boys who were hurling down abuse at Mandy Tuft who had once eaten a worm in the playground because two other girls told her it stopped you from getting cancer. Darren said nothing; but every time they said something he would burst out laughing; every time they made a mocking little gesture, he would ape it and look for approval. They would move to the right and he would move to the right; they would take a step to the left and he would do likewise. Jesus, Darren - if they stuck a finger up their arse would you do the same? Where's your dignity, man? Twice, trying to recapture former glories, he had visited his old school and hung out with us kids, a brave warrior back from the battlefront; but I wasn't buying it. I had seen him up above.

Still, for six years, I hadn't given the place much thought; there had been enough to worry me down below. I think I had assumed (arrogantly) that there was absolutely no way that I would be setting foot in the place – therefore, no point even thinking about it. Here now was a brand spanking new anxiety: the very real possibility that I would fail the Eleven Plus and end up having to go to the High School.

It was unthinkable.

I had no idea what lay inside that huge, grey building but my imagination was happy to fill the void. Endless, echoing corridors crammed with massive, sneering lads – all of them with nothing at all to do except focus their attention on the little fat new boy with the under bite and the funny lip. Mud laden rugby scrums; towel flicking and sweaty showers; great hairy dicks and swinging balls.

Jesus Christ on the cross, please help me.

Of course, Pete was eager to assist. In a moment of weakness, I had asked him if he'd found the Eleven Plus difficult and if he would help coach me. He told me that it was one of the easiest things he had ever done and that he would love to help me except the question books were hard to find and also, to be honest, it was the sort of thing that you were either good at or not. He looked closely at me and I could see him thinking hard, composing.

"I'm busy just now."

I knew he wasn't.

"I'll get back to you – okay?"

He found me later and what he said, as near as I can remember, was this:

"You see, the dilemma you have is that you have to extrapolate all the relevant, salient information from the conundrum. In order to be able to do that, you must first contemplate the ramifications of the various statistics and data you are presented with. Does that help? I've tried to make it as simple as I could."

I thanked him for his time.

Later, I sneaked into his room and saw, beside the dictionary, the statement he had presented me with. How much time had he spent looking up the words and memorising it?

He really was a wanker.

CHAPTER TWELVE

I began Primary seven and my teacher was Mr Palmer. I had a brand new school bag; pencils, rubber, sharpener; and a lethal looking mathematical compass which was, and remains, a mystery to me. This was the big one. The Eleven Plus year. My life had reached a major crossroads. Up to the right lay the Academy and all the splendours it had to offer; down to the left was the High School and the thought of it had all but ruined my entire summer holiday. I had a school trip to London at the end of the year but just now I couldn't even think about it, there were too many obstacles in the way.

We were allowed to choose our seats so me and Jimmy sat at the front – Jimmy, to be beside me, myself, to show Palmer a conscientious attitude. There were about twenty-five kids in the class, eighteen of us sitting the exam. Rip sat beside Jon Park who had joined the school the year before. You had to feel sorry for him on account of his neck. The doctor had made a blunder when he was born and yanked him out too quickly and as a result he couldn't hold his neck up straight and looked like he was always questioning you even when you said nothing. Stephanie Gillespie, sneaky bitch, had sourced and befriended the ugliest girl in Primary seven, Sally Clarke, and the result was a contrast that could give you a nose bleed, like Rita Hayworth holding hands with an Orangutan.

Palmer's class was like a little museum. The desks themselves were decades old with the initials of bygone students carved beside the obsolete ink wells. The sense of history you experienced was sometimes overwhelming. Who was A.W and did he still love J.H? Was he still alive, somewhere in the town, a downtrodden middle-aged nobody with dreams long since dashed? How much of his essence remained here in this grimy little desk?

There was art work on the walls displaying ability that I could only dream of: incredibly detailed renditions of local landmarks, shops and monuments. Prominently featured was an A3 sized pencil drawing of the town post office; if you got up close to it you could clearly see the glazed dimples on the window panes and the tiny weeds growing up through the cracks in the pavement outside.

But the back of the room was where the real treasures lay. A dozen or more dust covered jars of varying sizes. Within each, carefully preserved in alcohol, were things that once had been alive. I could have stared at them for hours. Frogs that stared balefully at you through milky blind eyes; strange little fish from the depths of some far off lake; a drooping stingray that looked like a sad old pancake.

My favourite was the baby crocodile. It was about six inches long, a perfect miniature version of some gigantic, tail swishing grandfather. The old Tarzan movies always featured a razor toothed croc. It would always feast on some poor native who had fallen out of his canoe. Tarzan would be too late to save him but would dive into the middle of it to save the white girl. You'd see him tumbling over and over with this huge rubber thing – then a close up of him with his knife (hair all tousled) as he plunged the blade into its heart – then you'd see it floating belly up.

Except this little baby crocodile was the real deal. I would give the jar a little shake, watch it float around in slow, sad circles. Had he been missed? Probably not. Were animals even capable of such emotion? Disney would have you believe that mummy crocodile had searched the swamp for weeks after his disappearance weeping crocodile tears (ha ha) and mourning her loss. No. But it certainly was a sad fate for an Amazonian crocodile to have ended up in a jar on the shelf of a Primary seven class in County Down, Northern Ireland; preserved for all eternity for all the wee Protestant kids to gawk at.

There were stuffed animals as well. Badgers, squirrels, a barn owl and a mongoose. All of them frozen artificially in some stereotypical aspect. Every time I looked at them I thought of Norman Bates. No one had ever seen Palmer's mother. Was she even now sitting at home in her rocker, eyes bulging with cotton wool, mouth pulled back into a toothy grin? Alas, no. Palmer lived with his wife and had two adult sons. But it was fun to imagine.

By this stage I was reasonably familiar with Mr Palmer. His speciality was geography and he taught one off lessons throughout the school – anything from sugar planting to mountain formation. His temper was not nearly as volcanic as Pete had wanted me to believe but he still was a man who commanded respect. He was not exceptionally tall but gave the impression of height because of his cadaverous frame; he possessed an amazing arm span and the ability to reach and grab you suddenly if he thought you were not paying attention. When I first saw him do this I was reminded of my Stretch Armstrong toy. The manufacturer's claim was that his arms could stretch to beyond two metres without breaking. This proved to be too much of a challenge for me and Jimmy and we tug of warred the poor bastard into exhaustion before tossing him into a ditch. Palmer's infamous ear twist would soon (along with the slipper, cane and strap) be outlawed and, clearly aware of this, he was twisting with gay abandon when I arrived in his class, desperately trying to satisfy the urge before it was permanently denied him.

"This is without doubt the most important year in your education thus far," he intoned. The other thing about him was that he had quite a nasally twang. "You will undergo two fifty minute tests, the results of which will have a monumentally influential effect on your lives!"

I gulped. I couldn't help it.

And the bastard swooped.

"That's right, McBride, you would do well to look nervous. Fifty minutes to get it right. Fifty minutes. What's your favourite television show, McBride?"

He called the girls by their Christian names and the boys by their surnames.

"*The Six Million Dollar Man*, sir."

Oh God, oh God, where are you going with this? How many zeros are in six million? That's easy – six! Too easy. Oh no, I know, how many *pounds* is six million dollars? That's what it'll be.

"I've seen it a few times myself," Palmer said.

My eyes widened.

"Yes, my five year old grandson is a big fan and I sometimes have to watch it with him."

Ah, sarcasm, that was another of his traits.

"That show lasts about fifty minutes – correct? That's how long you've got to make sure of your future. From the time Steve Whatshisname crash lands until he winks at the camera and the credits roll. That's how long you've got!" He scratched his chin thoughtfully, all the while impaling me with his eyes. "Did you see much of the Moscow Olympics, McBride?"

I nodded. We'd all been glued to the screen. The Yanks didn't go. Americans don't like Russians. Steve Ovett and Sebastian Coe. My favourite had been the little bald Ethiopian fella, Yifter the shifter. He ran the five and ten thousand metres. Everybody was gasping on the last lap and then – he just took off sprinting! Magic.

Yifter the shifter.

"Remember Alan Wells?"

I nodded again. One hundred metres champion. Who could forget his wife? She screamed his name when he ran –

COME ON, ALAN!!

– The other sprinters were too busy clamping their ears to dip for the line.

Palmer threw it out to the rest of the class. "Hands up! Who knows who Alan Wells is?"

Of the twenty-five, about eighteen put their hands up. Not bad. Well done, Alan.

"Yes, Brownlie."

"He won the one hundred metres, sir."

"Correct, Brownlie. Fancy you knowing about the hundred metres dash!"

Sniggers and giggles.

Despite my anxiety I glanced over at Stephanie; sometimes

her diddies wobbled when she giggled. But she hadn't joined in. Classy.

"McBride, if Mr Wells had run that famous race point ten of a second slower he would have been awarded a silver medal, not a gold. You would not have seen him standing to attention to God Save the Queen, he wouldn't be famous, he wouldn't be rich, and I guarantee you that eighteen hands would not have risen a moment ago. Point ten of a second, Mr McBride, the difference between fame and fortune and being a nobody. Understand?"

I nodded, although I wasn't sure what it had to do with anything.

He drew our attention to the chalk board. "The preparation begins in earnest here, ladies and gentlemen. Take a close look at this little problem."

A gardener started to plant 10 rows of cabbage plants at 10.15am. He planted the first 6 rows at the rate of 5 rows in 25 minutes, and the last 4 rows at the rate of 3 rows in 33 minutes. At what time did he finish the 10 rows?

It was a psychological blockage, it had to be. They can't have been that difficult and I can't have been that thick. I tried so hard. I swear to God I did. I'd scribble down the figures - scribble some of them out - scribble them back again - add them and subtract them. Get muddled. Flustered. Round about then I would think about the High School and imagine my trousers being pulled down and everyone laughing at my tiny thing whilst my head was being thrust down the toilet on top of a great big pile of deenge. Then I would glance hotly around at the rest of them and see on their faces how easy they were finding it. That done, I would return to my own page, feel the clamminess of my palms and pray to God that the ground would open up and swallow me whole. I didn't mind if the devil was there; I didn't mind if I never saw my parents again; just take me away please! And if that wasn't possible, then at least please do not look to me for an answer. Do not ask me. Do not ask me.

"Right, McBride, times up – what have you got? What time did he finish the ten rows?"

Along with the sarcasm and humiliation, there must have been some kind of teaching I'm sure. I don't remember. I zoned out. When you have completely given up on something any kind of lifeline becomes more hassle than it is worth. Why waste the energy when you are certain that the rope is going to snap or that the avalanche is going to kill you anyway?

Sometimes, on a good day, the clouds would clear for just a moment and the sun would find me. On those days, for some reason, I found it possible to predict that Mr Milroy travelled three miles extra on day four than he had managed on day two, allowing for the fact that he stopped off at a shop and purchased three cans of beans, two of which were half the price of the third which itself had been reduced by 40%. That was the worst of it: the knowledge that somewhere in amongst all the angst, I actually could do the damn thing. These brief glimmers of hope served only to torment; the clouds were always amassing.

Dad would have helped and he did go into Belfast to find some obscure little shop that sold the hateful verbal reasoning tests. I didn't want him to tutor me though. He was always tired from work but that wasn't it; whatever faults he had, he always found time for me. He was clever and had passed the tests himself; but passing them and teaching someone else were two separate skills.

The real truth was that I was terrified of him knowing how stupid I was. That would kill me. He knew the scores I was getting but to have my stupidity confirmed eye to eye, first hand? His look of frustration at his own inability to teach me and then seeing the disappointment on his face that I was not as clever as he had thought. I'd never be able to watch a movie with him again or share a sly joke under Mum's radar. It was unbearable. Much better to suffer in solitude. He could interpret the scores whatever way he liked and he did:

"You're like a champion boxer, Kevin – saving it all for the big night. Think of Ali before the second Spinks fight! He didn't look great in sparring and then – kapow!.. AND THE NEW HEAVYWEIGHT CHAMPION – KEVIN MCBRIDE!"

*

Every second Sunday we visited my grandparents in Carrickfergus. Granny only had a little table so she fed Mum and Dad first, then I had the pleasure of Pete's company all to myself. Mincemeat, potatoes and carrots. I would mash mine all together then use the fork to make railway tracks on top. Pete would look disdainfully at me across the table even though he had done the exact same thing right up until the Academy.

"Granny, we were learning about snakes the other day in school."

"Oh, I hate snakes, Peter – horrible things. Thank God for Saint Patrick."

"But they're really interesting, Granny. Did you know that a lot of them can dislocate their jaws so they can get more food into their mouths?"

"They can do what, son?"

Pete was happy to demonstrate by pushing out his lower jaw. "They are so greedy they can actually make their jaws go bigger to get the food down."

"I didn't know that. Kevin did you know that?"

"Can you imagine how disgusting that must look, Granny?" and he gave himself a little shiver, "horrible, greedy things."

Granda was a travelling salesman, still working into his seventieth year. He was never without his pipe and I used to watch him, mesmerised, as he compressed the tobacco with his thumb, clamped down, struck the match and inhaled. The resulting cloud of smoke was a wonderful sight to behold and the process of preparing and lighting his pipe afforded him time to collect his thoughts and weigh up the situation.

"I saw something on the news yesterday that fair turned my stomach," he took his pipe out, pulled a face at me as if he was about to be sick, and replaced the device. "It was about the dirty protest."

"Daddy!"

"What, Doreen? The boys need to know what's happening in their own country."

Dad sucked in his breath and disappeared further into his paper.

"They're just like animals, aren't they, Granda?"

That was Pete. Little suck up.

"No, Pete, they're not like animals at all. I kept dogs and weasels when I was a boy and never once do I remember them spreading their piss and shit all over the floor and walls."

"Daddy!"

"You know what the worst thing was, Del?"

Dad folded the paper with a look of resignation. There would be no more reading done today. "What was that, Bob?"

"The camera zoomed in on a prisoner – beard, long straggly hair, flowing blanket – who do you think he was made to look like?"

"Jesus?"

"Aye, did you see it too?"

"No, your description."

"Jesus Christ. The image of him, he was. That's the bloody B.B.C for you – trying to stir it up."

"I told him to turn it over," Granny said, in from the kitchen, "but, oh no. Like a dog with a bone."

"She'd made me a puddin' for after ma tea, Kevin. I couldn't get it down son. I had to leave it for a while – and you know how much I love ma puddin'."

"Was it chocolate pudding, Granda?"

He scratched his baldy head. "No, son it was caramel – oh, you cheeky little bugger!" He took the pipe out, fell back in his chair, and slapped his pinstripes. "Did you hear what he said? Did you hear what he said?"

I felt a warm glow. Except for Pete, they were all laughing and there was nothing like making an adult laugh - especially one born before the First World War.

Granda loved a joke. Once, I had spent my pocket money on a fake dog turd and we'd set it in front of the fireplace. He'd called to Granny to bring the shovel – the bloody dog from next door must have got in. Gnarled and grumbling, she'd stooped, scooped - and then seen the "Made in Japan" logo on the bottom. Granda laughed so hard his teeth flew out and there was a mad scramble to save them from the fire.

CHAPTER THIRTEEN

On Friday of the second week, Mr Palmer had some news for us.

"A new boy will be joining our class on Monday. I am quite sure that we will all make him extremely welcome." As he spoke, he surveyed the room, a gleam in his eye. "His name is Ronald Douglas and he comes from Waterford, in the South of Ireland."

Rip looked like he was sucking very hard on a polo mint. The rest of the class sat forward keenly. A new student, dispelling the monotony, was always of interest. Two years before, the whole school had been summoned into the assembly hall and forewarned that a Chinese boy would shortly be joining the school. The headmaster warned us that if anybody called him any names or did stupid things with their eyes they would have to answer to him. Several people told Rip that he had better watch out as Chinese kids were all taught martial arts from an early age and for the next few days Rip could be found practising Kung Fu kicks in the playground. As it turned out, the Chinese boy was quite nondescript and had never even heard of Bruce Lee.

But this was something else again.

"A lovely quiet class," Palmer remarked. "I've always dreamt of being in a class where you could hear a pin drop. Oh, it's so annoying – I forgot to bring a pin today."

Stephanie's beautiful tanned arm went up and I prepared myself for her sweet voice. "What's he coming here for, Mr Palmer?"

"Our town has a lot to offer, Stephanie."

Rip's hand flew up. "She means why's he coming to our school and not to St. Mary's or St. Theresa's?"

Palmer's eyebrows rose. "Is that what you meant, Stephanie?"

She smiled timidly and gave a tiny nod. God, she was divine.

"Let me make this very clear to you, Mr Turnbull, and anyone else who has any kind of a problem. This school welcomes anybody from anywhere. We are all about inclusion." He took a step towards Rip and pierced him with his eyes but the bold Rip stared right back at him. There was a stubbornness about him that you simply had to admire. "I have no idea what religion the new boy is but I do know that he will be made welcome in this class."

"Mr Palmer," Stephanie again, "he must be a Catholic if he comes from Waterford."

The class murmured agreement.

"You are showing your ignorance class. All sorts of religions live across the border. Turnbull, you're a great one for flags. Can you tell me anything about the Irish flag – the tricolour?"

Rip timed it to perfection. He waited for Palmer to look away before making a spitting gesture on the floor. There were a few titters but not enough to penetrate the concerned atmosphere that had been generated. "Don't know, sir, but I can tell you the history of the Red Hand of Ulster flag, if that's any help."

"No, thank-you. I already know it."

"Sir, there's a big tricolour painted on the mountains on the way to Newcastle," said Nicola Madeley. "My dad always says to look away when we're going to the amusements – but he's only joking."

"Correct you are, Nicola - but can you tell me anything about its history? Why for example is there orange in it?"

Blank expressions.

"The orange, in fact, is to represent the followers of William of Orange."

"Does that mean this new boy is a Prod?"

"I don't know – or care." He suddenly seemed to lose patience and interest. "I'm glad we've had this little chat because on Monday he will be here and we will be welcoming him into the class. No interrogation. What does that mean, Patterson?"

"Means don't be asking him lots of questions in an angry way."

"Correct you are, Patterson. Go to the top of the class – oh wait, you're already there. Tee hee."

*

Rip was in a serious mood in the playground. Usually he might kick a ball about or share a joke; all he could manage today was a weary smile. "This is the start of it lads. Wait and see. In a year, maybe two, this place will be fuckin' jumpin' with Bog Wogs – you won't be able to turn around without tripping over a Theresa or a Patrick or a Mary."

"Hey," Jimmy said. "My auntie is called Mary."

"Give the lad a chance, Rip." I said. "He hasn't even got his foot through the door."

"His left foot," Jimmy threw in, but Rip wasn't in the mood.

"I don't want to fall out with you lads but I did feel that you could have objected a bit more. It felt like it was just me fighting the Protestant corner," a glance up at me, "me and Stephanie Gillespie."

"Oh piss off, Rip, what did you want me to say? We're eleven year olds. What say do we have over who comes to our school?"

Jimmy looked uneasy. There had never been any serious problems between me and Rip but he had annoyed me with his mention of Stephanie Gillespie.

"Only eleven and look what's happening. He's turned two brothers against each other," he shook his head sadly. "I've never had an argument with you in all the time I've known you, Kev, and yet here you are telling me to fuck myself."

"I didn't say that, Rip." He looked genuinely downcast and I felt a ridiculous wave of guilt. "Look, I'm sorry. Tell you what, I've still got a bit of birthday money left over, how's about I treat you and Jimmy Cagney to the pictures?"

"Kev, you're the best. What about it, Rip?"

"No thanks, I don't think I'd be able to concentrate. I'm wondering what my family will say – big Jack. I can't help feeling I've let them down."

"That's crazy, Rip! What could you have said or done?"

He shrugged. "I don't know. Just feel I could have made more of a fuss about it. Did you see the way he looked to me? He saw me as kind a like the leader and he was seeing what I would say. All that stuff about the Irish flag. Caught me off-guard, lads. It's really me should be apologising to you."

News travels fast in an Ulster playground. Ian Russell, a lanky big eejit from the other Primary seven class, came bounding across the yard, a daft grin on his face. "Hey, Turnbull, Stanley Brownlie just told me the news. Taigs in your class now, eh? Would never happen in our class. Nah – we just wouldn't let it. Is he gonna be teaching you how to play hurling, do you think, or—" Rip punched him in the belly. The grin vanished as his face contorted and he slumped to his knees, clutching his stomach.

Rip seemed happier now. The sudden outlet of aggression had done him the world of good. He was on his tip toes, gesturing for Russell to get back up, like Ali standing over Liston.

I bent over Russell and began a little commentary. "Referee Arthur Mercante has a very close look at the fallen fighter... seven ...and eight...and nine ... he's out! He has been knocked out! Rip Turnbull is the new heavyweight champion of the world!" I held Rip's arm aloft and I clapped him on the back but only for a moment before it started to feel foolish. What I really wanted to do was thank Russell and give him a hug. But that wouldn't have gone down well. And anyway, he was a dick.

*

Dad looked tired at the dinner table and Mum was rushing everything because of her shift at the pub. Pay day was still a week away which meant beans on toast. I actually didn't mind at all and was shovelling them in, but he was clearly dissatisfied and was pushing them around the plate. I could read him well. He was spoiling for a fight. It didn't happen often but when it did it was like tip-toeing through a mine field in the dark.

"There's a new boy starting in Kevin's class on Monday," Pete said. "He comes from Waterford."

I was appalled and disgusted for about a second – the time it took for Dad to slam his huge claw down on the table making the salt and pepper leap into the air.

Pete started.

We all did.

"What the hell business is it of yours who's coming into Kevin's class?" He glowered at him. He was livid. "Is that not his news to tell? Why the hell would you be telling his news?"

Pete glanced at my mother but she kept her head down. God help him. Be wise, Pete, weather the storm. Don't say anything stupid.

"Daddy, I'm sorry."

Good lad.

"It's not me you should be apologising to."

"Sorry, Kevin," the tears brimmed over and there was nothing left for Pete to do but look down at the table cloth.

"Pete, do you want to go and wash your face and put on your Jim-Jams?" I could see Mum was furious with Dad but she was no fool. She would wait for the humour to return and then she would rip him apart. She watched him leave the table before tossing the dynamite to me. "So, Kevin, tell me about this new start."

I drew in a deep breath and told them all I knew, embellishing the conversation between Rip and Mr Palmer, including the fight between him and Russell. I kept going for as long as I could, aware that I could keep the argument at bay as long as I kept talking. The weekend depended on it. As I elaborated, I stole glances at them both, risking little humorous asides to help crack the tension. Dad melted first; you could see his shoulders relaxing and his breathing becoming less shallow; finally the twitch of a weary smile. Mum kept hers simmering on the back burner. She was brilliant at staying angry, baring grudges, keeping it warm and just under the surface. Nothing could alter her course. My dad was for it.

"That Rip's a right character," he said. "God only knows what he hears at home – that's where he gets it all from."

"Do you think the new boy is a Catholic, Mum?"

"Probably. I don't know. If he is, I hope you treat him with kindness."

Dad took it on the jaw. I watched the little finger of his right hand begin the tentative journey across the table cloth towards hers, waver, think better of it, return to the fold. Instead, a beaten man, he began to gather the plates.

"Kevin, go and sort your clothes out for the washing please."

I loitered for a moment behind the door so that I could save him if she became too vicious.

"What the hell was all that? You nearly made him wet himself!"

"I'll tell him I'm sorry. I'm really tired."

"And that's his fault?"

"Alright, Dor, point made. I'll make it up to him."

Any fool could hear the exhaustion but she was going to go for him now.

"He'd no business telling Kevin's news. That was just to annoy him."

She gave a disgusted little snort. "Ever asked yourself why that is? You've never time for him. You are always watching movies with Kevin, joking and carrying on, making sarky little comments towards him – yelling at him!"

I left them to it and trudged upstairs. I wanted to speak to Pete but wasn't sure what to say. This could be the day we looked back on in years to come. Remember when Dad yelled at you and I came into your room and we laughed about it? I knocked on his door.

"Who is it?"

"Me, Kevin."

"Piss off!" he hissed.

So I did.

CHAPTER FOURTEEN

Saturday mornings were always the same. I would remember that there was no school and be glad for a moment; then I would think about the Eleven Plus and breathe hot heavy breaths into my pillow; then I would remind myself that – although it was close – it wasn't quite upon me yet and there was still time to improve. Palmer always gave us verbal reasoning tests as weekend homework and I forced myself to do some of the ones Dad had procured for me in Belfast. Monday morning was always a past paper and then, after he had marked them, Palmer would give you your scores (oh, how I looked forward to that moment) and then you would spend much of the rest of the week going over the difficult ones on the board. I dreaded the Monday tests. I would try to push the thought of them to the back of my head until at least Sunday night (when the dread of it often completely overwhelmed me and kept me tossing and turning) but they would creep in throughout Saturday as well if I wasn't on my guard. I might be addressing my boiled egg when suddenly a voice from within would whisper: *if Kevin McBride has a boiled egg five days a week and each boiled egg takes approximately four minutes to boil, how many minutes would be required for a years' worth of boiled eggs, allowing for bank holidays and remembering that the timer loses seven seconds every second week?* Sometimes I would just sit there miserably and let it envelop me and by the time I sat down to do some practise questions – always Sunday, never Saturday – I was well and truly beaten. Other times, I would grit my teeth and put all my energy and focus into the attack on the egg and I would eat it with a steely determination that must have been strange to watch. He sure likes his eggs does our Kevin. Sometimes it would creep in when I was on the toilet, in the bath, or worse again, when I was watching television.

Pete had been through the bathroom before me. He'd peed on the seat, left the lid off the Colgate and made sure there was no toilet roll in the holder. He always got up earlier than me so he could control the TV. Before I would have raced him to the couch but I had bigger things to worry about now and allowing him pointless little victories seemed like a good strategy.

Mum was bright and breezy despite her late shift at the pub.

"What will it be, Kevvo? Frosties or Krispies?"

"Krispies, please."

Champion the wonder horse was galloping after some black clad baddies on the telly. The sun was kissing me through a gap in the curtains. Except for the damn exam it would have been a lovely morning. I poured the milk, held my ear to the bowl, heard them snap, crackle and pop.

"Found out some things about your new friend last night."

"Eh?" for a moment I had no idea what she was talking about. "The new boy?"

She nodded, clearly pleased that she had my attention. I also sensed, strangely, that she felt she had somehow short changed me last night at dinner. Presumably she had already spoken and breakfasted the sullen creature on the couch and been reminded of what a pain in the arse he was. "Davey Boyle used to do business with Grace Douglas – you remember, she used to own the sweet shop?"

I nodded. Who could forget that Aladdin's cave of wine gums, cola bottles, fizzy chews and bon bons? We used to go there for a treat on the way to the cinema. Old Mrs Douglas was friendly enough but she wouldn't let you mix your wine gums with your cola bottles which was a bit of a pain. She said it was too footery.

"Ronald Douglas is her nephew and he's coming to stay with her. Her brother married an American girl. They had Ronald, she went back to America, then the poor man died – and that's why he's ended up here." She beamed. "How's about that then? Didn't think your old mum would be able to find that out, eh? So you can tell Rip Turnbull to put away his sash – the new boy is at least half orange."

"Why's he with his auntie? Where's his mum?"

"She lives in Ohio. She offered to take him but he wanted to come here. "

"Instead of America?"

"Maybe he's really close to his auntie."

"I suppose."

There was a thought. A dead father, an old auntie who dealt in sweets and a mother in America. I hadn't even met him and already he was the most interesting person in the town. Boy, would Rip and Jimmy be pissed when I swaggered in on Monday with this information. In fact, to heck with that, I would arrange a meeting in the den today to let them know the good news.

*

It was too good of a day to spend it in the den. Rip had secured two crates of empty milk bottles and we carted them to the big field beside the old rugby club. He also had his Black Widow catapult and a huge bag of marbles. Nobody ever went there, even cows, and it was a good place to smash bottles out of earshot of adults.

My turn with the catapult. It was an impressive piece of kit, nothing like the daft "Y" shape elastic band thing Tom Sawyer used. This had a leather pouch and a half metre long stretch of industrial rubber that could propel a small stone or marble half a mile. For short distances it was like a bullet.

"Loose lips cost lives," Rip said.

I squinted, pulled back the rubber, aimed and released. Missed. Fifty feet away the row of ten milk bottles still sparkled mockingly in the sunshine.

"Really close, Kev." Jimmy held his thumb and forefinger an inch apart.

I reloaded. "What do you mean, Rip?" this time my aim was true and one of them shattered with a satisfying tinkle.

"That stuff your mum found out. That guy just spilling his guts over the bar. During the war, talk like that cost people their lives – you know, in France and stuff."

"Lucky bastard," said Jimmy. "I wish my old man would die and some sugary sweet auntie would adopt me."

"She's retired now," I reminded him. "Sure, the sweet shop is part of Woolworths."

My third shot, we were allowed three each, missed the far left hand bottle by at least a metre.

"Fuck!"

"My turn."

I passed the bag of ammo over to Jimmy.

"My neighbour had a dog once," Rip remembered. "He called it Tiger. Mad, dangerous thing it was – take your fucking hand off if you were stupid enough to stroke it. You know what the problem was? It was *half* Alsatian and *half* Rottweiler. The poor fucker didn't know what the hell it was – didn't know if it was coming or going."

Jimmy's first attempt obliterated a bottle.

"Mon, yerself, Jimmy boy!" He jumped up and down like a dancing leprechaun.

"Rip, we know nothing about his mother, maybe she's a Protestant too."

"I doubt it. But it's possible. I'll be able to tell as soon as I see him."

"You mean, if he's got a pointy tail and horns coming out of his head." Jimmy released and another bottle exploded. He was smoking.

"You're a funny wee fucker, aren't you Hood."

Pull back, aim – release - connect! Jimmy roared with delight; he usually wasn't this sharp.

"I'm fucking Lee Harry Oscar, that's who I am."

I looked at Rip but he didn't get it. "Do you mean, Lee Harvey Oswald?"

"Aye, what did I say?"

"Never mind."

"Give it here!" Rip took possession. "Can I just say now, I've twisted my thumb this morning – my aim mightn't be as good as usual."

He always said something like that.

Jimmy glanced over at me. "How did you twist your

thumb, Rip? Were you sucking it?"

The marble whizzed through the air and hit nothing.

"You cheeky wee bastard! You put me off – I'm taking it again. Still got three."

He took careful aim.

"Were you hitchhiking, Rip?"

Twang – whizz – nothing.

"I'm warning you, Hood. Do that again and you're for it."

Marble in – pull back – aim –

"Were you sticking it up your mum's arse again, Rip?"

And the damnable thing was that this time he found the target and the bottle came apart.

"You're a cheeky cunt, Hood!" He was chasing him round the field but you could see he was pleased and all three of us were roaring.

We spent the next hour wasting marbles and insulting each other's mothers, then we lay down in the long grass and cracked open our fizzy drinks. The sun was shining and we had our whole lives in front of us. High in the sky, an aeroplane was leaving a set of silvery tracks; cotton wool clouds drifting lazily across. A cow in the adjoining field called to its mate. There were even butterflies, *butterflies* in September. The Eleven Plus was creeping up behind me, about to pounce and ruin it all, but I managed, with an effort, to push it back. It could have me tomorrow when I was on my own. Sunday was the perfect day for being miserable, not Saturday.

*

Saturday night was movie night with Dad. They only showed the old double bills in the summer but sometimes you got lucky anyway and they would have a late night horror movie. I would always check the T.V papers earlier in the week so that I could read about it in my *Halliwell Filmgoers Companion*. We would pull the couch right up to the television and it was like our own private movie theatre. Just me and him. The shadows would swallow us up and we would plunge into the technicoloured world of a Hammer movie – Christopher Lee baring down on some gorgeous and expendable buxom wench, her diddies practically spilling out.

A few of the rich kids at school now boasted of having a video recorder at home. They sounded sensational. You could record things and then watch them over and over again anytime of the day or night. Better still, you could press a button and freeze the characters as if you had stopped time. The advantages of this were obvious. If a girl flashed her diddies and thought she got away with it because she had been so fast, you could go back and pause it so that you could take a really good look at them.

Even better than the freeze frame was the idea of the slow motion button. Malcolm Taylor, who knew I loved horror movies, told me that he had slowed down the part in *The Omen* where David Warner gets his head cut off. That blew my mind because the sequence had already been rendered into slow motion by the director. Taylor, therefore, had seen it in *super, super* slow motion. I was impressed enough to ask Dad about getting one.

"Maybe when they're a bit cheaper."

I couldn't help myself. "Malcolm Taylor says that you can rent them for a month to see if you like them. Just rent them, you don't have to buy. Then you can give it back and you haven't spent a fortune."

He took a long drink of his Guinness. When he set the glass down he would have a frothy brown moustache that he would lick off with his tongue. It was part of the ritual.

"Sometimes you can have too much of a good thing, Kevin. I look forward to these movies with you every week – but it would lose something if we were watching the same movie over and over every day. Don't you think?"

It sounded like an excuse but I could see that it had the potential to annoy him so I let it rest.

Tonight was my favourite actor of all time, Vincent Price, in a movie Dad had seen but I hadn't, *Theatre of Blood*.

"You are going to love this one, Kev. Saw it at the pictures years ago. Scared the Bejesus out of me!"

I laughed out loud. I loved it when he cursed. It was one of our special things. Something he did when Mum wasn't there.

"In fact, it was so scary - I crapped my pants!"

I laughed so hard I farted and then we both were howling.

And then the bubble burst.

"Do you think maybe we could ask Pete to join us tonight?"

What kind of joke was that?

His slightly pained, nervous expression told me that it wasn't one.

And I fucking hated him.

This was our time together.

Everything else – toast, toothpaste, toilet paper – was fought over. Did he not know how special this was to me? Maybe he saw it as just a duty. Not much preparation required: just press the on button, stretch out your legs, and say a few dirty words. I wanted to communicate all of this to him but, of course, I couldn't find the words.

"You know he doesn't like horror movies."

"Will we ask him, though? It won't hurt to ask. You don't mind?"

I shrugged. All of a sudden I was conscious of the elastic in my pyjama bottoms digging under my little overhanging belly. Girl diddies and rubber lip. Wee fat eleven year old in his pyjamas, all excited because he was being allowed up late on a Saturday night to watch a daft movie. Thinking he was the man because he had a box of Maltesers and a litre bottle of Pepsi. Piss pathetic.

Dad was creaking up the stairs. I could imagine the conversation upstairs. Pete would agree, of that there was no doubt; he might look bemused at first – he genuinely did not like horror movies - but then he would realise how much it would annoy me and he would accept.

I could hear them coming down. Two sets of footsteps. Big surprise.

"Here we are," Dad said. "You are really going to enjoy this lads. Vincent Price is brilliant."

"Alright, Kev." Pete plonked himself down slap bang

middle of the couch. It was too dark in the room to see his smirk but I could hear it in his voice.

Dad was really trying hard. "This is great, all of us together. We'll have to be sure to tell Mum."

Of course. Lazy bastard. Couldn't be bothered finding a special thing to do with Pete. Had to ruin mine.

No knockout is complete without a final little victory jig.

"This is a great movie," said the bold Pete. "I think I've seen part of it before – is it the one where he kills all the theatre critics?"

Oh you lying bastard! It's never been on the television before; you read that in the Radio Times. I felt myself go quite hot and a little light headed.

"This is the last word I'll say, 'cause I don't want to spoil it for you, but this movie is really going to help me because we're studying Shakespeare in English and Vinnie is a Shakespeare actor in this."

Vinnie? Oh, Dear God. His voice was dripping with glee. He was practically fucking vibrating. But Dad was missing these missiles. Either not hearing or choosing to ignore. Mum had nobbled him.

The B.B.C continuity announcer put on a spooky voice to introduce the movie.

"Well, I hope you have your crucifixes and silver bullets at the ready, because now it is time for that master of menace, Vincent Price, to send shivers down your spine in ...*The Theatre of Blood.*

Vincent Price could go to hell. I wasn't interested anymore. Didn't even want the rest of my Maltesers. In the darkness, I licked four or five, put them back in the box and pushed them aside. I seethed in silence, teeth gritted, the muscles at the side of my jaw throbbing. I wanted to tell him how let down I felt; how cheapened. I didn't want Pete to die - he would enjoy the attention too much, lying there all smug – but I wanted him never to have been born. Most of all, I wanted Vincent Leonard Price, born in 1911 in St Louis, Missouri, the youngest of four children, to hurry the fuck up and do whatever he had to do so that I could go to bed and never ever watch a movie with my dad again.

It was gratifying to imagine future conversations:

"Kevin, Boris Karloff is on tonight, do you fancy it?"

"No thanks, too tired and anyway I've gone off horror movies."

"Since when?"

"Just don't fancy them anymore. Why don't you ask Pete?"

That last bit would be too dangerous, and if you caught him in the wrong mood it might turn nasty. "Don't you worry, son, I will ask him. I'll not be asking you again." That sort of thing. I didn't want him to be cross and I didn't want to hurt his feelings. I just felt let down.

But then a wonderful, miraculous thing occurred.

Sometimes God can be kind and can throw you a line when you least expect it.

Theatre of Blood turned out to be actually quite terrifying.

What happened was this: Vincent Price was an eccentric Shakespearean actor called Edward Lionheart. He adored Shakespeare and throughout his entire career performed exclusively in Shakespeare plays. The theatre critics hated him because of this and wrote scathing reviews and finally – when they denied him the Critics Award – he jumped off a tall building into the muddy Thames. Dead. But here's where it got really good. Price wasn't really dead. He was saved by a group of down and outs, waited for a couple of years, and then began to kill the critics - inspired by grisly Shakespearean deaths.

And Pete was not enjoying it.

God help him, he tried not to show it, but there was no hiding place.

I felt him start on the couch when Michael Horden was surrounded and stabbed repeatedly, in the manner of Julius Ceasar.

He gave a little yelp when Denis Price was impaled and his body dragged through a graveyard, tied to the back of a horse.

And I began to enjoy myself.

"Right enough, Pete." I made myself sound bright and breezy. "This would be good for essays and stuff – knowing how they all died."

Even in the darkness, I could see him grimace and turn away as Arthur Lowe –
Who do you think you are kidding, Mr Hitler,
If you think old England's done?
- had his head sawn off as he slept.

"Are you enjoying it, Pete? Is it as good as you remember it from the last time?"

Price kept the best death for the English actress Coral Browne who later became his real life wife. By now all the remaining critics knew they were in danger and she had a sleepy police escort with her when she went for a haircut. Her regular stylist wasn't there – it was Vincent, with a big daft afro, camping it up; he lured her down the stairs whilst the sleepy policeman read some magazines in the waiting area.

"What do you think is going to happen to her, Pete?"

"I don't know," he nudged Dad. "What do you think, Dad?"

I knew by the silence that he was curled up on the sofa, dead to the world. That happened sometimes after a busy week.

"Just you and me here, Pete."

On screen, Vincent Price and his friends were attaching strange looking curlers to Coral Browne's hair and, for some reason, placing her feet in a steel bowl. He was flirting expertly with her, fanning her ego, keeping her well off guard.

"Kevin," it was like the smallest voice in the world, a little mouse's voice. "I can help you with the Eleven Plus, if you like."

Price tore away his disguise and thrilled at Coral Browne's look of horror as she recognised him. She was gagged so she couldn't shout for the sleepy policeman.

"Nah, you're alright, Pete. I've got those papers Dad got me, I think I'll be fine."

He yanked down the electric lever and she started to shake and jitter.

"Oh, Jesus Christ."

"Mind your language, Pete. If you take the Lord's name after midnight, the devil doesn't have to wait for you to die."

Smoke was coming from Coral Browne's hair. The policeman up above was starting to sniff a funny smell but still he didn't look unduly concerned. Price had set colourful magazines with enticing, low cut models on the front cover on the waiting room table.

Coral Browne's skin was starting to peel from her scalp as thick dark smoke curled up from her head. Vincent was reminded her of all the wicked, career destroying things she had said about him and if she still believed they were true. It was brilliant.

"Dad ...Dad...wake up! You're missing it, Dad!"

"Let him sleep, Pete." I was almost giddy with delight. "He sometimes sleeps down here anyway. I have to get myself to bed – up the stairs in the pitch dark. Creak creak."

"Fuck off!"

"What's wrong, Pete? Aren't you enjoying it?"

Coral Browne was dead and Pete had had enough.

"Stupid Vincent Price! Who the hell would believe a daft old poof like that could kill all those people and get away with it each time. It's a crap, stupid movie and anyone who believes it is fucking retarded. No wonder you can't ...do the ...Eleven ..."

"Why are you nearly crying, Pete? Have you got hay fever?"

He snorted contempt and made for the door.

"Beware the darkness, Pete!"

Dad was snoring lightly. It would have been wonderful to think that this very pleasing result might have been part of his grand master plan; but I knew it wasn't.

I was still upset with him.

And I was bloody scared too.

I was completely alone in the darkness with Vincent Price leering out of the screen at me. My heart was thumping. I kept turning my head, certain that there was something in the shadows behind me – probably under the table. Some sixth sense told it exactly when I was about to turn and it would dart back into the gloom. Waiting. Biding its time. I'd read a story once – or was it an episode of Scooby Doo? – where a make-believe swamp monster became real when so many radio listeners believed in its existence. Television could be just like that. I didn't know exactly how it worked but I knew that there was every chance that Vincent Price had used the television as a portal and was lurking right now in the kitchen waiting to jump out at me when I went in for a Wagon Wheel.

And Pete knew it too.

I grinned.

Vincent Price would never kill me. He was a lot of things but he wasn't stupid. I was a fan of his. You don't kill or torture your fans; they're the ones who watch your movies and put butter on your bread. Furthermore, if he had any influence with the supernatural – and I was pretty sure he did – he wouldn't allow the thing behind me to lay a claw or whatever else it had on me. That made sense too. The thing behind me had probably been sent to get Pete, knowing that he wasn't a believer, that he was disrespectful.

I relaxed a little and watched as Robert Morely had his two beloved poodles baked in a pie and force fed down a pipe into his throat. It was a great movie.

When it was over, I put the blanket over Dad and set aside his Guinness glass just in case he put his wrist on it during the night and bled to death. It was a quarter to one and my eyes were nipping. No Granny tomorrow, so at least I could sleep in before beginning my Eleven Plus practise.

Don't worry about it now, worry about it tomorrow.

Up the stairs silently.

Into the bathroom. Teeth. Toilet. Pissing around the enamel so it was noiseless.

This was going to be brilliant.

Shush ...shush. Tiptoeing down the landing; lovely soft carpet, kind to the feet.

Now wait.

Wait.

Wait.

Open his door a crack.

Keep it short; keep it fast; and whatever you do, don't giggle or you'll ruin it.

I could impersonate his velvet voice quite well, impressionists loved him.

"Peter? This is Vincent Price. (pause) I didn't like you calling my film stupid and calling me a poof. (very brief pause) I'm going to kill you, Peter McBride. I'm going to cut off your head when you sleep and throw it out the window."

"Kevin, fuck off!" He was groggy from trying to get to sleep, tossing and turning, trying to forget what he had seen.

But the wonderful thing was this: I could tell from his voice that he wasn't *absolutely*, one hundred per cent certain that it was me.

It was delicious!

It was pitch black dark.

"Kev? Are you still there?"

Tip toe away, avoiding all the loose floorboards.

"I know it's you, Kevin."

Into my room.

Slippers off. Into bed.

His voice, plaintive and imploring, swallowed by the blackness of the night.

"Kevin? Let's be friends. Do you want to get in with me tonight? We can tell each other jokes and stories.

"Kevin? Kevin?"

I slept like a baby.

CHAPTER FIFTEEN

Monday morning, second week of September. I blew on my fingers and levitated my hands over the radiator. Palmer had just left the room and a ripple of excitement and expectation went through the class. He had gone down to the office to collect the new boy. There were whispers and a few sniggers but the volume was low. He had demanded silence throughout his absence and his shadow loomed large at the front of the room. He had a habit – in fact he had only done it once – of lingering silently outside the door and then exploding inward to confront the person or persons who had disobeyed him.

But Rip could not resist. It was expected of him after all.

"They'll probably be fuckin' ages," he whisper hissed. "Take them half an hour to carry his crucifix up the stair!"

Some laughter, but muted, and you could see the disappointment on his face. It occurred to me then that he had prepared the line and again I felt that strange sympathy for him.

For my own part, I was glad of the distraction. They could take as long as they liked because after his initiation it would be Eleven Plus party time again. Yippedy dee! My stomach was enjoying its usual Monday morning churn. My bowels, completely uncooperative an hour ago were now winking and nudging me – reminding me that break time was an eternity from now and I would need to focus all my attention on them unless I wanted Stephanie Gillespie to witness an unfortunate little accident.

Could there be any more miserable subject than this fat, rubber lipped eleven year old with his numb fingers and a wad of toilet paper stuffed up his arse? I took a deep breath and squirmed uneasily in my wooden seat, reasonably satisfied that the paper cork was firmly secured. Jimmy winked at me and again I envied his complete lack of anxiety. He never seemed to worry about anything. Then again, not many eleven year olds did. Only me.

How would Ronald Douglas be feeling just now? What would

it be like to be in a brand new school, in a brand new town, in a brand new country? Christ, his head must be spinning. I had never been across the border before and knew little about it. Green fields, stone walls (we had some of those too) not as modern as us – a little bit backward. Irish dancing, fiddling, banshees – all that was from *Darby O'Gill and the Little People.* They played football and hockey but with funny rules and funny sticks. I probably knew more about Japan than I did the South of Ireland. That made me feel funny for a moment. Would you be able to tell by just looking at him that he came from a different country? What physical signs would there be? I shook my head in disbelief at my stupidity. It was good that I could at least still muster a smile. There would be no difference at all, you idiot, except perhaps a little paler and his eyes closer together.

The door swung open and in they came. The class did not gasp but there was certainly complete and utter silence.

"Class, it is my great pleasure to welcome a new student into the body of the Kirk," Palmer intoned. "This is Ronald Douglas and I'm sure you will all make an effort to make him feel very much at home."

All eyes fixated on the tall figure beside him. He was slim but not in a fragile way, more whippet like with a sinewy look about him. His eyes seemed perfectly spaced on either side of his nose and as he gazed around they gave the appearance of being bright blue and penetrating. And he had an air as well. The way he stood beside Palmer, surveying the class. He did not seem at all timid; no outward signs of nerves. Some might have said there was an arrogance about him but that was not so. I recognised what it was immediately. I could smell it from where I sat. It oozed from his pores. Something I lacked and always would. Natural confidence.

"Ronald, if you'd like to take a seat beside Mr Brownlie?" Palmer gestured towards the seat and table orbiting around Stanley. "Can you move over a bit, Brownlie?"

He sulked for a moment before shifting, Jabba like, several inches to the right.

"Now then, now then," Palmer pretended that his board marker was a cigar and my heart sank. It was his little joke. He always did a Jimmy Saville impersonation when we were about to start Eleven Plus work. "Now then, boys and girls, boys and girls. We are going to have to say good-bye to several of our friends – Turnbull, Gamble, McGloughlin, Chambers – Mrs Patterson has some language work you will enjoy in room 7b. We shall see you after break."

Rip and his comrades departed and Palmer began to pass around the test.

And my heart started to wallop in my chest; my bowels, furious at the discovery of the toilet roll, were pressing against the blockage and calling on their friends to join the scrum. My hands now felt clammy. Jesus, they were numb with the cold fifteen minutes ago. How could your fingers sweat? Was that even possible?

"You can now turn over and begin. Absolute silence please."

Two trains connect with each other every day at a junction. Train "A" leaves a town 176 miles away at 9.am and averages 48 miles per hour. Train "B" leaves a town 98 miles away at 10am and averages 30 miles per hour.

   a. *Which is the first train to reach the junction and at what time does it arrive?*
   b. *How long would a passenger have to wait for the other train to arrive?*

Oh God, please help me!

Settle down. Try the next one, it might be easier.

A clock, which loses half a minute every second hour, is put right at 9.am on Monday. What time will it show at 2.pm on Thursday?

Listen to them scribbling. They all know how. I know some of them find it tricky – I'm not that stupid – but they all know *how*. They can climb over the barrier. A few scrapes, a few bruises; but I fucking can't! I am stuck here in the mud.

Okay, still don't panic. Deep breaths. Leave this one for

now – just make sure you come back to it later.

But the next one is just as bad.

And the next.

BLANKETY BLANK, BLANKETY BLANK – DAH DAH –
BLANKETY BLANK, BLANKETY BLANK – DAH DAH – COME ON A
SUPER MATCH GAME, SUPER MATCH GAME – *BLANKETY*

BLANK ...*BLANKETY BLANK!*

Oh, Jesus Christ, please help me!

Maybe the next one. At least it looks shorter.

The average of 4 men's ages is 30 years, while the average age of 3 of them is 33 years. What is the age of the fourth man?

"What's this, Joe? Surely it can't be? McBride's corner are throwing in the towel! They're stopping the fight, Joe. Angelo Dundee is dancing! Clay's gloved hands are aloft! The fight is over! The fight is over! Get in there, Joe!"

Now would be a good time to die. A heart attack. Unlikely at my age. A brain haemorrhage, then? A kid in Newry had died from that. If it could just happen now I wouldn't have to even look at this thing again. The toilet roll up the arse would be a little embarrassing but it would be worth it to end this hellish misery.

The sound of their scribbles was deafening. And now, every several seconds, another: the scratchy, superior sound of the page being turned over. Questions one to seven had been tackled, onward troops, here come eight to fourteen. And I still had not put pencil to paper. There was a hot, urgent flush rushing up my body. Maybe this was the blood clot on its way to my head?

How was Darby O'Gill managing, shall we risk a little look?

Ah yes, faith and begorrah, there he is, scribbling away like Shakespeare, a wee half smile on his face. Of course.

*

I wasn't in the mood for much at lunch time. I felt flat, zapped, barely enough energy to eat my Mars bar. Joyless chewing. All that lovely chocolate and caramel wasted; may just as well have been munching on a carrot. I wasn't up for company either. I had positioned myself in the middle of the yard, tucked in behind the brick furnace where the caretaker burned boxes and paper. Jimmy was over at the bars with a small group of younger boys. He had a deck of cards and was showing them a magic trick he had taught himself from a book he had borrowed from the mobile library. He was branching out a little, trying to add a little variety to his routines. "You have to mix it up a bit, Kevin. I can't just let myself be a one trick pony. Ha ha! Get it?" He had recently got into Tommy Cooper and I could see him now doing his Tommy Cooper impression to the bewildered audience. And I felt a sudden, overwhelming sense of self-disgust – so much so that, unprecedented, I binned the remainder of my Mars Bar. How was it possible to feel so much anger and resentment towards my best friend just because he was fumbling and bumbling through some silly magic trick?

Ah, but look at his wee face, Kevin. There's your answer. Look how gay and carefree he is. Happy little chappy. The last thing on his mind is the Eleven Plus. He's completely forgotten about it. He's moved on to the next thing. No torment. No angst. No dirty wad of toilet paper up his bum.

Idiots tend not to worry.

Tis true. Except, the thing is, whilst I can't be absolutely certain about this, I'm pretty sure he scored higher than you in the little test you've just done. Sorry.

They all seemed carefree, that was the thing. The pig tailed skippers by the faded hopscotch lines, the Georgie Best wannabees trying to get the ball, kids chasing after each other playing tag - *tag* for Christ sake! There was Rip, up at the top of the yard, chief of a secretive cluster. His head was bowed and he had his left hand shielded over his mouth lest some lip reader had his telescopic lenses trained on him.

And where was your man? I had almost forgotten about him. How was he feeling? I squinted and scanned the playground with a bit more purpose. All the laughing, grinning faces. Please God, at least let him be miserable like me. If not miserable, at least not happy. Give me something.

There he was. Up near the top of the playground, near to the banks that sloped down from the High School. Not the best place for him to be. He was by himself. Good. His height and solitude made him conspicuous and I watched as several of the High School thugs congregated above him. Any moment now they would run out of things to talk about and start looking around – and down – for a focus to fill the conversational void. It was just too easy.

Oh, move away, you big daft bastard. Can't you sense them up above?

Clearly he did not. He was surveying the playground, hands in his pockets, and it was difficult to tell what his emotions were by looking at his face. No smile, no frown. If he was bawling like a five year old, would that make me feel better about myself? Maybe. I didn't know. I really was turning into a bitter, hateful little fucker – that I did know.

I saw one of the High School boys nudge his companion and gesture down. There would be a little kudos for him, a finder's fee, even though the target was in plain view for all. Better still if he could initiate the barrage.

Oh, go get him, Kevin – help him out! If nothing else, it will take your mind off things for a while.

I began to stride towards him. Running would be too obvious. I needed to catch his eye so that he didn't turn around when they yelled down.

"Hey, Wadlow!"

Too late.

Ronald turned and craned up.

But the opening salvo had caused some confusion up above.

"Who the fuck is Wadlow?"

"Robert Pershing Wadlow," the boy said with a hurt expression, "tallest man ever. I saw it on *Record Breakers*."

"You fuckin' poof!" the leader of pack stepped up to the wire and yelled down. "Hey Giraffe Boy! Fucking Stretch Armstrong – up here!"

"Let's move down," I suggested to Ronald. It's not really a good place for you to stand."

"Hey, Monkey Gub – can't your boyfriend speak for himself?"

I bristled at that but knew better than to respond. Even a surly glance might be enough to rile them; some of them had hair pin trigger tempers. It was close to the bell and it was very rare for them to climb over the fence but I had seen it happen before – and for very little.

"They're just dicks," I whispered, "let's go." I placed a hand on his back and gently pressed – but he resisted and for a moment it was like pushing a boulder. What the hell was this? "Come on, Ronald – they're not worth it."

Rip and a few others nearby were watching with a keen interest.

"Hey, Rip!" from up above, "better tell your lanky pal to fuckin' watch himself!"

"He's not my pal!"

The bell sounded then, nice timing, and we lined up.

I took a deep breath. "Listen, Ronald, don't worry about them – they're not worth shittin' on."

Nothing. I was staring at his shoulder blades.

"Ronald," I tapped him on the shoulder. "What's your problem?"

Just then there came the rapping of Palmer's ten pence on the uppermost window of the staircase and the buzz died down. He did this every day. Rap on the window, then point his finger at no one in particular – except, like that old guy in the posters, you always thought he was pointing at you.

"Next time, I'll fucking leave you to it – how's that?"

Still nothing. Ungrateful bastard.

"Pssht!"

It was Rip, behind me, I hadn't even noticed him.

"What?"

He gave me a double thumbs up and a grin.

*

I thought I might give the den a break that evening and lie on my bed but the thought of Pete poking his head in and out was too much. He would be attuned to my mood and would be dancing or singing or smiling happily at how wonderful the world and life in general was. So I had my tea (sausage and mash) and was round at Jimmy's just after six.

He could hardly sit still.

"What's up?"

He looked quizzically at me. "You're joking?"

"Oh, yeah – I forgot."

Rip was bringing Jack's video recorder and an Electric blue porno.

"How could you forget?"

"I dunno. It's the Eleven Plus. My head's filled with it. Sometimes I can't think about anything else."

"This'll take your mind off it, Kev. Rip says it's brilliant. Wet T-shirt contests. Massive big honkers! You see their fannies too."

"Right."

"He better not let us down. I've been really looking forward to this."

"Better watch your mum or dad don't suddenly arrive."

"Naw," but it stopped him from rocking for a moment. "I'll wedge the stick behind the handle; won't happen anyway – look, here he is!"

Rip swaggered in brandishing a Woolworth's bag.

"Did you get it?"

He held the bag aloft.

"Good for you, Rip!"

"But not the bluey – sorry."

Jimmy's face fell. "What then?"

"Something even better! Something that's gonna put a smile on this miserable bastard's face."

I tried to muster something. "What is it?"

"Horror, tits - and fannies!" He allowed himself a smile, a pause, a swelling of the chest, then: "*Carrie*, Stephen King. Kevin McBride's favourite author."

"Why couldn't you get the Electric Blue?" Jimmy asked.

"Ungrateful little fucker. This is a brilliant movie – tell him, Kev.'"

"It's a really good movie, Jimmy."

I had never felt less like watching a movie in my life.

"What's it about?"

Rip leapt in. "This weird girl is washing her tits in the shower – and you fuckin' see everything. Then she gets her period and you see the blood pissin' down her legs. The other girls – all of them bare arsed – laugh at her and throw fanny pads at her. But here's the thing: she can fuckin' move things without touching them – what's it called, Kev?"

"Telekinesis."

"Aye. So she gets her revenge on them by locking them in the assembly hall and burning it down."

"You've just told me the whole movie, you dick!"

"Yeah, but you still want to see them in the shower, don't ya?"

Jimmy started to grin and reached for the cassette. Rip held it out of his reach for a moment, made him dance for it, before handing it over. As Jimmy fumbled it into the loading deck, Rip sat alongside me and gave my leg a quick squeeze. "That was brilliant tellin' that streak of piss to fuck off. You know, when I yelled up "he's not my pal," I meant him, not you – right?"

"Sure."

"Good lad." He snuggled himself into the couch. "Fuck me, I'm gonna enjoy this – is that her ready, Jimmy boy?"

Eight teenage girls each have a shower after a game of netball in which five of the balls cost the same amount as the total of the other three. Four of the girls have hair measuring between twelve and eighteen inches; three of the girls have streaks in their hair and one of them is ginger. How much shampoo is left from a 500ml bottle if three of the girls use half as much as the other five who each spend an average of four and half minutes under the water?

Maybe I'd done better than I thought. That was the little

glimmer of hope that always came to me in the dark of the evening. Maybe I wouldn't be at the bottom of the pile this time. Maybe, unbeknownst to me, something might have clicked in my head; some cryptic methodology like the time I had accidentally managed to complete the Rubik's Cube. It was possible. The trick then would be to try and back track to see how I had managed it and if I could harness it and repeat the feat. This then would be the new anxiety, always a new one ready to replace the old: if I had done better would the improvement continue or would it just be a fluke? Jesus. Maybe it was better just to fail miserably and be done with it.

CHAPTER SIXTEEN

Tuesday was swimming-pool day. A chance to sneak a look at Stephanie Gillespie's diddies whilst averting attention from my own. Stanley Brownlie was vital for this enterprise and I sometimes wondered, on the rare occasions when I wasn't completely bogged down by my own problems, if he found my sudden overt chumminess suspicious. If he did, he didn't say.

Military timing. Palmer had spent his formative years in the army and he had no truck with dawdlers or untied shoe laces: leave at 10:45; arrive swimming pool at 11:00; swimming lesson 11:15 – 11:45; back in time for lunch. God help you if you forgot your swimming gear and to forget it twice in a row was unthinkable. In Primary six, Dennis McKay had done just that and you could hear Mrs Thompson yelling at him all the way down the corridor as she frog marched him to Mr Flynn's office. He hadn't been slippered but Dennis later confided that Flynn had pushed him out of the office with such force that both of his feet had left the ground. The week after, in the swimming-pool changing rooms, he had shown us the dark bruise in between his shoulder blades. He never forgot his gear again.

We were marching through the town. Onward Christian soldiers. Rip was behind me, Jimmy in front, Brownlie by my side. Jimmy was telling him all about the movie we had watched and he was wide eyed at his lurid description. It was safe enough to tantalise him because we knew his parents didn't let him out at night beyond their street so there was no way he was ever going to be anywhere near the den. He waited patiently until Jimmy finished and then, as was the way with school-boys, he tried to top what he had just heard with a story of his own. Stanley's story, if such it could be called, involved him finding his brother's stash of hard core porno mags; he didn't get much of a chance for a flick because his mother was hobbling nearby but what he did see would stay in his mind forever.

"Go on…"

"She had no clothes on and she was on a trampoline. She bounced right up and opened her legs wide – and that's when they took the photo!"

"Fuckin' 'ell!" Rip said. "Can you bring it in?"

The request, not unreasonable and quite predictable, seemed to fluster him.

"Thing is, he came back on leave and the next time I looked they were gone. He must have sold them or passed them on. I could try to find it for you, if you want."

"Forget it," Rip waited for him to look away before doing a silent Joey Deekin impersonation.

We were in the middle of the town now, passing by McDowell's the butcher, who got his curtains and carpets at Whyte's the drapers, who got his shirts and off the peg suits at Moffet's who got his petrol, as did they all, at McKnight's filling station. Palmer was at the front of the line, occasionally whizzing round to check on behaviour, but otherwise head held high, arms swinging. By his side, no real surprise, was our southern fried friend. Palmer had taken a shine to him.

"I fuckin' hate Palmer," Rip's hot breath was in my ear. "He's nothin' but a Fenian lover."

"But he's not Catholic, remember."

"Well, he fuckin' should be. And another thing, I bet ya he swims like Johnny fuckin' Winemiller."

"Weissmuller."

"Yeah... wait and see."

Rip himself, whilst not a shallow end dweller, was not the greatest swimmer in the world. He made plenty of noise, no doubt about that, and he splashed about a lot and could dive bomb (forbidden, of course, but he did it anyway.) But when you actually looked closely at his technique you saw that he wasn't really swimming at all, in the real sense, and he was never completely out of his depth. Aware of his lack of swimming finesse, he held court in the changing rooms, flicking people with his towel (again, strictly forbidden) and perfecting armpit farts. His favourite thing to do was to tuck his thing and balls in between his legs and strut about pretending to be a girl. Bizarrely, if you refused to look at him or laugh, he would call you a poof.

At the pool, Rip was rather more reserved than usual. It was almost certainly to do with Ronald and not knowing exactly how to behave around him. A certain etiquette. How long did you have to be in someone's company before you felt comfortable enough to point at your tucked in testicles and yell: *Look at me fanny! Look at me fanny!* There had been the usual mad dash for the cubicles although everyone always left the first one free for Rip as a sign of respect. Ronald had missed out and I felt some sympathy for him. He was trying to change into his trunks under the cover of his towel. Was there anything in the world so lonely and desolate than a new boy trying not to show his private parts in a swimming-pool changing room?

I left him to it and quickly undressed myself, marvelling at how unselfconscious Stanley seemed to be. He was like Moby fucking Dick. His breasts hung freely and his belly kind of melted and dripped down over his trunks in great big globules.

I could smell the chlorine already, in fact you could smell it as you approached the building. In the distance, if you cocked your ear, you could hear the echoing, splashy noises of the other primary school who were booked in before us and who always, we imagined, left their dirt and spit and pee for us to swim in. And then there was the delicious, yet somehow terrifying, thought of the girls – especially Stephanie – stepping out of their knickers and bras (okay they were silly wee pretend ones but they still counted) on the other side of the building.

A swimming-pool is 25 metres long, 10 metres wide, 1 metre deep at the shallow end and 2 metres deep at the far end. Billy, who is 9 years and 4 months old, turns on the big tap to fill the pool at 7:00 am on Tuesday morning. The tap provides 2.6 litres of water every 5 seconds. How long must Margaret, who gets the number 16A bus to work, wait until the pool is ¾ full?

Rip was wrong about Douglas. He was in the shallow end, his tall white figure looking vaguely ridiculous amongst the other non-swimmers. What do you know? Confident just on dry land it would appear.

Stephanie Gillespie was the world's most beautiful mermaid. She was in the deep end (as was I, although at the other side) chatting and laughing with Shirley McKnight. Her hair was pinned back and there were little splashes of water on her forehead and cheeks. Occasionally, she would arch her back and her chest would peer momentarily above the water line, check you were still watching, then go back under. She. Was. Gorgeous.

The two lazy attendants – one for the non-swimmers, one for the swimmers - were idly chatting before beginning the lesson. Safely up in the café, Palmer would be sipping his coffee and doing his Daily Mail crossword. I felt like I was on auto-pilot. It had occurred to me that morning to feign illness and ask Mum for the day off. She was usually fine like that. A quick check of the throat and then back to bed. Sorted. But that would only be postponement. Until Palmer gave us our scores it would be better just to try to go about business as usual. Keep the mind busy. It was just possible to keep the Eleven Plus monster at bay and under control if I kept myself occupied. Alone, in my bedroom, I would be at its mercy.

Rip caught my eye and I knew by his funny little smile that he was urinating. He finished, looked in surprise at the clear surface, and shrugged his shoulders. This was a regular and affectionate little dig at Jimmy who had solemnly told us that they now added a chemical to the water that shamed people by rendering their urine bright purple.

Who was this edging towards the deep end with an expression of studied concentration? Douglas. Clearly grown tired of waiting down in the shallow end, here he was on a wee wander, a little expedition of discovery. Typical. That bloody cock sure confidence I had seen yesterday. Can't swim a lick, but happy to finger nail his way around the pool. Again, I felt that irrational wave of resentment that seemed to be becoming a regular feature of my personality: what right did he have to be up here in vicinity of Stephanie Gillespie? I had been in the shallow end for two long years before my doggy paddle graduation. I had earned it. I purposefully stepped back against the tiled edge. I wasn't shifting. He would have to swim around me. Good luck with that, Ronnie.

Shirley McKnight giggled shrilly, a high-pitched grating sound that was clearly designed to draw attention to herself. I looked over and saw that she was laughing at Stephanie who – get this – was doing a little dance in the water, some unknown rhythm that involved her shifting her lovely shoulders up and down and clicking her fingers and mouthing some lyrics I couldn't make out. Oh God. You know we're looking, Stephanie, how can you be so beautiful and so cruel at the same time? She was so lovely it made me feel queasy because I knew I would never be worthy of her. I knew I would never have the nerve or the equipment to ask her out. I didn't even want to ask her out. What I wanted was for her to remain single for the rest of her life and to pine for me the way I pined for her. That was all.

Where was Douglas now? I scanned the pool but amongst all the splashing bodies I couldn't see him. Wait though – his head suddenly bobbed up and the look of utter panic on his face galvanised me in an instant. Even as I swam towards him I was remembering when the same thing had happened to me about a year earlier: tiptoeing towards the deep end, then suddenly the momentum carrying me forward out of my depth whilst at the same time angling me beyond reach of the side.

I grabbed his torso and in less than two seconds we were at the side with him gasping and coughing up water. I looked wildly about. No-one had seen his distress or my gallant act but if he didn't stop hocking up the Atlantic that would all change.

"Take it easy, you're fine; try to take big deep breaths."

He nodded. I could see fear and relief in his eyes; his body was shivering and his fingers were white from holding the lip of the edge.

"Don't panic, you're perfectly safe now, but don't make a big deal of it or they'll never let you forget it." And now there *was* a little bit of interest being shown; I could sense a few curious looks, a few more seconds and there would occur an almost telepathic ripple of communication that would have all eyes focussed on us. "Go back to the shallow end –it's safe there."

He nodded and gave my arm a little squeeze. All the gratitude in the history of the world was in that squeeze and I felt like the Ready Brek Boy with a warm orange glow all around me. I hadn't saved his life, that was laughable, you couldn't possible drown in a public swimming pool. Drowning was a noisy, splashy, frantically attention grabbing spectacle; but I had saved his dignity, that I was sure of. To be dragged, coughing and spluttering, from a pool under the watchful gaze of twenty-five eleven years olds was a fate almost worse than death. Children never forgot such things. They were the fodder of rainy lunch times, sleepovers and depressing school reunions.

I was pleased with my morning's work. The Eleven Plus monster was snarling in a corner but it clearly didn't like the strange glow around me. I knew it wouldn't last but it felt nice. In the changing room and on the short walk back to school, I could feel Ronald's eyes on my back.

*

Palmer had a thing about accents. He had travelled the world in his younger day and brought back stories about what he had seen, what he had done and, above all, how they had spoken. He had studied English language at university and had a joy in phonetics that few of us could understand. We didn't mind. All we knew was when he launched into his Australian or Canadian accent he was in a good mood and there was fun to be had. Little surprise then that he welcomed the new voice to the class.

It was the afternoon, hair long since dried, and we were doing maths. Decimals into fractions. Easy enough. No cause for panic.

"Thirty-three point three three," Palmer intoned. "What would that be as a fraction?"

A dozen or so eager hands aloft, mine amongst them. Answer one now and there was less chance of being asked later when you were stuck.

"Yes, Douglas?"

"A turd, sir."

A pause.

Disbelief. A couple of giggles.

"Again, please."

"A turd, sir – 33.33% is a turd."

An avalanche of roars this time and – you guessed it – there was the bold Rip at the fore, holding his sides lest his spleen burst.

Palmer smiled to himself and waited for the merriment to subside.

"Here's a thing," he pushed his glasses from the tip of his nose back up to his eyebrows. "Mr Turnbull thinks it's comical because Mr Douglas has an Irish accent, does he? Does he not realise that the world is full of English speaking people who pronounce words differently from him? In South Africa, for example, they pronounce "fighting" as "farting." So, if they were lucky enough to have Mr Turnbull as a pupil there they might be heard to say, "Is that Mr Turnbull farting again in the playground, oh dear, that poor boy is always farting."

Giggles and titters. Kids respected Rip but what Palmer said had been quite funny.

Rip was livid. You could see the muscles in his jaw clenching and unclenching. His eyes were darting here and there, taking note of who was giggling; but there was a certain safety in numbers and it was a difficult task for him. I felt sorry for him. Alright, he had been guffawing but it didn't seem fair to single him out when everyone else, me included, had been laughing.

*

I was trudging home with Jimmy, the orange glow had long since left me and my mind was on the Eleven Plus once more. Palmer had promised the results for tomorrow morning. He said he had already marked half of them and there was still a lot of work to be done and my heart had plummeted because he clearly looked at me.

"You're still coming tonight?" Jimmy asked.

"Sure."

"I've got a couple of new tricks to show you. Do you think Rip will be there?"

"Not sure."

"Did you see his face? I had to bite my lip to stop from laughing."

"Hey, Kevin, Jimmy – hold on!"

We turned and there was Ronald, red in the face from trying to catch up.

"I didn't get a proper chance at lunch time. I just wanted to thank you properly for today."

Jimmy looked suitably perplexed.

"Your friend here saved my life!"

"Rubbish, Ronald," but the orange glow was returning; I could see it chasing after me along the pavement and passed the Toyota showroom, like that big ball that came after Patrick McGoohan. Pretty soon there would be a lovely, if only temporary glow ...ah yes, there it was again. "I didn't save your life, Ronald. What I did do, maybe, was stop you from getting laughed at."

"Me life flashed before me." Ronald insisted, and all of a sudden, this new boy who hadn't spoken fifteen words in the last two days, gushed fourth. "I was up to me stomach, then me chest, wasn't going to go further than me neck – when suddenly I'm under! No way of going back – it was as if the water was sucking me to the bottom. I grabbed for the wall but the wall's disappeared and then I can feel meself starting to fall and I think – Jaysus, Ronald, this is it!"

"Are there no swimming pools where you came from?" Jimmy asked.

"Sure, but me dad wasn't really into swimming. I'm thinking to meself: nobody's seen what's happened. You're about to drown, Ronald Douglas."

"You were never going to drown," I said mildly. "Mind you, I'm surprised that the level of the pool didn't drop by at least half a metre the amount of chlorine you swallowed."

Ronald afforded this a generous laugh and so did Jimmy although he still looked lost. We had reached the top of Christine

Lane and there was the awkward business of ending a pleasant exchange.

"Where does your auntie live?"

"At the top of the old Dublin Hill."

"Really?" We knew the hill well. There was a graveyard halfway up and the hill itself was one of the longest and steepest in the whole county. "How do you get up there?"

"Walk."

"Blimey," Jimmy said. "No wonder you're so skinny."

"You walked all along with us even though you have to go back and climb that hill?" I was pretty impressed.

"Yeah, I wanted to thank you."

Another awkward pause, and then, there was nothing else for it. "Me and Jimmy – Jimmy's actually – have a den. It's great. It has a big old television, pool table, sofa and everything. There's a toilet in it too."

"It was meant to be a Granny flat but then my granny died," Jimmy added helpfully and I thought what a great guy he was. He had read my mind and there was no need to pull him aside and ask him for permission.

"We hang out there in the evenings – just for a chat and a bit of telly. Would you like to come down tonight?"

He was clearly pleased. "Sure I would. I'll need to check with me auntie first. What sort of time?"

"After tea. Usually about half past six to half past eight."

It was agreed. We gave him Jimmy's address and told him just to knock on the door.

"Blimey, he talks really fast, doesn't he?"

I nodded. "You didn't mind me inviting him – I should have asked you first."

"Shite. The den's yours as well. The way he speaks is funny – it's like he's singing, only he's speaking the words. And he says me instead of my – did you notice that?"

"Aye, me did." We both grinned.

"Do you think Rip will be happy?"

"About what?"

"About us asking him to the den?"
"I don't know."
But of course I did.

CHAPTER SEVENTEEN

Rip was not speaking. He was rocking back and fourth in the old rocker I had given the den. It belonged to my Great Uncle William, Granda's brother, but he had passed it onto me because he had bad piles and could no longer sit in it comfortably. Rip's knuckles were white but he was pretending not to be annoyed. Every now and again he would give a little shake of disbelief followed by a tiny nod which translated: *why should this surprise me?*

"We didn't have time to ask you, Rip," Jimmy repeated. "Wait'll you hear the way he goes on. He talks like a machine gun – doesn't he, Kev?"

You could see Rip thinking about the machine gun image and how he might use it to his advantage, but it was too difficult to twist and then the moment was gone and he was crosser than ever.

"He's actually really nice, Rip. He mightn't even turn up – he said his auntie might have something on."

Rip shrugged and held out his hands. "Lads, it's none of my business who you invite to the den. Just because I brought a few posters and Jackie's old dumb-bells doesn't mean I have any rights."

The dumb-bells were gathering dust in the far corner by the window. Rip had brought them to compliment the Conan the Barbarian poster that now adorned the wall. He had read somewhere that Arnie had once been a puny nobody like everyone else and had started pumping iron by using humble dumb bells just like these. Me and Jimmy had a bash but our hearts weren't really in it. Rip had kept it going for weeks until one of the two kilogramme discs fell off the bar and landed on his toe. He had hopped and yelled and used such language that the following day Mr Richmond from next door came round and told Jimmy's dad that one of his Chihuahuas had dropped dead of a heart attack.

"Apparently, they are easily upset." Jimmy explained.

"Is Rip in trouble? What did your dad say?"

"He shut the door in his face, and later on he said he would kiss Rip's toe better."

Mr Hood didn't like Mr Richmond or his Chihuahuas.

"And what's all this shite about you saving his life? I was in the pool and I didn't see fuck all!"

"I told you, I just helped him out a little."

"And he says you saved his life? Don't you see what he's doing? He's trying to slime his way in."

"Aw, come on, Rip." Jimmy said. "Think what it would be like if you were a new boy in the south."

"Never happen, mate!"

"Just suppose. You wouldn't know anybody. They'd all be doing their Irish dancing and you wouldn't have a clue how to even tie up the shoe."

"Look, look, I came down tonight just to hang out with my two best mates. I had no idea all this was happening."

All this, were the cans of Coke and Mars bars we had put on the coffee table.

Rip stopped rocking and his back stiffened as he looked out of the window. He gestured to the door with a little nod. "Here's your bum chum now."

Three hard knocks.

"Christ, Jimmy, you better get it before he stoves the fucker in!"

Jimmy flew to the door. I felt strangely nervous and to be honest, no offence to Rip, I would have preferred just for this once for him not to be there.

"Alright, lads, sorry I'm a bit late – that hill takes ages to walk down."

"Better down than up, though," Jimmy blurted, "Me and Kevin sometimes take the bikes up on a Saturday. Its murder going up but what a buzz going down – isn't it Kev?"

"It is, aye." Rip didn't own a bike but you couldn't not talk about bikes just because he was there. No way. "You can get up to fifty miles an hour on the way back down – and that's without peddling."

"You can't even peddle because you're going so fast – it's brilliant. You're really lucky where you live, Ronald."

I checked Rip. He was eyeing him warily but seemed okay. So far so good.

"This is a grand club you have."

"It's a den." Rip's first contribution.

"A den, sorry. Hey, sorry about class today. The teacher shouldn't have said that thing about the farting. Everybody was laughing at my turd and I didn't mind. Just a bit of fun."

Rip shrugged.

"Help yourself to a Mars bar and a can of Coke. This is where it all happens – we can give you the big tour in a moment, it'll only take about ten seconds. There's the T.V, we don't have a video yet but Rip borrowed one the other day. Toilet's out the back."

"Brilliant! Do you do your homework here?"

"Not really, it's more of a fun place. We usually do our homework at home and then come here to relax."

"Okay."

I cracked open a can and took a slurp. It gave me something to do and a moment to think. "Are you settling in okay? We all know your auntie. We used to get our sweets at her shop before we went to the pictures."

"Is that right? She's great. She doesn't really bother me much. She's got loads of friends that she visits."

Rip was making little effort and it was grinding on me because it was clear that Ronald was. I decided to ignore him and concentrate all my efforts on our special guest. After a little gentle prompting he told us a little about himself – some of which we already knew. He had lived all his life in Waterford where his dad taught history. His mother, an American art teacher, had met his dad on an exchange programme and had taught alongside him before the slow tranquil life in Waterford had begun to bore her.

"I was only three when they divorced – don't remember much."

Divorced? Like Burton and Taylor. Right here in the den.
"Don't you miss her?"
"Sometimes. I miss my dad more…"
We knew not to ask. Even Rip.
"When's the last time you saw your mum?" I asked, safe enough.
"At my dad's funeral."
Shit.
"She wanted to take me back with her but I didn't want to go."
"What?" I couldn't help myself. "I'd give anything to go to the states."
"Why?"
"Why? Are you serious? Hollywood, Evel Kinevel, Lee Majors, Stephen King – what's not in America is not worth having."
Finally Rip found his voice. "You had the chance to go over there and instead you came up here? Why?"
Ronald considered carefully. "This is where my dad came from, where he was brought up. He used to tell me stories about all the places he had been in the north – camping and caravanning when he was a boy. The Mourne Mountains, the Fermanagh Lakelands, the Walled City of Derry."
"Londonderry."
"Sorry, Londonderry. It was our plan to visit them all … before he got ill. My dad said that there are parts of Northern Ireland that you never see on the news – some of the most beautiful places in the world."
"Shite," said Rip. "If there are I've never fuckin' seen them. Your Da' was away a long time, my friend, things have changed."
"You mean the Troubles?"
"Aye, that's what I mean."
"Dad was fascinated by the Troubles."
"Fascinated?"
"Interested."
"I know what fascinated means."

"Ho ho, this is really getting interesting now," Jimmy enthused, rubbing his hands together. "Our Rip here is a real expert on the Troubles. Catholics versus Protestants. Did you know that Kevin knew you were a Protestant even before we met you?"

"Really?"

I could have cheerfully throttled Hood. "Yeah, sorry, my mum works in a pub and when we heard you were coming she asked a couple of people..." it sounded so lame.

But Ronald seemed delighted. "That's the sort of thing I'm talking about. Even before you met me you knew my religion. That was the most important thing to know. I might be an axe murderer – but you'd rather know what religion I am."

"Hold on a wee minute," Rip sat forward in his chair. This was his baby so he was going to ask a question or two. "Exactly what is it about the Troubles that you and your dad find so fascinating? People being blown apart and burnt alive? Bullets in kneecaps? Policemen shot in the back?"

"That's horrible," Ronald said. "But what interested him – and me - is how it all started."

"What, the I.R.A?"

"Yes, but what led up to it all."

"The I.R.A," Rip repeated slowly, like he was talking to Lennie from *Of Mice and Men.* That's what started it – their killing and bombing and destroying."

"I understand what you're saying, Rip – but I'm talking about what caused the I.R.A to do those awful things. You know, the treatment of the Ulster Catholics for the last fifty years – not being able to vote, no jobs, no houses – the way they were kept down!"

Rip was stupefied. "Well, if they don't like where they live, why don't they piss off back over the border?"

"Because some of them have never been over the border, Rip," Ronald said with a faint smile. "Ulster has been their home for generations."

"Shall we stick on the telly for a bit?" I suggested. "See

what's on?"

Ronald stayed for about another half hour before thanking us and saying goodnight. He thanked me again for what he called, *the business at the pool,* and Jimmy, as I knew he would, told him he was welcome back anytime. As the words left his mouth, I could feel Rip tensing.

"Well, he's not fuckin' shy, is he?" Rip shook his head in disbelief. "Jimmy Cagney, I'll say this just the once! If you're gonna open up the den to every fucker that walks by – I'm away pal. I come here because I know I can relax and don't need to be on my guard."

"Aw, come on, Rip, he's nice enough."

"Is he?"

"Is it because he started to talk about the Troubles?" I asked.

"Aye, I knew you'd pick up on that, McBride – you think that's what annoyed me?"

"Is it?"

"No, it's not."

"He seemed to know a little bit about it."

"He knew fuck all! He's read a couple of books. We've lived in it!"

"What annoyed you, Rip?"

"I'll tell ya. He's new here, right? He knows that people are wondering about him, right? And yet he fuckin' strolled up to the den – I watched him – his hands were in his pockets, all relaxed like, as if he was gonna feed the ducks. It's a wonder he wasn't whistlin' Zippedee fuckin' Doodah!"

"Come on, Rip, it's not like he's Kunte Kinte?"

"I didn't want him to look scared; just a little – I don't know – respectful. He's no idea who's in charge here."

"I like him." Jimmy said.

"Me too."

"Lots of people liked Hitler," Rip said and he nodded to himself, pleased with what he had said. "Yes, lots of people liked old Adolf – before he, you know, started to kill people and stuff."

*

Palmer liked the drama of it. He liked to keep us in suspense. You could see he had the tests with him – a big transparent plastic pouch – and you could clearly see his red markings; but he liked to milk it.

My hands felt clammy again and I could feel the pulse of my heart in my throat. God, I hated this so much. I loathed every single thing to do with the Eleven Plus with such intensity that it made me feel giddy.

"Right, ladies and gents, let's make a start."

This was it.

"Some improvement in some quarters, elsewhere ..." and he glanced in my direction - the bastard. Oh, just give me the fucking thing and be done! "Hood, be a good chap and pass these out. Remember, it's nobody's business what anybody else gets, just concern yourself with how you can improve your own score."

That was a joke. Already there was a buzz about the room as kids shared their scores with one another – "What did you get? What did you get?" –before long every single person in the room would have a fair idea of the pecking order. No real surprises. Spazzy David Malcolmson with his stupid National Health specs (we know your parents can afford proper ones, Malcolmson, you're not cool, you're just a dick!) at the top of the pile with Rubber Gub McBride in charge of the Z squad special needs. I followed Jimmy round the room as he handed them out – Malcolmson got his, Brownlie, Douglas – here came mine. Ronald nodded to me and I nodded back but that was all I could manage just now.

Nine.

Oh, Jesus.

Nine out of fifty.

Shit, shit, shit.

Palmer had encircled the mark with such force that there were little perforations in the paper, like the "rip along the dotted line" application forms Dad sometimes brought home from work. Oh, dear Jesus. That was it then. Game over.

I felt a presence hovering at my side, eyes peering over half-moon glasses.

"Beyond poor, McBride – would you agree?"

I nodded hotly.

"I need to speak to you up at my desk."

I pushed back my chair and it seemed to me that the whole class was holding their breath. Was Stephanie looking at me? Was she focussing on my lip, or my fat arse, or the way my belly hung over my belt? Or was she perhaps trying to decide who had the biggest diddies: me, Brownlie, or her good self? At least I was in the top three for that.

Joy of joys, I wasn't alone up at Palmer's desk. I had the distinguished company of Christopher Nicol and Sam McGill. Chris was only doing the Eleven Plus because his mum had insisted; he collected lolly pop sticks – the ones with the jokes on them – and had over one hundred, even though there were only ten jokes. Sam, who was grinning at the novelty of being up at the desk, was one of those kids who was always a beat behind everyone else when you were reciting the times tables:

Class: Six nines are fifty-four...

Sam: ...ifty-four...

Class: Seven nines are sixty-three...

Sam: ...ixty-three...

"Okay, class, I have a little bit of business here. You can quietly read your books for a moment."

Palmer looked carefully at each of us in turn. "Boys, this is bad. McGill, please take that stupid look off your face, there is nothing funny about this." He ran his finger down the column of numbers that ran parallel to the register and I positioned myself so that I could see. McGill had scored seven and Nicol had scored eleven. I was disappointed; disappointed that Sam had scored less. I was throwing in the towel.

"I'm assuming that you three still want to pass this thing?"

I nodded, it was what was expected of me.

Palmer thought for a moment. "Let me impress upon you: if I don't see very rapid improvement pretty darn fast, you three don't have a snowball's chance in hell of passing the Eleven Plus! Do I make myself absolutely clear?"

We nodded again.

"Go sit down."

Jimmy gave me a pat on the shoulder as I sat down and I shook him off without a thought to his feelings. I was High School bound. I glanced over at his paper and saw that he had managed twenty-one. Bully for you, Jimmy Cagney.

"Malcolmson's pissed off big time," he whispered. "He's not tops. Look at the face on him."

I turned round half-heartedly and saw his miserable kisser. Hope you die soon, Malcolmson, you're the last person in the world I'd want to be.

"Guess who the champ is?"

"Who?"

But I knew already.

"Ronald! Guess how much?"

"Oh, do be quiet, Jimmy."

"Forty-eight!"

Forty-eight??

He nodded, delighted with my expression. "Palmer wrote "absolutely excellent" on it – I seen it!"

Good. Maybe, since he didn't have to do much revision, he could take some swimming lessons.

Palmer wiped the board clean and now would begin the long and enjoyable post-mortem of the test. He would focus on the ones that the majority had found difficult – poor Ronald was about to be bored – and the first one of these concerned a donkey that was capable of rational thought and had to choose between different lengths of carrots according to the length of journey it was about to walk. There might have been something to do with heavy children and light children as well.

His droning voice faded.

I felt as if I was floating. It was a strangely liberating feeling. I thought to myself that this is what a condemned man must feel like when there is no escaping the electric chair. Blissful acceptance. No more struggle, torment and worry. It was a foregone conclusion. All he had to do was sit comfortably, accept his fate, and sizzle like a sausage – his shit and piss boiling under the voltage. I could feel a smile spreading like margarine across my face and I knew how stupid it must look but I couldn't stop it. And I thought of what Palmer had said –*you don't have a snowball's chance in hell* - and I really took to the image, imagining the devil reaching into a freezer, pulling it out, and the snowball dissolving in his cruel, twisted claw. Then, I saw myself decked out in the High School uniform. I was behind the wire and I was yelling down at my quivering former self: *Hey, Funky Gibbon! How did you get that rubber gub – did your ma fuck a monkey?*

"MCBRIDE!!"

I jolted out of the chair, almost wet myself.

"ARE YOU IN THERE, SON?"

"Sorry, sir!"

"Sorry? I've been calling you for the past half-minute. You're a space cadet, McBride. You should be strapped in with Armstrong and Buzz. Not five minutes ago you were up at my desk and I was telling you how important it was that you buckled down – and here you are in a wee world of your own with a big daft grin on your face!"

"Yes, sir. Sorry, sir."

"Well?"

"What, sir?"

"OHH!" Palmer looked in disbelief to the heavens. "THE DONKEY, BOY! – THE DONKEY!"

Oh yes, of course, the donkey.

A strange sensation. That sense of floating again – but also a rising, not entirely unpleasant, feeling of hysteria.

"WHAT DID THE DONKEY SAY, MCBRIDE?"

He was purple in the face and I thought his eyes were going to pop out of his head. And suddenly, I knew exactly what to do. I took a deep breath, filled up my lungs and replied:

"HEEEEEEEEEE-HAWWWWWWW!!"

The class exploded in laughter. It was almost worth all the sleepless nights, the misery, the worry, the toilet paper up the bum. Almost. I had perhaps two seconds to enjoy it and then he had me by the ear.

Oh, suffering Jesus!

Pete, you sad excuse for a sibling, wherever you are, please accept my humblest apology.

I was yanked from my seat and it felt like my left ear was internally attached to my left testicle.

"Wise guy, McBride? Funny thing is, you're not so wise when it comes to doing the tests – are you, son?" He hauled me out of the class, their laughter still ringing in my ears and Rip yelling after me: "You're a legend, Kevin! A legend!"

*

Mr Flynn did not think I was funny at all. He glared at me and made me stand in front of his desk whilst he pondered what to do with me. *Carrie* was still fresh in my mind and I looked for the ash tray that I could topple with my telekinesis but there wasn't one on the table, only those stupid swinging ball things and they weren't for moving. I could see his string vest through his shirt and it wasn't difficult to imagine him fingering fluff out of his belly button. I also had the notion that he and Palmer, the only male members in the school, didn't see eye to eye. Was there some sort of rivalry there that I could exploit? Could I be bothered? Palmer's attack on my ear - it was red and throbbing - had robbed me of that lovely floaty feeling and now I felt dejected and dispirited beyond belief.

"Dearie me, McBride. Mr Palmer didn't have time to fill me in with the details but it seems you were very impertinent," his face registered distaste, "something about a donkey?"

"Sorry, sir."

"You know what impertinent means, McBride?"

"Very rude, sir."

He nodded. "I knew you would know it. You have always struck me as a cleverish boy - but struggling with the Eleven Plus."

"Yes, sir. Sorry, sir."

"Not really Mr Palmer's fault. Good teacher wouldn't you say? You need to work harder – concentrate. Stop gazing out of the window. The town will still be here tomorrow, don't worry."

"Yes, sir. Sorry, sir."

"Brother at the Academy."

"Yes, sir."

"Peter, isn't it?"

"Sir."

"I'm sure you'd like to follow in his footsteps?"

"Yes, sir.

"Maybe you could get him to help you?"

"Yes, sir. Sorry, sir."

He dismissed me with a flick of his fingers but called after me. "Take your time and wash your face before you go back. Tell your teacher you're very sorry. I've slippered boys for less, Mr McBride. Don't want him thinking you got special treatment just because you're the son of the Quiz King!"

As I slowly made my way back up the stairs, I wondered how many times I had said sorry in his office and how many times I had apologised to Palmer on my way down. The Amazing Apology Boy. Was that the way it was always going to be? Weaving my way through life, dispensing apologies left, right and centre – sorry about that, can I apologise to you for that? I'm sorry for troubling you, but ...sorry, sorry, sorry. And if there wasn't an opportunity to say sorry, at least be good enough, young man, to have an apologetic expression permanently plastered on your fat face. Dad was a bit like that with workmen around the house. He felt guilty that he couldn't do the work himself and, even though they were being paid, he would jump up when they entered the room and apologise for being in their way. He would constantly ask them if they wanted tea or coffee and then he would yell in to Mum to switch on the kettle. It was a bit pathetic, to be honest, but the difference was that he was clever. His youngest son, it would appear, was as thick as shite.

Another thought: Flynn had not called me Kevin. He had started off with McBride, to show I was in trouble, then later on had switched to son and then Mr McBride. He hadn't called me Kevin because he could not remember my name. And he was not alone in that, sometimes other teachers called me Keith or Kenneth. So, here I was, the Amazing Apology Boy, whose real name no one could remember, who was failing the Eleven Plus and about to apologise, yet again, to Mr Palmer for making the sound of a donkey. Could it get any worse?

Yes, it could.

CHAPTER EIGHTEEN

I was finding it difficult to sleep.

Vincent Price, Evel Kinevel, Steve Austin and eighteen dead soldiers decide to rent caravans in Millisle for the summer. Eleven of the soldiers opt for an orange caravan, whilst Vincent chooses peacock blue and Steve settles for lemon. Evel asks for stars and stripes but is told by the caravan sales manager, who is called Jack and is 47 with three children whose average age is 12 and a half, that they do not come in that colour. Two thirds of the remaining soldiers choose either pink or green whilst half of what is left have to settle for H-Block brown. It is 55 miles to Millisle and Evel, averaging 57 m.p.h, sets off at 7:55 am with Vincent riding pillion. Steve Austin leaves 17 and a half minutes later on foot; he can reach a top speed of 60 m.p.h but needs to rest every ten minutes for 130 seconds or else his bionics will overheat. Eight of the dead soldiers start their journey eleven minutes after Steve Austin but stop halfway there to erect a roadblock which takes 25 minutes and needs to be manned by 2/5 of the remaining soldiers who begin their journey – in three separate black taxis – 19 minutes later. Ten miles from the camp site, Evel runs out of petrol – he had not calculated for the weight of Vincent Price – and they begin to walk. Vincent, impatient to get there, pays a boy – Philip Pelan, who is 9 and is the third of 5 children, 3/5 of whom are not boys - £4.92 for the use of his pogo stick.

On Friday, Mr Palmer announced that he was stepping up the pace of the Eleven Plus practise tests. Due to the imminence of the actual exams, we were going to sit an additional test – "I will analyse the results for Monday" – then we could hit the ground running as it were. My heart sank. Mondays were always going to be awful, but now that was Friday scuppered as well. And it would make no difference to me. A hundred attempts and I still wouldn't get it.

In a school there are twice as many girls as there are boys. 50% of the boys and 25% of the girls are under 11 years of age. If there are 486 children in the school how many of them are not under the age of 11 years?

It looked gettable, certainly friendlier than some of the others, and I even made a little start at working it out. But then I muddled myself, the figures melted into each other, and all I could hear was the scratch, scratch, scratching of the pens and pencils all about me.

Again, as before, I thought about dying. How could my fear of failing the Eleven Plus be less than my fear of dying? It didn't make sense. Boris Karloff and Bela Lugosi would be there to greet me into heaven.

"Look, Bela —it's that sad little boy who watches our movies."

Bela would smile, extend his caped arm and in that glorious Hungarian accent say, "Hello, Kevin — we bid you ...welcome."

"Kevin?"

I looked up and saw Palmer smiling down on me.

"Are you not feeling well?"

His tone was kind and that was the killer. I could feel the tears prickling. Pity was the one thing that always got me. Don't cry, Kevin. For God's sake, don't cry. Laugh if you must. Snarl.

Palmer stood, held a finger to his lips to dismiss one or two enquiring looks – although most were lost in the paper – and gestured for me to follow him outside.

"Kevin, we're not going to fall out over this because you are too nice of a boy and you come from a good family." He put his hand on my shoulder and that's what broke me. "You're just not coping with this, son. Do you want me to withdraw you?"

I was finding it hard to breath; big fat tears were rolling freely down my cheeks.

"There is still a way for you to get to the Academy, you know. You could go to the High School – work hard like I know you can do – then get transferred to the Academy in second or third year. It's happened before."

I could well imagine.

"Who's the new boy?"

"Kevin McBride."

"How come he didn't join in first year like the rest of us?"

"Thick bastard couldn't pass his Eleven Plus."

"Jesus. So what's he doing here now? And why's he sticking his lower lip out at me? Cheeky fucker."

The tears continued unabated. Where were they all coming from? *Poor wee, Kevin – his bladder's too near his eyes.*

Palmer looked quite upset himself. He plucked a tissue from his cardigan and handed it to me. "Nothing's worth this, Kevin – let me phone your dad."

"No, sir, please, sir – no!"

"He'll understand – of course he will."

I spent the next half an hour sitting on the toilet, weeping and wondering if it was some kind of nervous break-down I was having. The graffiti on the cubicle door wasn't very comforting - neither original nor diverting.

Fuck the Provos.

Pope John Paul's a faggot.

Celtic eat shite.

My tears finally stopped and I did feel better if somewhat drained. The mirror showed a puffy faced, red eyed reflection that required some attention. Crying in school was second only to peeing your pants. I splashed cold water about me and towelled myself dry. Better. A little. Utter silence. In less than a minute the bell would clatter, the same bell that had called them out for the last fifty years, and you would hear the squeak of sneakers and the squeals of them as they thundered down the corridor. I had my story ready.

There it was.

Here they came.

Who would it be? Jimmy or Rip?

Neither.

"Are you okay, Kevin?" Ronald made no move towards the urinals and I thought that was pretty classy; he'd only come into the toilets to seek me out, not because he needed a piss.

"Stomach cramps!" I kneaded my belly. "Something I've eaten. I'm gonna kill my mum."

He nodded and I knew to stop.

"What are you doing tomorrow morning?"

"Huh?"

"Are you doing anything?"

"Why?"

"Do you want to come to my house – my auntie's house?"

"What for?"

He shrugged. "You invited me to the den ..."

I didn't have the energy to make an excuse.

"Don't worry, forget it."

"No, I'll come."

And for some odd reason I felt a little bit better.

CHAPTER NINETEEN

Margaret Elizabeth Donaghy was dead. She had been lying in this secluded spot for one hundred and thirty-five years under the shade of a tree, looking onto the traffic although in her day it would have been horses and carts instead of cars. The graveyard, half-way up the old Dublin Hill, was a favourite hang-out for me and Jimmy. It was a good half-way stop when you were humping your bike up the hill and some of the graves were brilliant. Although not the oldest, this was our favourite. She had died in 1845 and the inscription, still perfectly legible, read: "Beloved daughter, forever in our hearts. Sleep well beautiful angel." She was seventeen years old. I'd been here loads of times with Jimmy, but never with Rip; it wasn't the sort of place he would appreciate. We wondered what had killed her so young. Jimmy suggested the plague but then we remembered that the big famine was round about then. That was probably it. Poor girl starved to death because there weren't any spuds to eat. We loved to talk about what she might have looked like, what colour her hair had been. It was fun to imagine, like having a girlfriend but without the embarrassment and bother of wondering what to do with her. Only seventeen years on top of the ground and all these years underneath. It was a thought. Strange to think that she had once walked in the town where we walked. There would be old buildings that she might have touched – the library, the town hall - places me and Jimmy had been to. Funny to think of it.

I checked my watch. It was ten minutes to ten. I was never late anywhere but you didn't want to be too early either. That looked a bit desperate. Ten minutes would be just enough time to push my Grifter up the remainder of the hill. I said good-bye to Margaret and left, maybe Ronald might like to visit her later. He might find it *fascinating*. I wasn't really sure what to expect up at his house, probably a video of some sort, but I wasn't giving it much thought. I was trying not to think too deeply about anything just now. Palmer had not phoned Dad; either he had forgotten or he was leaving it till Monday. I wasn't sure how I was going to play the situation and actually this little expedition was just what was needed. It was possible, I supposed, that Palmer might phone him today. If that was the case Dad might be waiting for me when I came home.

"What's all this, son? Mr Palmer phoned the house. I had no idea you were doing as badly as this?" And Pete would be whizzing around like a top. It didn't bare thinking about so for the moment I simply didn't.

I made it to the top of the hill, puffing and panting, and mounted the Grifter. It was a good solid bike, great for flying down, but really heavy and cumbersome for going up. Three gears, colour coded, and in the right hand grip – none of this reaching down to tweak with silly little levers. Granda had gone halfers on it with Mum and Dad. He had connections in the bicycle trade.

"Hope it doesn't get bashed falling off the back of the lorry!" Dad had joked, but Granda hadn't found that one funny. It had been delivered to his house on the Tuesday before my birthday and we had arranged to pick it up on the following Sunday. The anticipation. Having to get through the rest of the week knowing it was sitting there waiting for me. He had phoned me on Tuesday night – they hardly ever phoned – and described it down the line.

"Is Kevin McBride available? Just to let you know, I have recently taken delivery of a rather large object which is currently residing in the box room."

"Tell him it looks like a motor bike!" Granny yelled from behind. She sounded really excited. It was a big purchase and there had been much in the organisation of it.

I found Ronald's house (much bigger than ours but not newly painted) and rang the doorbell. I was nervous without really knowing why and was starting to wonder how long I would have to stay before making some excuse to leave. Through the opaque glass, I saw the approach of a slightly bowed, middle-aged figure. Deep breath, Kevin. Polite smile. Here went.

"Ah, you must be Ronald's friend?"

"Hello ..." I gulped. I had very nearly called her Mrs Sweetie. I couldn't think what else to say. I couldn't say *pleased to meet you* because I had already met her before.

"I used to buy sweets from you in your sweet shop."

Oh, for fuck's sake.

"Come in ...come in. Don't worry about your feet, the carpet's bogging anyway."

I followed her down the hallway. Maybe I should've parked the bike round the side. Nah, it was probably safe enough up here on top of the hill.

"We were in the middle of a game," she said over her shoulder. "Would you like to join us?"

A game? Jesus.

"Hi, Kevin!" Ronald smiled at me from the settee and pointed to the chair opposite. He gestured the board game on the coffee table. "Sorry not to get the door. She cheats, you know, I didn't want her to see what I had."

I nodded awkwardly. Scrabble. God. And there were some jaw-breaking words on the faded old board: *Explicit, Sordid, Munificent, Eloquent.* Fuck. Deep breaths. I'll just say I have a headache. Puffed out from the ride up the hill. Easy. Sorted.

"I don't need to cheat." Mrs Sweetie squinted at her letters. "P-I-T-H-Y – pithy, there I'm out!" She toted up the score. "You lose again, 362 to 257." She clambered up off her seat.

Ronald stood up and, like an eejit, so did I.

"Do you need a hand with anything?" he asked her.

"Maybe the bags," she smiled at me. "Nice to see you again, Kevin – tell your dad I was asking for him."

"I'll be back in a sec. Kevin."

I relaxed a little. Clearly Scrabble was their thing and her invitation had only been out of politeness. It was a really big living-room and the old flowery suite was really comfy – the chair anyway - but there was also a musty, dusty smell to it as if the room hadn't been aired in a while. Big unkempt garden out the back, I could see it through the window, and a long dining table that had seen better days. There was an impressive Grandfather Clock in the corner – and suddenly I had Rip's tuneless voice in my head:

My grandfather's cock was too tall for his pants so he used it to hose down the wall.

"Sorry about that," Ronald bounded back into the room with a sheepish grin. "That's her away now."

"Where's she off to?"

"Och, she's got millions of friends. Golf today. She meets people for coffee, book clubs, knitting circles. She has the life of Riley."

"She seems nice."

"Nice? Jaysus, Kevin – she's bloody bonkers!"

He said it with such fondness and enthusiasm that I found myself grinning.

"Mind you, the last thing in the world she expected was to have an eleven year old boy living with her."

"She doesn't seem to mind."

"She doesn't. But the thing is, she's no notion what to do with children. She has an idea that they go to bed a bit earlier and you're not meant to curse around them – but that's about it, she's brilliant."

"What do I call her? It's Mrs Douglas, isn't it?"

"'Tis. But she'll slap you if you call her that. Gloria – that's her name."

"And I can call her Gloria?"

"Course."

"Wow." Mum would never allow for that, you never called people over forty by their first names - even cleaners; but then she would never know.

"Do you want to see something special?"

"Sure."

"Follow me."

He led me up the creaking stairs and along the landing. It was intriguing, but I had a fair idea now what he was up to. A train set, or Scalextric, or Subbuteo. Something on a grand scale that his auntie had bought him but that required another boy to play with. That was what the invite was all about. There was nothing sneaky in that. It was what we all did.

"Can you keep a secret?"

"Depends what it is."

He paused at the second door on the landing.

"This door is always locked."

"What's behind it?"

"Ah! Can you keep a secret?"

"This had better be good."

He grinned, produced the key from his pocket, and swung open the door.

I gazed around, my eyes widening even as the smell washed over me and I was transported back to every joyous occasion I had ever experienced. Cinema trips, outings, birthdays, Christmases. Oh, that smell. The sweetness of it, the sugariness. You could feel it reaching for you, enveloping you. And then a thought occurred to me with such sickening speed that it almost jolted me back a step: no way am I sharing this with Jimmy and Rip, no fucking way! This is my thing. It's nothing to do with them. Bring them into it and it will cease to be special.

I licked my lips. I couldn't help myself. The room, intended as a small bedroom, was filled with jar upon jar of sweets. Dozens of them. Wine gums, midget gems, gob-stoppers, chocolate eclairs, jelly beans, chocolate limes, American hard gums, and on and on and on. Suckable sweets, chewable sweets, sweets that melted on the tongue, sweets that you hardly ever saw in other shops and that tasted all the more yummy because of their rarity. The only thing missing was a chocolate river and a grinning Oompa Loompa.

"How?" I stammered, "I mean ...why?"

Ronald was beaming at my reaction. "Gloria has a really good relationship with the wholesaler. When she sold up the shop she didn't want to stop dealing entirely so he still supplies a small order direct to the house."

"Who the hell eats them all?"

"She gives a lot away to charity – you know for prizes and things like that. I help her to make up big jars and then they raffle them off after you've guessed how many sweets are inside. Whist drives, fetes, quizzes, jumble sales. "

Of course. Dad had brought a huge jar home last year from one of his pub quizzes. This was where it came from. I was still in a bit of a daze. The smell of sugar and glucose was overwhelming.

"Would you like some?"

"Really?"

From a drawer, he handed me a white paper bag. "Help yourself. Don't make yourself sick, though."

"Gloria won't mind?"

"She told me to offer you."

"Right ...right..." I looked around me, suddenly depressed at the choice available and the size of the bag, but realising that I would back for more at some stage. Wine gums, fudge, and cola cubes. That would do. Ronald helped me screw off the lids and there was a little plastic shovel so that we didn't have to touch them with our fingers. We carefully screwed the lids back on, you had to keep the contents air tight otherwise they lost their freshness.

"Aren't you having any?"

"Not just now."

"Of course, you're probably sick of sweets."

Sick of sweets? My God, imagine that?

We bore them downstairs and I flopped back down on the chair, munching happily and totally relaxed. Guilt would come soon as my belly filled and I thought of all the calories adding to my bra size. But that was for later; just now I was enjoying the sugar rush and kept firing them in.

"Ronald, this is some place."

"Tanks!"

I burst out laughing.

"What?"

"The way you talk is so funny. I'm not making fun of you – I swear to God – I just love the way you talk."

"Ah, sure well God Almighty, I'm glad you find me funny. Maybe we can find the pot o' gold at the end of the rainbow and we can dance an Irish jig, you, me and all the little leprechauns." He leapt to his feet and did a little hop, skip, half kick thing and I nearly choked on a wine gum. It was the kind of thing that would never be funny in class or even in the playground – but it was hilarious here. I could describe it to Dad later, or to Jimmy, but they wouldn't get it and would be laughing just to be nice.

"There's something else I want to show you?"

"Yeah?"

This was turning out to be the best visit ever.

"Here..." he moved to the table and pulled out a chair for me. Then he gestured towards the paper and questions that lay in front of the salt and pepper. I recognised them immediately from the way they were formatted – I didn't even have to read them to see what they were.

"What's this?"

"I thought I could help you."

"Did you, now?" it was mad, but I suddenly felt like Hansel being enticed into the gingerbread house by the wicked witch. "I didn't ask for your help."

"I know."

"Is that what the sweets were all about?"

"No. The sweets are all about sweets. I told you what she does with them."

"You know what I mean."

He looked genuinely wounded and I was completely unsure what to make of the situation. It flashed before me that maybe Palmer had engineered this whole meeting – matching up his star pupil with the boy who so badly needed help. That would account for him not phoning Dad.

"Did Mr Palmer put you up to this?"

"Palmer? No!"

"What then?" There was no way on God's green earth I was going to show him how impossibly thick I was when it came to these hateful things. He knew my score – everybody did by now – but I wasn't about to show him how such a fantastic score was achieved. No way.

"I can do these. Me dad taught me how, although it's the kind of stupid word play that I can do anyhow. I came here and I knew nobody. You helped me in the swimming-pool and you invited me to your club."

"Den."

"To your den. I'd like to help you with this. If you don't want my help – fine, but I'd like to."

I was breathing heavily and I could feel the congealed sugar pick-axing into my teeth. His offer was sincere and so was he; but what good would it do for him to see how stupid I actually was.

"Thanks, Ronald – but it's pointless. I'm absolutely shit at this and there's not enough time before the tests."

"Wrong. There's a month. If you let me help you – and not just today, you can do it."

I didn't look convinced. I wasn't.

"Kevin, I watched you yesterday in class. You were beaten before you even started. Little shakes of the head, gazing round you, scribbling things out as soon as you'd written them down."

Christ, that obvious? No wonder Palmer had swooped.

"I can tell by talking to you that you are way cleverer than 9 out of 50. You're selling yourself short because you're overthinking it. That's something me dad said."

I managed a sort of grunt, didn't really want to argue with his dead dad. Rude.

"Give me half an hour. You don't have to do anything. Just watch me."

"Watch the master?" but the sarcasm felt dirty and uncalled for.

"Deal?"

"Go on then."

The first question, hand written, was a familiar one.

In a school there are twice as many girls as there are boys. 50% of the boys and 25% of the girls are under 11 years of age. If there are 486 children in the school how many of them are not under the age of 11 years?

"From yesterday? You remembered it?"

"So what? Parrots and monkeys remember things too. Stop overthinking!" he reached for a piece of paper and a pencil. "Here goes. Remember, I'm not going to make fun of you and I'm not going to laugh at you. If I do either of those things you can stick this sharp pencil in my ear.

"First we start with the fixed number which is 486.

There are twice as many girls as boys, so that's a ratio of 2:1. Still with me?"

"Not really."

"Think of them as slices of cake. Two slices are girls, one slice is boys. That makes three altogether – yes?"

I nodded, peered a bit closer.

"We want to find out what one of those parts is. We know that three parts equals 486 so a little bit of simple division is called for: 486/3 =162. So now we know that one part or slice of cake is 162. So there are 162 boys. To find the girls, we double it and that makes 324. We should now have enough information to answer the question so we go back to the start. 50% of boys are under 11; 50% equals a half, so 162/2 means that 81 boys are under 11 years of age. Take away 81 from 162 and you get 81. Exact same thing with the girls: 25% equals a quarter, so divide 324/4 and you end up with 81 girls under the age of 11. Take away 81 from 324 and you get 243. Answer: there are 81 boys under 11 and 243 girls under 11."

"Jesus Christ. You honestly think that's easy?"

"It looks horrible, Kevin. All the numbers, the backwards and forwards of it; but if you read the question carefully and take it step by step it becomes easier- like a jigsaw."

"I hate jigsaws."

"So do I. Can I show you another?"

"As long as I don't have to do anything."

"You have to watch and listen."

"Go on."

He went through the process again with a similar kind of question.

"Don't be annoyed with me just because I can do them."

Jesus, was I that easy to read?

"Hating me isn't going to help you. Remember, you can do things that I can't."

He showed me another one.

And then another one.

"Here's a type you'll recognise. This sort of one always comes up."

My best friend is tall and dark. I am nine and he is ten. He is one of these four boys below. Read the following sentences and write down my best friend's name.

Harry is younger than me. He is short and dark.

Dick is ten. He is a tall boy with fair hair.

Tom has dark hair. He is older than me and is a tall boy.

Jack is a tall boy with dark hair. He is nine.

"I fucking hate these ones."

"Remember, don't give up before you start. First thing we do – and you'll recognise this from class - we make a table. A lot of the work has been done for us, we just need to lay it out so we can see it clearly. Sometimes you have to work with the information you are not given as well as the information you are given."

Name	Age	Height	Hair Colour
Harry	?	Short	Dark
Dick	10	Tall	Fair
Tom	10	Tall	Dark
Jack	9	Tall	Dark

"Okay, I can see it now – Tom is the best friend!"

Ronald grinned at me.

"Smart arse!" but I smiled too and I could feel a funny tingling in my toes. Something was happening.

"There are only about five different types of question. All

of them look horrible from a distance – loads of information, stupid facts, figures, statistics – but when you lay them all down flat they're nothing special."

He demonstrated another one.

Then another.

And another.

"Palmer teaches it different."

"No, he teaches it the same – but you don't get peace to learn. There's people fartin' and pulling faces behind his back, interruptions and distractions. He can be sarcastic too and that's no use for someone like you or me – we just switch off and stop asking questions. Am I right?"

He was. Spot on.

"Can I show you another one?"

"You quite like these, don't you?"

"Sad, isn't it?"

I could hear the tick of the old Grandfather Clock but time did not feel like the enemy now; in fact, the sound was quite soothing and relaxing. It was just me and Ronald. The way he sat back with his fingers intertwined, head bowed, took away much of the pressure. It felt like he could wait forever without getting annoyed.

"It's more difficult in class. Harder."

"Knowing you have the ability to do them is the big thing. Blocking out distractions will follow naturally and we can work on timing. Just now time does not even exist. Forget that 50 minute shit Palmer keeps talking about. It's not helpful at all."

I nodded, feeling sharp and alert. It was as if I had been given brand new glasses to replace my cracked old ones.

We continued for the next hour or more and by the end of the session I was taking the lead with the pencil. That strange tingling in my toes had worked its way all the way up my body; a delicious combination of sugar and adrenalin fizzing through my system. I felt like I was fluttering, about to start flying around the room like Dick Van Dyke. And the best thing was that the part of me that loved to worry had been taken completely by surprise.

Ronald's offer, a potential solution to my problem, had been so unexpected that I could feel my mind frantically searching for an anxiety replacement. It settled on an old favourite – Dad lying in his coffin, victim of the heart defect that had claimed his own father at an early age, Mum bowed over with grief – but there was no real substance to the image and it was easily vanquished.

As my confidence increased so too did my ability to solve the horrible things. I still hated them, and some of them I simply couldn't do at all; but I was on my way and it was a fantastic feeling.

And I still had the hill to go down on my bike.

KEITH MCKIBBIN

CHAPTER TWENTY

Saturday night was fight night and I had never felt more up for it. It was the world middleweight championship. England's Alan Minter (champion) against the mighty Marvellous Marvin Hagler. Wembley again. It had been building up for weeks and because the Eleven Plus had robbed me of looking forward to it I was making up for it now.

"You're in great form tonight," Dad said, cracking open the second of his six Guinness cans. The radio commentator – it wouldn't be on the telly for a day or two - was describing the electrifying atmosphere at Wembley. Minter, under pressure, had remarked that he did not intend to lose his title to a black man and the papers had gobbled it up.

"It's the Eleven Plus, Dad, I think I've finally cracked it."

"Yeah? Good lad – that's great!"

"Ronald showed me a few tricks today."

"That was good of him."

"The way he explained it was so clear."

Dad nodded and twiddled with the radio knob. "His dad was a teacher, wasn't he?"

"Yeah," I took a slug from my Coke can and looked carefully at his shadowy figure. "Dad, do you think I can miss Granny's tomorrow?"

"Huh?"

"Ronald's invited me up again. There isn't much time before the Eleven Plus."

There was a distant roar as Hagler started to make his way towards the ring.

"You're a bit young, Kev, to be in the house on your own."

"But I wouldn't be, Dad. I'd be up with Ronald for the whole day and his auntie would be there. Please, Dad – it's important."

After a little more cajoling he agreed and we settled down to enjoy the fight. Mum might be annoyed but I could live with

160

that. What would be more difficult was if either Granny or Granda died during the week. Pete would love that. He would spend the rest of his life talking about how wonderful it had been to see them that last Sunday and all the great things that had happened that day. But it was a risk I was willing to take.

We were cheering for Minter. He wasn't really a racist, just caught on a bad day. But I did feel bad for poor Hagler. He didn't have any hair and the crowd booed his National Anthem. Then the fight started and Alan began to bleed. Hagler was catching him with everything – lefts, rights, upper-cuts – and the crowd had to watch their man being ripped apart. They weren't best pleased. In the middle of round three, blood pouring down his face, the referee called it off. Hagler held his hands aloft. He had little time to savour the moment before the beer bottles started landing on him and his corner men.

"Jesus Christ!" Dad said, his drink nearly spilling as he leant forward towards the radio. "Are you listening to this?"

I nodded, even though I knew he wouldn't catch it in the gloom.

Hagler's team shielded him and the security managed to get him safely from the ring and back to his dressing room. He wasn't even able to get his belts in the ring – the best part about being a champion. Later, we would get to see the television highlights and we laughed at Harry Carpenter at ringside – "And there is chaos here, absolute chaos. I'm smothered in beer and so are all my colleagues around me – aaaooowww! I've just been hit on the head by a bottle!" – but just now we were stunned and I could imagine millions of American heads shaking in disgust.

"There's no bigot like an Englishman!" Dad said, and he meant it.

*

On Monday morning I was outside the school shortly after the caretakers. I wanted to catch Palmer before he got to class. It was vital. I had spent all of yesterday with Ronald, eating sweets and practising Eleven Plus questions. It was all starting to come together. I was so relieved and excited that I could have yodelled.

On the way home, I began waving at people I thought I knew. Some of them waved back and others honked the horn. Then I started to wave at people I didn't know. Some of them waved back, some didn't, and one nasty looking character gave me the fingers. I did a little soft shoe shuffle as I neared the house; it was the first time I had ever danced in the street. At home, I almost kissed Pete on the head. He was walking up the stairs and I was already on the landing. I could easily have done it and I almost did. He knew I was happy and he hated it. He started to sing the *Funky Gibbon* and I joined in which made him sing louder and then stop altogether. Then he went into his room and slammed the door behind him. I had been so giddy that I hadn't slept well. *This* was how Hagler was meant to feel. On top of the world.

Shortly after 8.15, Palmer's old Escort came farting up the hill. He looked surprised to see me but took immediate advantage, thrusting books and a Woolworth's bag in my direction.

"Here, make yourself useful, McBride."

"Yes, sir. Sir, it was about what you said on Friday."

"What – oh, yes, I never got round to calling your dad – sorry, very busy weekend."

We were climbing the stairs to his room and I was struggling to keep up.

"Please, sir, can you give me one more chance. I've been working really hard with Ronald Douglas..."

"Douglas?" he gave a little snort of approval, "that shows initiative – good for you."

"Thanks, sir."

"And you think this new association will be enough to win the war?"

"Yes," I nodded with determination. "Yes, sir."

He set the books down on his desk. It was just me and him in the room. Me and him and all his stuffed animals.

"Let's see how you do with today's test before we decide anything – deal?"

I waited for Ronald outside before the bell sounded.

"Did you see him?"

"Yeah. He said he wouldn't phone him if I did better on today's test."

"Grand. How do you feel?"

"Nervous."

"Why?"

"In case I fuck up. This is it." And even as I said it, I could feel the old nerves creeping back over me: a little nausea, that hot heaviness, the usual shit.

Ronald spoke evenly. "Don't sell yourself short," he said. "There is no way in the world that you could possibly score worse than you did last time. No way. Just remember the techniques — the way of writing them down. Take control of them, don't let them control you. Focus on your own work and nothing more. Forget how easy the others are finding it, forget how much further ahead they are than you, forget how much more wonderful you think they are. Right?"

"Yes."

"You're sure, now?"

"Yes."

And for the most part I was able to remember his advice. The questions were just as difficult as last week but it was as if I was looking at them from a slightly different angle and the numbers were coming at me one at a time instead of all at once. I did get stuck, several times, but I didn't panic and I didn't focus on what the rest of the class were doing; I remembered the techniques Ronald had taught me and tried to unpick them. Only three left out and I managed to get to the finish. This time I felt that the clock, if not exactly my friend, at least wasn't actively against me.

"Well?"

It was break time.

"Pretty good I think. Deffo better than last time. The one about the staples was really hard."

"Multiply the size by the length — then slot all the boxes into the big box."

"Yeah, that's what I did – but I think I've messed it up."

True to his word, Palmer had them marked and ready to return the following day. He was no slouch, I'll give him that. I followed him around the class as he handed them back.

"What happened last night?"

"What?"

"I thought you were coming round to the den."

"Jimmy, I was knackered. I spent the whole weekend doing Eleven Plus questions."

"With Ronald?"

"Yeah ...shush, here they come."

Palmer set both our papers down and winked at me. "Don't get sloppy, McBride – but well done."

I had scored 27 out of 50.

I was pleased but also a little disappointed. For the first time ever I had outscored Jimmy and he patted me on the back. I glanced around and gave Ronald a little one fingered salute. I held up two and then seven fingers, he held up four and then five. His standards were slipping.

"Now then, now then, boys and girls, boys and girls. Some very positive signs of improvement I am delighted to say. Now, before we look at the paper, I would like to do a little seating rearrangement – Hood swap with Douglas, please!"

Jimmy looked devastated.

I was shocked. I hadn't anticipated this.

"Come on, Hood – you'd think I'd asked you to give up one of your kidneys, hurry up!"

Jimmy slowly gathered up his things. I could see how wounded he was and his desperation not to meet my eye. Ronald was already standing alongside him with his jotter and pencil case. I managed a nod and then spotted Rip observing the scene with a sad little smile. Jesus.

"I think you'll be really good for each other," Palmer leant over. "You can help each other out when it comes to paired work. Right everyone, eyes front!"

I couldn't wait for the bell to sound so I could sort things out with Jimmy. He was on the grass banks by the gravel pitch and Rip was feeding him cheese and onion crisps.

"Jimmy, that wasn't my idea – it was Mr Palmer's."

"I know."

"You know Ron's been helping me?"

"Ron?" said Rip.

"Ronald's been helping me."

"I could've helped you, all you needed to do was ask."

Christ, his bottom lip was quivering. What was this?

"Jimmy, it's not like that – it's just, he's really good at explaining things," I wasn't helping myself, "his dad was a teacher."

"My dad's an accountant."

"My dad shovels shit," Rip said and let out a roar.

He was really getting on my wick.

"Don't be like that, Jimmy, you know how much I've been struggling with this stupid fucking test."

"Come on, Jimmy Cagney," Rip placed a hand tenderly on his shoulder. "I'll buy you a Coke at the Tuck – don't worry."

"Wait," this was bad timing but there wasn't going to be an easy moment any time soon. "Jimmy, I'm gonna have to skip the den for the next wee while. I really need to get some serious Eleven Plus practise."

He didn't seem surprised.

Rip did his stupid little smile again. "And so it begins…"

And suddenly I had had enough. Couldn't Jimmy see how important this was to me? Stupid, thick Rip and all his shit – even though Ronald wasn't a Catholic.

"Why don't you go and fuck yourself, Turnbull – it's none of your business. I knew Jimmy before you."

He came at me fast and pushed me hard on the shoulder - but I pushed him just as hard back and then we were nose to nose like Hagler and Minter.

"Wanna fuckin' fight ya cunt? A'll fuckin' kick the shit outta ya!"

His breath was rancid; I'd never been so close to him

before, toothpaste and Rip were not the best of friends – mouthwash a complete stranger.

"Leave it, lads!" Jimmy squeezed in between us. "This is stupid – just forget it."

I was shaking with adrenalin but Jimmy had burst the bubble. Rip leered at me and made a point of spitting a huge gob onto the gravel, it stretched and dangled from his mouth and landed on the toe of his shoe.

"Fuck it."

It had all happened so quickly that there hadn't been time for the masses to gather - a couple of little clusters that was all. Far off to the right, near the bicycle sheds, I could see Ronald an interested spectator. He had kept his distance. Wise man. The bell rang then and we drifted towards the doors, the three of us well apart.

"What happened there?"

"Nearly had a fight with Rip."

I was still trembling.

"Jaysus – over the seat thing?"

"Yeah."

I felt rotten for the rest of the morning. Jimmy and me had been best friends since the first day of school. Was this the end of that, just because of a stupid seat? I hadn't asked Palmer to uproot him although the benefits of having Ronald beside me were obvious. Palmer would know the difference between an off task whisper and a genuine attempt to help; it would be like an extension of the stuff we had been doing at Ronald's house at the weekend. Still, poor Jimmy. He always smelt so good and now he had to sit beside yer man and his smelly pits.

At lunchtime Jimmy sought me out and I was so relieved I could have hugged him. No sign of Rip and that suited me just fine.

"I'm sorry, Kev, I was acting like a real girl. It was just when he moved me it was such a surprise. I love sitting beside you and now I'm sitting beside," he puffed out his cheeks and pulled his jumper out in front of him as far as it would go.

I laughed louder than it deserved. "Don't think bad of Ronald, Jimmy, it wasn't his fault either."

"No, no – Ronald's a good guy," he looked around as if to find him so that he could apologise to him as well. "In fact, I was thinking maybe he might like to come to the den again?"

The den? What for?

"Or I could come up to his with you? We could ride our bikes up – does he have a bike? We could visit Maggie's grave, maybe practise the Eleven Plus together?"

I thought of the dynamics – three instead of two. The way I behaved with Ronald was completely different than with Jimmy – it was like I was more grown up. I thought about Jimmy's daft jokes and how I sometimes laughed just to make him happy and how Ronald would look at me if he saw me doing that. I thought about his silly magic tricks and the farting noises he made to fill in the silence; and yes, God help me, I thought about the sweets. I thought about these things only briefly but long enough for him to read my mind.

"Never mind, Kev, it was just an idea."

"Yeah, yeah, we could do that, Jimmy – maybe not today but soon."

"Sure."

*

On October 2nd we watched the young Larry Holmes hammer the hell out of Muhummad Ali. Ali was attempting yet another comeback but this time he was out of luck. He tried the rope-a-dope again but Holmes wasn't buying it. He just kept punching him. Again and again. During round five, Pete came into the room and did a stupid little shuffle on the carpet. Dad's glower sent him scuttling. Towards the end, the dye that Ali had used to cover his grey began to drip down his face. I wasn't crying but I was close. Dad was sad too. He had grown up with Ali. It was the end of an era.

CHAPTER TWENTY-ONE

"Have you all been watching the news?" Palmer asked, with that little smile that said he was up for some fun. "Put your hands up if you know who Ronald Reagan is."

A sea of hands, even Sally Clarke thought she knew.

"Sally?"

"He's an actor, sir!"

Giggles.

"Why are you laughing? You are exactly right, Sally. Go to the top of the class – oh, you're there already. Yes, Wilson?"

"He's gonna be the next President of the United States of America."

"You are almost certainly correct, Wilson." Palmer surveyed the class. "Why would the most powerful man in the world be interested in our little country? I heard him on the television just last night saying that if he was to become President – and it looks like he will – he would be keeping a very close eye on the events in Northern Ireland."

I could sense Ronald itching to speak and I squeezed his arm underneath the desk.

"Come on, class – help me out here," Palmer made a big show of looking flabbergasted. "Why would the mighty United States of America be at all interested in our six little counties? Turnbull?"

Rip shrugged.

Ronald flew out of the blocks.

"It's because there are millions of Americans with Irish ancestry, sir!"

"Ancestry? What a fantastic word. What does it mean?"

"It means they can trace their family tree back to Ireland, sir."

And here was the funny thing about Ronald that I had noticed before. When he spoke about Ireland his eyes lit up and he sat forward as if it was the most exciting thing in the world; I'd seen a glimpse of it that night in the den.

"So what are they all doing over there?" Palmer asked. "Are they on their holidays, Turnbull?"

He was singling Rip out and that wasn't really fair. There was a class full of people.

"Can you enlighten us, Douglas?"

"A lot of them emigrated to America, sir, in times of trouble and especially during the potato famine – hundreds of thousands."

Palmer beamed. "Here is a boy who knows his Irish history – who knows what he is talking about. Mr Reagan's great grandfather came from Tipperary."

Jimmy's hand shot up.

"Hood?"

"It's a long way to Tipperary, sir!"

Even Palmer chuckled at that one and I felt good for Jimmy. He caught my eye and tipped me a wink.

But the laughter was short lived.

"The Yanks don't know nothing about the Troubles! They think it's just the Brits and the Catholics – they don't even know what loyalists are. They haven't a clue!"

Rip was shaking with rage.

The whole class was looking at him.

"Very interesting," Palmer mused. "You are almost certainly right, Turnbull; most Americans have a very simplistic view of the Troubles – and when you think about it, it is a very complex problem. Nothing is black and white. For example, everyone has heard of the famous Battle of the Boyne?"

Lots of nods. Rip looked dangerous.

"Protestant King Billy against Catholic King James. Here's a funny thing though. Did you know that the pope back then, Pope Alexander VIII, was a big fan of King William; actually, when he defeated James, the pope sent William a message of congratulations."

"No, he didn't."

"I think you'll find he did – am I wrong, Douglas?"

Ronald shook his head and I wondered how someone so clever could be so dumb.

"Orangemen would have you believe that good king Billy fought to overthrow the pope and popery at the Boyne. Not true. Pope Alexander was fighting against King Louis XIV of France, Louis supported King James II against William, and since William backed the pope against Louis XIV, the pope was more than happy to support good King Billy against James at the battle of the Boyne. In fact, the pope and the whole of Catholic Europe – except France – celebrated his victory at the Boyne. They even sang a special hymn, a Te Deum, for him in St Peters in Rome."

Nearly all of the class had switched off before he had finished but I kept my eyes on Rip. He hadn't understood much of what was being said; but he understood. He said little for the rest of the day (even less than usual) and occasionally I would see him watching Palmer with a primitive resentment that was quite unsettling. He reminded me of a chained animal who cowers in a corner but with lip curled back, waiting for its owner to misjudge the length of the chain.

*

"Why do you think Palmer hates Rip so much? All that today was just to annoy him."

We were making our way slowly up the hill to Ronald's house and it felt like my schoolbag was full of bricks.

"Didn't you find what he was saying interesting – that the pope was on the side of William of Orange?"

"What has that got to do with anything?"

Ronald stopped and I was really glad of the break.

"Jaysus, Kev, people are dying all over this place – shot, blown up, knee capped – millions of pounds worth of damage and destruction, and most don't even know the history or the reasons behind it all."

"And you do? All those books in your room?"

"A little, yeah. I've always been interested. I used to have these big long conversations with Dad … before he got ill."

I could see he was a little upset so I thought I should

change the subject.

"This hill is like Everest. We should keep an eye out for George Mallory and Sandy Irvine."

"Who?"

"You don't know who they were?"

"Go on."

"They disappeared in a snow storm when they were trying to climb Everest. The 1920's I think. They were last seen close to the top and then disappeared forever. Nobody knows if they made it to the top or not. It's one of the great mysteries."

"Oh, yeah, I've heard of them."

But I could tell he hadn't and it pleased me.

"I know he's your friend an' all – but you do know Rip's a bigot."

"A bigot?"

"You know what that is?"

"Of course ... a stupid, ignorant person. But that's not really his fault."

"A bigot is a person who won't listen to any other ideas if they are different from his own – especially ideas on religion, politics and race."

I felt uncomfortable. I knew things would probably never be the same with me and Rip but he wasn't as bad as all that. He had shown me kindness in the past and he was funny. "People here have different opinions, Ronald. Rip has his, you have yours and I have mine. That's the way it is."

"Yes, but whose opinion would you rather hear – one based on fact and common sense, or one based on sectarian bigotry?"

Sectarian? Jesus. I thought of the scrabble board and felt a fleeting panic; then I remembered the way he helped me with the questions. He wasn't trying to catch me out.

"Rip's not all bad. He'd stick up for you if you were in trouble." I realised how childish that sounded. "I think he just listens to the wrong people sometimes."

"I'm not so sure he'd stick up for me, Kevin."

We were at the top of the hill and I was straining to see if Gloria's car was in the driveway. Mum said I could stay until tea time and I didn't want to waste time being polite and awkward with her. I was desperate for some American Hard Gums but I didn't feel like kissing her arse for them. The hill had tired me out.

"You're definitely a strange Protestant."

He burst out laughing.

"What's that supposed to mean?"

"Well, most Protestants I know, they...I don't really know what I mean. Do you want a united Ireland?"

"What's that got to do with anything?"

"That's why Catholics are fighting Protestants. Isn't it?"

"That's not why the Troubles started, Kev – there's way more to it than that. That's like when Mr Palmer said that America had a simple view of what's happening. There are lots of reasons why the Troubles here started and it wasn't because they wanted a united Ireland."

I shrugged. "I thought it was."

"Aren't you interested in how it all began, Kevin – why people are dying and being killed? Doesn't that interest you?"

I really don't think he meant it, but the way he looked at me and the way he said it made me feel like a bit of a shit. It was as if *I* had been blowing people apart and shooting them in the kneecaps.

"To be honest, I've never really thought about it."

"No offence, but don't you think it's about time you did?"

Gloria wasn't in although she came back later. I spent over two hours with him, going over old Eleven Plus questions and chomping on American Hard Gums. We sat shoulder to shoulder in the living room and I had to keep reminding myself that less than two weeks ago we had been strangers. I did think a little bit about Jimmy and where he would sit and how he would fit in. It was impossible to imagine. I felt a little bit guilty – but just a little. We weren't like Siamese twins. It wasn't healthy that we were always in each other's pockets; it was only natural that we should start to find new interests and new friends. God, if it hadn't been for Ronald I would be heading up to the High School on the other side of the town from Jimmy. I still felt a bit bad though. I'd make it up to him later.

Dad honked the horn just after six and I packed up my stuff.

At the door I couldn't resist it.

"His name was Odell."

"What?"

"He was the guy on that Everest expedition – the one who saw Mallory and Irvine near to the top."

"Oh, yeah."

He gave me a little smile and I gave him the same smile back and then we both burst out laughing.

"Why were you laughing just then?" Dad asked as we pulled out of the driveway.

"Just a sort of a joke – can't really explain it."

"Right. She's really nice that old girl – I should have chatted with her for a bit, I just couldn't be arsed. Do you think that was rude me just honking the horn? I'll chat the next time. She's always donating big sweet jars to the quizzes."

"When she saw you at the window she said, "There's the Quiz King!"

"Shit, did she? I'll definitely come in next time."

The lights were on in the den as we passed by Jimmy's house.

"Are you gonna go there after tea?"

"I've still my homework."

"Isn't that what you were doing with yer man?"

"That was Eleven Plus stuff."

"Right."

Rip would probably be over to keep him company later on. I couldn't be bothered with him. Jimmy would be fine. I'd see him tomorrow anyway. I was getting tired. And I was hungry again.

"What's for tea, Dad?"

"Beans, burgers and chips."

CHAPTER TWENTY TWO

There was another Ronald Reagan movie on. *King's Row*. It was set in this small town in the past and Reagan had an accident and had to have both his legs amputated. Bad enough. But the twist was that his legs had been perfectly okay and the doctor cut them off just because he didn't like him. At the end of the movie Reagan's pal tells him the truth about what happened and – get this – instead of being annoyed, he becomes happy again and says, "Where did Gordon think I lived, in my legs?" All through the movie, I kept thinking about Archie Daly over the hedge (although by now they had moved to a bigger house with bigger doorways) and wondering if the modern day Reagan had heard about him. It was entirely possible, especially after what Palmer had said. It sent a wee shiver through me but it was a nice shiver. That was years ago but Reagan had been a politician for years. One of his helpers might have come up to him and said, *Look at this Mr Reagan, some poor guy in Northern Ireland has lost his legs.* And Reagan would say, *Wow, that reminds me of that movie I was in, King's Row.* And the helper would put his finger on a huge big map and say, *Look, Mr Reagan, this is where it happened.* And, Reagan would say, *Golly Gosh,* and he'd be looking down at my back hedge.

"I hope he makes a better President than he did an actor," Dad said. "I mean, who the hell's gonna say *where's the rest of me* when they lose their legs? That's not what I would say." He grinned at me and waited for me to ask.

"What would you say, Dad?"

"Jaysus! Where have me bloody legs buggered off to?" As he said it, he leant back on the sofa, kicked his legs into the air and let loose an enormous fart.

I roared and looked over to Pete to join in.

Pete reached for his text book and began his homework.

My Eleven Plus scores steadily improved and Palmer was as happy as I was: 27, 29, 33, 35, 37, 38. Nothing was guaranteed but my confidence had soared and I actually started to look forward to the damn things. All thanks to Ronnie. Sometimes we could work together for ages and the only sound would be the ticking of the old Grandfather Clock. It was a great place to learn and to settle your mind. The television was dead in the corner and I didn't miss it at all. Except for the news reports, I don't think the telly was ever on in his house. He was patient and he taught me well. He seemed to enjoy it. When I got stuck he never did it for me, instead he would point me in the right direction and allow me to work it out for myself. That was the way for me.

"You'll make a great teacher, Ronald," I told him, then added, without really thinking, "your dad would be so proud of you."

Immediately it was out of my mouth I knew I shouldn't have said it.

"I'll be back in a minute."

His voice sounded strange and I knew he was close to tears and I cursed myself for a fat, rubber-lipped fool. I had been trying to compliment him but it was a cheesy thing to say and he had been caught off-guard. How to handle it now though? I could do a real chicken thing: scribble him a note and slip away, sort it out tomorrow when things had calmed down. But I was better than that and he deserved more.

I creaked upstairs making as much noise as I could so he could hear my approach. The bathroom was empty, down the hallway was his bedroom. I paused outside, settled myself, then knocked twice.

"Come on in."

"Ronald, I'm sorry, I shouldn't have mentioned your dad – that was stupid of me."

He dismissed it with a wave of his hand but his eyes were red and he was sitting on his bed as if he was out of puff.

"I'll head off, see you tomorrow?"

"No, no – stay for a bit longer, I'm sorry; it just comes over me sometimes."

I sat down on the chair by his desk. I should have felt

awkward but I was relieved and pleased with myself for the making the effort to come upstairs. I couldn't think what else to say but that was okay too; it was kind of up to him to make the effort now.

"These were all his," he said, gesturing the bookcase which groaned under the weight of a hundred or more history books. "Every time I look at them I think of him."

"He sure liked his history."

"He did. American, Spanish – but Irish mostly."

What a surprise.

"Would you like to see his picture?" he reached across to his drawer and handed me a Polaroid. "Sometimes it makes me sad to look at him but I like to remember him the way he was before he got ill."

What to say. I held the photo gingerly and wondered what he would do if I accidentally ripped it. Then I told myself to stop being such a dick. I looked for some resemblance that I could comment on but there was none. The man in the photo had a beard and was plump in a healthy way. A lot of weight to lose. Something about the way he leant back on the fence suggested an easy going manner and he looked kindly.

"I like the way he smiles," I said, handing it back.

"Thanks."

And then, because I had put so much thought into it and I didn't want him to think I was being cheesy again, I took a risk. "You can tell a lot about a person by the way they smile. Some people just twitch their lips and they think that's enough; others smile wide but if you look real close their eyes are dead. *That* is a proper smile."

"Thanks, Kevin." And this time he smiled, a proper smile. "We used to have these brilliant conversations at night. The way he could tell a story, Kevin – Jaysus, he'd have you on the edge of your chair begging for more."

"What did you talk about?"

"All sorts of things about Ireland – the way people used to live, the way they were treated, the way they treated others.

History and politics – but never boring; he brought it all to life, Kevin. That's what a good history teacher does. There was a student at his funeral – I can't remember her name – but she told me that she used to hate it when the bell rang in his class. Can you imagine that?"

"Tell me some of the things."

And that was all the encouragement he needed. He was off and running.

He told me about the plantation of Ulster almost four hundred years before when Scottish and English Protestants were given all the land owned by Catholic Chieftains. As he spoke, he leant forward and those eyes of his drilled into mine, checking for understanding and agreement.

"Britain needed a Protestant foothold in Ireland. They had Catholic France and Spain to the right of them and Catholic Ireland to the left of them, so the poor O'Neills and the O'Donnells had their land taken from them."

"Jesus Christ," I said, and meant it.

"It stretches far back. Ever wonder why Catholics are so bitter?"

I'd never really thought of them as bitter, it was the Protestants who appeared to be constantly pissed off.

You could see the pleasure it gave him to remember these conversations and there was something very appealing about the way he himself told the stories: his passion and enthusiasm were infectious. My comment about him making a good teacher might well have been cheesy but it was no less true. He didn't bore with details and lengthy description; but he told you enough so that you could imagine you were there, angry and simmering at the way your family had been treated. We spoke about the Battle of the Boyne, of which I did know a little, and then he explained how the Catholics in Ireland had been mistreated right up until the Easter Rising of 1916.

"Do you know anything about it?"

I shook my head.

"Why would you? They don't teach it in schools here."

"In 1916, a group of rebels finally decided to try to end British rule in Ireland. They took over the General Post Office in Dublin – I've put my finger in the bullet holes outside– and announced that Ireland was finally free. It only lasted six days but what a stand they made. By the end of the week, the British had sent 16,000 men to do battle with them. They felt that the Irish had stabbed them in the back because they were busy fighting the Germans in the war – even though thousands of Irish Catholics were fighting alongside the Brits. Finally, heavily outnumbered, the rebels were forced to surrender. And how do you think the Irish people reacted to them when they were dragged through the streets?"

"Cheered them?"

"Nope. They hissed and spat at them. Called them murderers, traitors. It might all have ended there. But then the Brits messed up. They executed them all without a trial. That's when people started to sympathise and write poems and songs about them. One of the rebels, James Connolly, had shrapnel in his chest and his ankle was hanging off. He couldn't stand – so you know what they did?" Ronald didn't wait for me to answer as he leant forward, smiling grimly. "They tied him tight to a chair so that he could face the firing squad. Let him have a little sit down before they shot him in the face."

CHAPTER TWENTY-THREE

From then on our routine was set. We would hammer away at the Eleven plus questions then chill out in his room and talk about the Troubles and the conversations he'd had with his dad. I was amazed at how caught up I became. Part of that was down to his story telling skills but it was also the fact that I had never really thought much about history before (apart from Winston Churchill and his big cigars, giving everyone the fingers). History was in the past. It just never occurred to me that so much of the present was shaped by people long dead and turned to dust. Stupid, I know; but I was only eleven.

Ronald told me about the War of Independence which had happened after the Easter Rising and about the Government of Ireland Act which led to the creation of Northern Ireland — with the understanding that a Protestant majority would be guaranteed. The problem with this — and I could hear the voice of Rip — was that the Catholic minority multiplied far quicker than the Protestant majority.

"Each year there were more Catholics and less Protestants. It was important that Protestants kept control of Ulster so those in charge started to twist and tweak the rules."

"What do you mean?"

"Well, the way people voted. The only people who could vote in local elections were ratepayers and their partners — that meant you needed to have a house to get two votes. So who do you think most of the new houses were given to?"

"Not to the Catholics."

"Correct. The whole voting system was rigged so that the Prods kept control of the councils so that they could look after each other. Derry always had way more Catholics than Protestants — about 2/3 to 1/3 now — but between 1922 and 1972 they never had a Catholic mayor!"

"That's not fair at all," I admitted, "but it's still no excuse for some of the things the I.R.A have done."

"You've lived here all your life, Kevin. How do you think Catholics have been treated in Ulster – do you think they've been given a fair shake?"

"Well ….no; but not every Prod has a dream house."

"It's not just housing or votes, Kevin. All of the decent jobs go to Protestants. Your dad works in the civil service, yeah? Ask him. 90% of the Civil Service is Protestant, and the 10% who are Catholic get all the shitty jobs at the bottom – running and fetching, tying parcels and licking stamps. And what about the R.U.C?"

"What about them?"

"Come on. Who do you think the *Royal* Ulster Constabulary have more sympathy for – Catholics or Protestants? How many Catholics do you think are in the *Royal* Ulster Constabulary, the police force in charge of security?"

"Not many."

Ronald counted on his fingers, "so, not able to vote, poor housing, shit jobs - if they had a job at all, and a police force that is always going to favour the Protestant majority. Is it any wonder things finally exploded into violence?"

"Still, Ron, it's no excuse for some of the horrible things the I.R.A have done. You know more about it than me - but you need to live here to really soak it up. What about Mountbatten and his grandson and all those soldiers killed on the same day?"

"Awful, horrible; but ask your dad about Bloody Sunday in 1972 – ask him tonight. The paras killed thirteen unarmed people – some of them shot in the back; your dad's a fair man, see what he says about that."

"Well, what about the Le Mons Hotel firebomb?" This was one of Rip's favourite I.R.A atrocities: a function at Le Mons House Hotel in Comber County Down. It was firebombed by the I.R.A. Twelve people were killed and twenty-three injured. Rip loved to talk about the blackened bodies and the smell of burning flesh.

"Terrible," Ronald conceded. "That will have done their cause no good at all. But Kevin, the U.V.F and the U.D.A have blood on their hands as well."

"Yeah, but that's different, that's in self-defence."

"Are you joking?" he laughed. "The U.V.F and the U.D.A kill people just because of their religion; a lot of the people they torture and murder have nothing to do with the I.R.A – they're just Catholics they've hauled off the streets. The I.R.A kill people they see as legitimate targets - army, police, prison officers – it's horrible when they kill ordinary people, but they don't set out to."

"Really?"

"Yes, really. The I.R.A rely on money from America. How many Americans are going to be sympathetic if a little girl or a little boy gets killed? It happens – but not on purpose."

I remembered what Palmer had said about the simplistic take the Americans had about the Troubles. It made sense. It would be difficult to avoid killing people you didn't want to kill when you were trying to kill someone else. You couldn't exactly tap Louis Mountbatten's grandson on the shoulder and tell him it might be an idea not to go out on the boat today. My head was starting to throb. That happened sometimes when Ronald really got going.

"In May 1966, Mrs Gould was the first person to be killed in the Troubles. She lived beside a Catholic pub which the *U.V.F* attacked with petrol bombs. Mrs Gould was a *Protestant*. The first killings of the period were carried out by the U.V.F by petrol bomb and bullet. The first explosions were by Protestants. Protestants shot the first republican and killed the first policeman – Constable Victor Arbuckle."

Arbuckle? Don't say it. Don't say it.

"Do you think he was any relation to Fatty Arbuckle?"

"What?"

"It's a really unusual name."

"I don't think so."

*

That evening, after tea, I asked Dad if there were many Catholics working in his building.

"God, that's a good one. Em, there's Patty the porter – he's a nice guy; Kieran works in finance, there's quite a few now, aye. Why?"

"I was just wondering. Something someone said at school. What about Bloody Sunday?"

He burst out laughing.

"What is this: *Question Time?*"

"Sorry, Dad."

He thought carefully for a moment. "The whole thing was horrible. It was an illegal march in Londonderry; they were throwing stones and bottles at the army, then some idiot started shooting at the army – then all hell broke loose."

"The army opened fire on them?"

"Yeah – but wouldn't you if a big crowd was shooting at you?"

"But I heard some people were shot in the back. They can't have been that dangerous if they were running away."

"I don't know. Anyway, there was a big expensive whatyamacallit – an inquest. All the soldiers were cleared, I think. I don't really like the army, but if people were shooting at me ..."

"What were they marching for?"

He shrugged and reached for the T.V Times. "It was a Civil Rights march, I think. Housing, the vote, whatever. Awful. One of those situations where everyone's to blame."

*

"They were marching against internment," Ronald told me at break time the following day. "All the eye witnesses say that the army weren't shot at – they were the only ones doing the shooting."

"My dad says-"

"Your dad's clever – all those quizzes – but mine studied it, read all the accounts, interviewed people..."

I let it drop. His dad probably did know more about Bloody Sunday than mine. Mine knew every Grand National winner since 1900 and every Heavyweight Champion since James J Corbett. That made me feel a little better.

"Do you know what internment is?"

"Go on."

"It means pulling people off the streets and out of their homes and throwing them in prison without having to charge them with anything. In 1971, that happened to 450 men the British thought were terrorists."

"Were they?"

"Nearly all of them were released after several days. And how do you think they were treated during those several days? Cups of tea and ham sandwiches?"

"If they thought they were terrorists."

"Here's a question for you: how many of the 450 lifted were Protestants?"

"You're gonna tell me none, aren't you?"

"Correct."

Sometimes it got a little bit annoying, that he knew so much and I knew so little; but for the most part I really enjoyed talking about the Troubles with him. He made it sound so interesting, so *fascinating,* and it made me feel grown up that we were talking about politics and bombings and people being kneecapped.

Jimmy had made a point of sitting opposite us in the canteen and I found it a little bit awkward. I think Ronald sensed it too because he finished his pudding quickly and made off to the toilets. That made it a little easier. I focussed on my apple pie, deliberately taking longer than usual. I couldn't think of anything to say but I didn't want to get up and leave him on his own.

"How's tricks, Jimmy?"

"Not bad – I've learnt a couple of new ones, would you like to see?"

"No, I didn't mean ..." I caught his grin and I grinned back. "You dick."

"What about you? Are you all set for the big one?"

"I think so, I hope so. Ronnie's really helped me, Jimmy." I didn't care if that was mean, it was only the truth.

"I have a message for you."

"A message?"

"Guess who from?"

"Lon Chaney, Man of a Thousand Faces."

"Nope. From Rip."

"Ah. What does he want?"

"He wants to see you."

"Pistols at dawn?"

"Eh?"

This always happened with Jimmy. Just when the thing was warming up.

"What does he want, Jimmy?"

"Tonight at the den – if you can make it. He wants to say sorry to you. Please try to make it, Kev. Ronald can come too."

The way he added that bit on, I knew that Ronald wasn't wanted.

"Okay, Jimmy." It was easier to say yes than to come up with an excuse on the spot. I really didn't want to hurt his feelings. I figured I could do with a break from the Eleven Plus anyway.

*

"Are you sick or something?" Mum asked.

I had left one and a half sausages, some alphabet spaghetti, and there was still bread and butter in the middle of the table.

"Think of all those poor wee Ethiopians with the flies and the swollen bellies."

But I could tell she wasn't that annoyed, just making conversation.

"Are you going up the hill, Kev?"

That was what Dad said when I was going to Ronald's.

"Watch the road."

He said that too. Every time.

"I'm not going there tonight. Actually, I'm going round to see Jimmy." I watched them closely to see their reaction.

"That's nice," Mum said. "He'll be glad to see you."

"Watch the road."

There were forty-two paving slabs from my house to Jimmy's. We had counted them years ago; it had been part of a game to do with marbles and chalk that I couldn't properly remember. The thick hedge that ran alongside his house had been where we played walkie talkies one summer. His uncle had bought him them from England. They looked great in the package, held in the hand of a stripy faced S.A.S hard man, but they looked completely different when you got them out. Two big plastic bricks connected by thirty metres of string. You had to pull the string taut and then you were meant to be able to hear each other down the line. To be heard, you had to speak so loudly that people on the other side of the street had given us funny looks. They were rubbish, but we'd played with them for the whole of one afternoon because his uncle from England had got them for him. That had been four years ago.

I paused at the door of the den and took a deep breath; then, because I hadn't been for a while and without really thinking it through, I knocked three times.

"Come on in, Kev!"

Rip's voice. That annoyed me a little but I swallowed it down.

"Thanks for coming, mate," he extended his hand. "I knew you would."

I shook his hand but I had stiffened immediately and was on the defensive. Rip and Jimmy were not on their own. Slouched comfortably on the battered old sofa, where I used to sit, was Rip's special guest from months ago. Jimmy was on the chair to his left. He smiled wanly and I knew that he hadn't known that he would be here.

"You 'member me mate, Sam?"

I managed some sort of snort.

"Right there, Kev?" Sam gave me a grin and a little two fingered salute. "Come on in and take a seat."

My heart was hammering and my cheeks were going red. That had not happened in a long time. Fuck him.

"Kev, I'm sorry for all the shite that's happened. I forgot how important that stupid fuckin' test is to you."

"Alright." I made a point of glancing from him to Sam and

back again.

Are you so fucking retarded, Turnbull, that you think I'm going to open up in front of this dick? Jesus Christ, are you that stupid?

"Think of all the great times we've had here, Kev – all the laughs."

"Right."

"I'll be honest with you here, mate – I can't fuckin' stand yer man. There's just somethin'..." Rip thought hard about it. "He just gives me the fuckin' creeps. And a've heard some of the things he tells you, Kev."

Oh, shit.

"He's a real fuckin' Lundy, Kevin."

"A what?"

"A Lundy – a traitor to the Protestant cause."

"What are you talking about, Rip, he is a Protestant – that was your big thing. He's not a Catholic and you're still not happy."

Sam reached down and pulled the ring off a can.

"Is that beer?" I made a big deal of peering down at the can. "Jimmy – does your mum and dad know about this?"

Sam snorted, licked and sucked the froth off his fingers. "Settle down, wee man – calm yersel.'"

"Kev, the only thing worse than a Catholic is a shit Protestant," said Rip. "I'd rather he was a fuckin' Taig, it would be easier."

"He's a fuckin' arse wipe," said Sam.

And I found my voice.

"Who the fuck do you think you're talking about? That's my mate. You don't even know him. And what the fuck are you doing here anyway? Did you invite him Jimmy – no I didn't think so -" that was as far as I got and then he was off the couch and his hands were round my throat. I could feel his nails digging in and – even though I had gone to the bathroom ten minutes ago – I felt hot piss trickling down my leg.

"Leave it, Sam!" Rip and Jimmy managed to haul him off me. He was like a snarling animal, yet, shocked though I was, I could see that he was putting it on a bit. I scrambled away into the far corner and put my hands round my neck to check the damage. It stung like hell. I looked down at my jeans. There was a little damp line but you wouldn't notice it unless someone pointed it out.

Sam was back on the couch, studiously avoiding eye contact with Rip. He had the air of a man who has been duped and will never allow himself to be duped again.

"This is your great mate that you wanted to make up with? Jesus Christ, Rip – I wouldn't fuckin' piss on him if he was on fire."

Jimmy was on the floor with me. He had raced into the toilet and wet a towel for my neck. His face was grey. He had no idea where this was going either. He plopped down beside me and for an awful moment I thought he was going to hold my hand, but instead he sat so close that our shoulders were touching. That actually felt quite comforting.

I wondered what my first words were going to be. I had no idea. When I did speak, I was just as surprised as everyone else at what came out.

"When my dad sees what you've done to my neck, he'll fuckin' run round here and kick your shit in."

"That right?"

He took two steps towards me but I could see the venom was gone.

"Aye, that's right." I was annoyed that my voice sounded so high, so I added, "ya cunt."

Sam spat contempt. He didn't seem sure what to do next. I was on the floor. Stupid bastard had played his ace too early.

"Sam, let's go," Rip set an arm on his elbow.

"What? That lanky big bastard?" he leant down towards me. "Yer Da comes fuckin' near me and I'll get his fuckin' legs broken!"

"Please go," Jimmy pleaded.

"Come on, Rip – leave them to their shitty wee hut."

He kicked at the door, but it opened inwardly and the frame held firm, so he had to use the handle.

"Leave these two faggots. They can suck each other's dicks."

Rip was dawdling.

"Hurry the fuck up!"

Rip moved towards the door. You could see him thinking what to do. He knew he had to follow him but he didn't want to leave us with nothing. What he managed was a quick thumbs up and a little nod. Then he was gone.

Jimmy helped me onto the sofa. It was like some kind of crazy dream. I felt zonked. Yet beneath it all was the realisation that this horrible situation was not nearly as bad in reality as the thought of it would have been. Being attacked and Dad threatened? That was the sort of thought that would suck all the joy out of living. My mind would dine off that worry for a year and now it had happened so fast that there hadn't even been time to get nervous. There was a part of me that felt short changed and it was this part that now looked for ways to prolong the drama and make it worse.

"I can't tell Dad about this. He would chase after him and then..."

"He's a real fuckin' dick head. I don't know why Rip hangs about with him."

I looked at Jimmy to see if he was serious and he was. He just didn't get it.

"Does he come here all the time?"

"Only sometimes. He just appeared tonight. Rip couldn't say no to him - he really wanted to speak to you."

"Yeah, but he's so fuckin' stupid he went ahead anyway – with him sitting there."

"Oh, fuck, he's left his beer – look!"

We were both thinking it.

"Just set it outside."

"Mum might see it. Dad might drink it."

That was a joke but I wasn't in the mood. I wondered if I would ever be in the mood again.

"Does my neck look bad?"

"Not too bad – a little red. I'm really sorry, mate – I tried to get him off."

"I know you did, Jimmy."

"Jesus Christ. Why did all this have to happen?"

I tried to stand up but my legs wouldn't let me. They weren't damaged, they just had no power. Give them another minute. I could wash my face here and check the damage. As long as you couldn't see his nail marks I might be able to get away with it. I could tell Mum and Dad that I had fallen into the brambles on the way over. That's if they noticed straight away. I could button my pyjamas right up to the top and tuck in my neck – as long as the marks weren't too obvious. My school tie would cover them tomorrow and by bath night – which was Wednesday – they would have faded a little.

For a while it was just nice to sit beside Jimmy and enjoy the silence. The beers didn't bother me now because I didn't think he would be back for them and even if he did I would enjoy ignoring him. He wouldn't bother me just now. The scene was played out. I had forgotten just how comfortable this old couch was. How many hours had we both sat here watching daft rubbish on the television? I tried my legs again and this time they were okay. The marks weren't as bad as I thought they might be and I washed my face and checked my underpants. Then I said goodbye to Jimmy and left him sitting on the couch that had once belonged to his mad granny who was now nothing but old bones beneath the ground.

It was the last time I set foot in the den.

*

I told Ronald of course. I had to. Rip would have told his loyalist chums all about him and the conversations he had overheard. It was too easy to imagine Sam jumping us as we walked to or from school; actually, that was unlikely given the amount of traffic and people. I suddenly had an image of Tommy the old crossing guy thumping him full pelt with his giant lollipop and it made me smile. Oddly, the incident had not made me collapse in on myself; it had scared the shit right out of me – but it had also sharpened my wits considerably. And the awkward problem of Jimmy and the den had been solved for me. Who could blame me for not wanting to go back when I had almost been strangled?

Still it was scary.

"He called me a what?" Ronald said in the playground.

"Shush! Keep your voice down – you don't know whose listening," I thought hard. "I think he said Lumley, like Joanna Lumley from *The New Avengers* – yeah, that's it."

Ronald shrugged and shook his head.

"I don't know either – but it wasn't a good thing. He said it meant you were a traitor to the cause."

"And that's when he tried to strangle you?"

"Yeah."

"Jaysus."

We were in the corner nearest the back entrance. It was a good spot because you could see the whole of the playground and it was as far away as you could get from the High School fence. I kept a wary eye for Jimmy and Rip. Jimmy had said hello this morning and I had said hello back – there were no hard feelings between him and me and there never would be. But Rip? I was determined that I was never going to speak to him again. That would be difficult, especially if Palmer put me in a group with him, but I was going to try to at least be as short with him as possible. His attendance was poor so that would help. Ronald agreed not to speak of the Troubles during school which I knew would be a challenge but since I was spending most evenings with him at his house I figured he should be able to manage it.

*

On October 27th, seven I.R.A prisoners in the Maze prison went on hunger strike. It was on the telly but it wasn't big news.

"What's Special Category Status?"

"It's what they're fighting to save."

"By starving themselves?"

"Yes. There's not much else you can do when you're stuck in prison."

I tossed a wine gum into the air and managed to catch it in my mouth.

"So what is it?"

He watched me munching and I could see him thinking carefully.

"The I.R.A don't consider themselves to be ordinary criminals – people who steal and murder just for themselves; they think of themselves as political prisoners, prisoners of war."

"Like *The Wooden Horse?*"

"Eh?"

"It's a brilliant black'n'white movie. They hide in a wooden horse and dig a tunnel when the others are exercising above. Him from *Mary Poppins* is in it – but he's much younger."

"Right. Anyway, the I.R.A and other organisations were given Special Category Status years ago – political status. That means they're treated differently from ordinary prisoners: they can wear their own clothes, they don't have to work in prison, they can have more visitors. But that's been taken away now and they're being treated like all the other prisoners."

"And they're starving themselves because of that?" I was incredulous. "If you're in prison you're in prison – what's the difference?"

"The difference, Kevin, is gigantic. It's how people see you. Think about it like this: if two men are shot by two different people then both of those people should go to prison for life – right? But suppose one of the men shot was a horrible person who had kidnapped and tortured children, and the other one was just an ordinary person. Should the two prisoners be treated the same way?"

"I'm lost."

"The I.R.A don't see themselves as terrorists, Kevin, they see themselves as freedom fighters – fighting against the things that we've talked about: housing, votes, jobs, being treated like dirt for years." He leant forward and looked at me with such intensity that I stopped chewing. "What do you think the dirty protest was about?"

"About the Special Category Status?"

"Yeah. Did you never wonder why grown men were spreading their shit on their walls?"

"I thought it was because they hated the Brits and wanted to be as nasty as they could."

"Nasty? By spreading their own shit on their own walls?"

"Why then?"

"When the rules were changed they refused to wear the new uniform – said they would have to nail it to their backs. So they gave them prison blankets to wear."

"The Blanket Men."

"Yes. Then they refused to leave their cells to wash and go to the toilet. The prison officers had to empty their pots of shit– all gets nasty, shit gets spilt – and that's the start of the dirty protest."

"All because of a uniform?   And now they're starving themselves – because of a uniform?" I thought of Ronnie Barker and poor Richard Beckinsale. They looked comfy enough. Of course, there was more to it than that. I understood some of what Ronald was saying, it was about identity - but still. Starving yourself? Spreading shit on the walls?

"You remember Mr Palmer telling us about Anne Frank and her attic?"

"Sure."

"You remember what he said about the clothes they had to wear – the Jews?"

"A star and a circle."

"Right. It's not exactly the same – the Jews were happy about being Jews – but the idea of being branded is the same," he tapped his shoulder. "This means I'm a Jew – I'm not allowed to go to the movies or even ride a bike."

"But, she didn't put shit on her walls – she put posters up."

"I know. I said it wasn't exactly the same."

CHAPTER TWENTY-FOUR

It was early November. The night before the first test. I'd been with Ronald for a while in the afternoon but we hadn't overdone it. Wouldn't do to leave all the fight in the gym. I was staring up at the ceiling, counting the cracks by the light of the moon. I could feel my eye-lids getting heavy and that was great; I'd been worried that I would be tossing and turning all night. This was a good sign. Nervous but reasonably confident; it wouldn't do to be over confident, the gods didn't like that. Arrogance was like a red rag to the gods of chance and fortune; if you got too big for yourself there was nothing that gave them more pleasure than pricking your bubble. Jimmy. Rip. That dick-head Sam. If I did fail, he would still be at the High School when I arrived. That thought would have tormented me before but now – thanks to Ronald – I had managed to control it and constantly push it away. Yet, it was still the last thought I had before I fell asleep. Rip was lost to me. I would be all on my own. Just me, my brand new uniform still with the tags, and my lip. That was if I failed.

"And in the red corner, fighting fit and raring to go, is the reigning heavyweight champion – Sugar Ray McBride!"

Dad cheered and applauded as I sat down. Mum had made me a special breakfast of scrambled eggs and bacon to bring me luck. Toast too.

"How do you feel this morning, champ?" Dad held his fork across the table as if it was a microphone, it was something he had done for years but it was actually a bit annoying just now. "Do you think it will be a K.O or will it go the distance?"

"Leave him be, Del. Just do your best, Kev – that's all we ask."

"You should be razor sharp after all the practising you've been doing with yer man."

Dad was all serious now.

"Are you walking up with Jimmy?"

"I'm not sure," I felt guilty; they didn't know that I hadn't walked to school with Jimmy for weeks. "I want to get there real early."

"*Really* early," Pete said, but nobody paid him any notice.

At the door, she hugged me and Dad gave me the double thumbs up. I was starting to feel it now. It didn't matter how much I had practised with Ronald or how much I had improved. This was it. Two fifty minute tests that would decide my future. Clever Clogs or Dumbo. If I did well on this one the pressure would be off a little for the second one; if I messed this one up then it would all depend on the next one. Fuck.

The school wasn't even open yet but there was a little cluster of Eleven Plussers outside the front door. Stanley Brownlie, Leo Scott, Sally Peters, and, Stephanie Gillespie. I nodded at Stanley, twitched a smile at Leo, stole a glance at Stephanie. With all that had happened over the past few weeks I hadn't really been thinking about her as much but here she was and I was glad that she hadn't suddenly grown all ugly. I remember once sitting beside Jimmy and painting a picture – Primary three I think, another house but the best one I'd ever done. I spent ages on it. It had complicated vines and ivy up the sides and front, a flickering candle in one of the windows and a shadowy figure downstairs that really kept you guessing. You couldn't tell for sure if it was the mum, the dad, or something more sinister. Jimmy agreed that it was the best thing I had ever done. We left them to dry at the front and I could hardly sleep that night thinking about my masterpiece and wanting to see it again. Next day it was gone. All the other paintings were there at the front, dry and ready to hang, but mine had disappeared. Then I looked closer. There was my name at the bottom of a painting – a terrible painting of a black house with green down the side, an orange smudge in the upstairs window and a big black splodge downstairs. After the initial shock and disbelief I had laughed myself hoarse and Mrs Lawther sent me outside to gather myself.

But Stephanie just got lovelier with each day. She'd shampooed her hair last night in preparation for the big test and as I watched her brush it behind her little ears away from her face, I could smell fresh green apples in the summer sunshine. Everything about her was just so: the spotless white shoes (if she lived to be one hundred she would never step in dog shit) the perfectly fitting jeans that hugged her bum, the pink cardigan top thing that didn't quite meet the jeans so that they gave you a little half inch of tanned tummy and perhaps even a wink at her belly button. And her diddies. Jesus. If you looked away for half an hour and then looked back they would have grown. They were beautiful, especially when you viewed them from the side – oh fuck!

She'd caught me looking at her! I'd been staring right at her diddies and she'd turned and looked me straight in the eye. I looked out over the town and prayed for Ronald or even Jimmy to hurry the fuck up. My face was burning. I must have looked like a traffic light.

"Hey there, Kevin – are you all set?"

Jesus H Christ. She'd moved over beside me. She was talking to me. She'd said my name.

"Oh, hi there, sorry I didn't see you – I was miles away. Yeah, I'm a bit nervous. What about yourself?"

She pulled a face and she was so close I could have counted the freckles on her nose. Then she gave her head a shake and her earrings, tiny little unicorns, swung back and forth. Oh, please, God help me.

"I'm so scared. I keep thinking, what if I forget everything Mr Palmer has taught us."

"Yeah, I know what you mean," I had brushed my teeth vigorously that morning but I pulled back a bit just in case. "Ronald's been helping me practise."

"You're scores have really improved over the last few weeks."

Bloody hell, she noticed.

"Well, good luck."

"Yeah, you too, Stephanie."

Good boy, good boy. Well done for saying her name.

More people were arriving now and I saw Ronald getting

out of his auntie's car at the far side of the school. Without anyone seeing, I quickly checked my nose and the corners of my mouth. Nothing there. Thank God for that. She had looked at me. She had come over to speak to me. She had said my name. I tried to remember if she had ever spoken to me before. She must have done. I had been in her group a few times before and she had spoken to me then; but it wasn't really the same, that was because she had to and it would only have been to do with the task we were given. This was *her own choice*. And she knew how much I had improved; that showed she was a little bit interested in me. Was it possible that she had been secretly watching me, building up her confidence, waiting for a good opportunity to speak to me?

Oh for Christ sake, listen to yourself. She'll be buying you a fucking engagement ring next. The only reason she came over is because there was no one else to talk to – Fats Brownlie, Sally Clarke, Jon Park – as soon as others arrived she was away like a rabbit. Waiting for an opportunity? Did you fuckin' ever?

Maybe. But she still didn't need to talk to me. She could have just said nothing and gazed out over the town the way I always did. She'd made an effort, and that was something.

"Sleep okay?" asked Ronald.

"Yeah, you?"

He nodded. "This is it."

"Yeah."

"How you feeling?"

I took a deep breath and saw that Stephanie was deep in conversation with one of the girls from the other Primary seven class.

They're talking about you, Rubber. She's saying how she finally plucked up enough courage to talk to you and how wonderful she now feels. Jesus.

"Ronald, my boy, I feel pretty damn good."

*

We had a different teacher give out the papers. His name was Mr Boyle and he was a Primary seven teacher from another school on the far side of town. They swapped teachers to make sure it was all fair and no one could say there had been cheating. Palmer would now be talking to Mr Boyle's kids at the same time as Mr Boyle was talking to us. It was a funny feeling.

"I'm sure you are feeling very nervous, but try not to be."

He was really nice.

"All you can do is your best – but what you must remember to do is read the instructions carefully."

I had the pencil in my hand even though he had said not to lift them. He walked down with a smile, gently took it from my fingers, and set it at the top of my desk.

"Pencils get all sweaty and sticky," he explained to me and to the rest of the class. "Best not to hold them until we start."

God, he was lovely. What a swap this was. I wondered what they were making of Mr Palmer across town; but then of course he would be on his best behaviour as well. They probably thought *he* was lovely. He would want the other school to see what a decent guy he was, the same as our friend here. Mr Boyle probably yanked ears in his own school.

It was almost time to start and I could feel my old friend panic racing up the stairs to join me. Big deep breaths. The Stephanie thing had been a little bonus but it meant nothing and I couldn't let it distract me. Everybody was now in place. I glanced around and gave Ronald and Jimmy a little nod. This was it.

"Okay, boys and girls. You may begin now and the very best of Irish luck."

*

I had a few dodgy moments. It was like I had fallen back in time to before Ronald and was drowning in all the figures and stupid percentages. But then I would take a few deep breaths, settle myself, and come at them again with a different attitude. The page turning didn't bother me at all. Just because they were ahead didn't mean they had them right. I zoned them out and focused hard on the questions the way Ronald had shown me. Some I still couldn't do – but just because they were *really* hard, not because I thought they were hard.

The best part was recognising and nailing questions that had once been impossible.

In an election, 3 candidates, McCready, Rankin and Orbinson, receive a total of 49,768 votes. Rankin has 780 more than Orbinson. McCready has twice as many as Rankin. How many has McCready?

No fucking problem.

If the 17th of September is a Monday, what day is the 13th of October?

Really? Is that the best you can do?

A cyclist leaves his house at 3pm to cycle to a camp site 33 miles away. He arrives at 5.30pm. At what time must his brother on a motor bike, travelling 3 times as fast, leave the house to arrive at the camp site at the same time?

Come on, is that all you got?

CHAPTER TWENTY-FIVE

It was late November and we were all gathered round the television, even Mum, desperate to find out who had shot J.R Ewing. She had made sandwiches and there were nuts and crisps. Pete had come down from upstairs but he had brought his book with him to show he wasn't that interested.

"Won't be Bobby or Miss Ellie," Dad said again. "Don't care how bad you are – you don't shoot your brother or your son."

"It'll be Cliff Barnes or Sue Ellen," said Mum. She was really getting into it. "Who do you think it'll be, Kevin?"

"Pam maybe, I'm not sure."

The strange thing was that I had been looking forward to this episode for months but now it was here it all felt a bit silly and over the top. They weren't real people after all, just actors, and they were following a script. Larry Hagman had negotiated a contract that made him one of the highest paid television actors on the planet. And here we were eating sandwiches and wondering who shot him but didn't really.

"I liked Larry Hagman in *I Dream of Jeannie*," Pete said, and he set his book aside.

"That was a good show." Dad reached for some nuts and shovelled them into his mouth. "Here's one for you, Kev. Who do you think would win a magic fight between Jeannie from *I Dream of Jeannie* and Tabitha from *Bewitched*?"

I grimaced with disgust as he asked me. I couldn't help it. The nuts had been clearly visible throughout and one of them had leapt from his mouth onto the carpet.

"Oh dear," he gave me a strange, hurt look. "Kevin's getting a bit too big for my silly questions – that's a shame."

"I think it would be Tabitha," Mum said and she put her finger on the tip of her nose and made it twitch.

They all laughed. But I just thought it made her look stupid.

CHAPTER TWENTY-SIX

It was Bing Crosbie's daughter.

CHAPTER TWENTY-SEVEN

On the night before the second Eleven Plus test, Granny and Granda stayed over. They hardly ever did. Mum and Dad slept on the bed settee and Granda told us stories about some of the characters he had met on his travels. He was hilarious and it helped take my mind off the test.

Mum had a great idea in the morning. We were in the kitchen and she was half whispering even though the door was closed.

"How's about Granda lifting you to school for luck?"

She caught me completely off-guard.

"Mum, I want to get there really early."

"Fine, I've already brought him his breakfast in bed."

"You've told him already?" I glared at her, I couldn't help myself. "So why are you asking me?"

Toast popped up from the toaster but she didn't even blink.

"Who the hell do you think you are talking too, mister? What's with the bad attitude lately, Kevin? I know you're nervous about this test but that's no excuse."

"I'm not nervous."

"So why are you being so damned rude?"

I was hot and bothered. Stupid bitch. Why did she have to complicate things? Granda would drag his heels and they would all be there to see him drop me off. They would see his hat, and his braces, and his pipe. The thought made me feel guilty and I hated her more. But he was nothing to do with the Eleven Plus. It was a completely different bloody thing.

"Granda's taking you and that's that. Make sure you thank him."

I told him to drop me at the bottom of the hill instead of at the top by the gates. His little car had problems with the clutch and I didn't want him to stall or whatever coming back down.

It was 8.30 am.

Stephanie Gillespie would be lost in a sea of faces now.

"Thanks, Granda," I reached for the door handle.

"I'm sure you'll do fine, son. Of course, there was no such a thing when I was a boy."

"Yeah, I know," my arse was half out the door. "I'm gonna have to run, Granda."

"No, no," he checked his watch which kept excellent time, not like those daft Japanese digital ones. "Doreen said it wasn't till nine – you've loads of time."

He was reaching for his pipe! Aw, Jesus.

"Education. Really important, Kevin," he pressed down with his thumb and struck a match. "I left school when I was fourteen, you know."

The cat's piss story. I've heard it before.

"I wasn't sorry to go. Hated the masters, cruel bastards all. Sorry."

I tried to jolly him along.

"What job did you get?"

"I was a butcher's boy in Belfast. I used to run errands, scrub the floors, parcel the meat."

Hurry up, man. The cat's piss.

"Seven shillings and six pence a week," he rolled his window down a little further to expel the smoke. "Thought I was the boy, so a did. Christ, I was a grinder. Every morning, I would clean the cat's piss off the outside window –"

"Granda, I'm gonna need the toilet before the test."

But he was lost in his smoke and his memories.

"I can remember one morning a boy yells across the street, Hey Bob, is that yourself? I looks up and it's a lad I knew from Derry – Albert Carson, we used to fish and climb for apples; and now he's all dressed up like he's off to his own funeral. Where are you off to? says I. I've got a place in Queens, says he, I'm learning to be a solicitor. Good for you, says I, and I reach back down to my bucket to wet the rag so I can clean the rest of the cat's piss off. He waves over at me the next day and the day after that; but then I begin to see him with other boys – all dressed fancy – and he stops waving at me, he doesn't even look across the road. It's as if he's forgotten I was there," he took a long draw of his pipe as he gazed back through the years remembering the slight. "Funny the way people can be."

I took my hand off the door handle and nodded in agreement. There was plenty of time before the test and it would take me less than a minute to walk up the hill. When he looked at me there were tears in his eyes and I wondered if the smoke had blown back in on him or if his eyes were just a bit watery today the way old people's eyes sometimes got. And I thought of a young boy in short trousers on his hands and knees, scrubbing away and waving at people and being polite and it made me feel a little sick. I felt like the world's biggest shit because my granda loved me and had told me something private – something more than just the comedy of the cat's piss – and I hated Mum for putting me in that position and making me feel bad about myself just before the test.

*

"Well?" Ronald grinned at me and pumped my hand as we left the classroom for break time. "What did you think?"

"Okay. Good. The question about the dartboard was a real bastard."

There had been a question about the least amount of darts a darts player needed to finish from 371. I watched the darts all the time with Dad. We booed Eric Bristow, *the Crafty Cockney*, and cheered John Lowe, *Old Stone Face*. I'd read the question carefully twice and was trying to work out trebles and doubles to accord with a standard dartboard. The answer was seven darts. There were several possible ways of doing it but the one I had gone with was: treble twenty, treble twenty, treble twenty, treble twenty, treble twenty, treble seventeen, and finally, double ten. I was pleased. Then I noticed the dartboard they had provided which included numbers completely alien to a normal board – 27, 55, 79 ....I could have screamed and nearly did.

"Did you fix it?"

"I think so. I hope so."

"Well, that's it over. How does it feel?"

"Good," was all I could manage just now. It did feel good, but where was that incredible feeling of relief I had been looking forward to? I just felt tired. Maybe I was worried that I hadn't done enough. "It's a bit of an anti–climax."

"Yeah."

"Alright, lads?" Jimmy joined us. "I always feel a bit sorry for Uncle Climax, nobody ever mentions him," he grinned and offered his open crisp packet.

I took one, even though I wasn't fussed on Prawn Cocktail. "How did it go, Jimmy?"

"Okay – what about you two?"

"Not bad, I hope." I said.

"Time will tell," said Ronald.

"Yeah."

You could see him searching for something else to add, wanting to be a part of the aftermath but not knowing how. He offered his crisps again before remembering he had just done that; then, too late, wiped sweat off his brow to show how relieved he was that the test was over.

"Touch wood, we'll all be in Academy uniforms next September."

Now there was a thought. Who would I sit beside next September if I had the choice? How did they work out classes – was it alphabetical or did they go by primary report? Jesus, here we go again. Out with the old, in with the new.

"There's Rip – better see what he's up to."

He seemed visibly relieved to be away from us and I relaxed a little.

Rip had had the luxury of a sleep in whilst we toiled. He glanced briefly in our direction before making a huge show of clapping Jimmy on the back and asking him how he got on.

"S'pose that's the last time I'll be seeing you up at my house," Ronald said. "Now that we can put away our verbal reasoning books."

"Don't be a dick."

"Oh, that's right – I forgot your sweet tooth. As long as there's a tooth in your head, eh?"

I pushed him hard enough that he almost lost his balance.

"Allo, Ronald," he put his lips around his teeth in a drawstring. "It's me, Kevin. Any chance of a gob stopper?"

I burst out laughing. It was nice to see him not so serious for once. However, I made sure to control my laugh – not to be too raucous – because Stephanie and her friends were nearby. The way I felt just now I thought I could probably handle talking to her. It would all be about the test and what questions were the hardest, boring shite, but at least it would keep the conversation going. I could talk about the dartboard question; then I could say that Clint Eastwood liked to play darts to relax (it was possible) then I could mention that there was a Clint Eastwood movie on at the cinema; then I could ask her if she fancied seeing it with me. Easy. We wouldn't need to worry about expensive sweets – Ronald would sort me out – although we could share a big romantic popcorn box. I could hold her hand at the scary parts, that would come naturally, and I would have a few jokes and stuff prepared to keep her laughing on the way home. That just left the goodnight kiss and the problem of where to put my rubber lip. Tricky. But then black people managed without a problem – although to be fair they had two, one to balance the other.

CHAPTER TWENTY-EIGHT

We were glued to the telly. It was December 18th and the hunger strike in the Maze had collapsed. They had been starving themselves for fifty-three days. *Fifty-three days.*

"Has Thatcher given them what they wanted?"

Ronald gave me a pained look and held his hand up for silence.

"I don't know. It looks like she might have."

She had not. It transpired that the prisoners had been fooled and outplayed by the government. There had been an assurance that a settlement document was on its way from London but before it arrived one of the prisoners, Sean McKenna, became gravely ill. He was transferred to the Royal Victoria Hospital and the leadership, fearing his imminent death, were forced to agree to unseen terms. With the strike called off the government were in a strong position. They decided that prison uniforms were to be abolished – one of the demands. But they were being replaced by prison issue "civilian style clothing" which was just another uniform. The hunger strike had been for nothing.

CHAPTER TWENTY-NINE

Ronald was away for the whole of Christmas. His auntie had a cottage near Killarney. That was the Christmas I got my Evel Kinevil bike toy. It was triple wrapped in paper so I knew that it was my big present – and the fact that it had been kept to last. Mum and Dad were watching me closely and I didn't disappoint, whoops of joy and fist clenching *yeses*. It was a pretty cool present though. The sort of present that I would have killed for three years before. It was a little doll decked out in the famous stars and stripes uniform complete with helmet. You placed him on his bike and then put the back wheel in what they called the energiser, then you wound it up - it made a fantastic grinding noise - and pressed the release button.

"Guess who else got one?" Mum asked, sniffing the air to see how the turkey was doing. "Jimmy. I bumped into his mum in the town."

Ah. Get ready for it.

"Know what would be nice?"

"What?"

"Not today – too busy, but maybe sometime during the holiday, you could invite him round to play?"

To play? Jesus. Get out the building blocks and the Teddy Bears.

"That's a great idea, yeah."

Every Christmas I always told myself I would stop when I was full and wouldn't keep going just because more food was available. Every Christmas I couldn't do it. I just kept on munching. On Christmas morning, with the excitement of presents, I just more or less had my usual breakfast. Then it started in earnest. Granny and Granda came to ours and brought with them an assortment of mince pies, apple crumble, strawberry tart and chocolate cake – all of which needed to be eaten within the holiday period (Granda's connections got him good discounts on all sorts if the produce was approaching its use by date.) Custard, whipped cream, strawberries. The turkey was gargantuan – that was the word Dad used every year and expected everyone to applaud him – and all the trimmings: roast tatties, ham, carrots, mashed potatoes, Brussel sprouts, all drowning in a sea of black gravy.

And I kept on shovelling.

I would end up feeling like that fat girl with the chewing gum at Willy Wonkas. And I would say to myself: enough now, Kevin, this is actually quite painful, you are as full as full can be, you won't be able to eat another thing for at least a day.
Then half an hour later I would be reaching for the biscuit tin.

Mum invited Jimmy round on the day after Boxing Day. We played in the hallway with our Evel Kinevils and it was good fun – although the carpet was a bit too thick for him to really get going. You could set books up at an angle for him to jump and I ransacked my old toy box for matchbox cars for him to fly over. Jimmy was really getting into it with an American style commentary and I had to ask him to tone it down because I could hear Pete tutting from the living room.

"I wonder how much money he makes on each one?" Jimmy asked.

It was a good question.

"He probably gets a percentage – about 5% for each one sold."

"Not much."

"It is for doing nothing," I said. "All he's doing is lending his name to it; then he just sits on his arse and waits for the cheques to fall through the letter box."

"Yeah, but he had to make his name first. All those broken bones. If he hadn't fallen off all those times he wouldn't be so famous and no one would be playing with his toy. He earned it – even if he didn't make them himself."

He was right; and I was annoyed because it was something I should have said. Not him.

"Still, that's a lot of money he's made. Let's say they've sold a million – probably more but let's just say a million – at eight pounds each. That's eight million pounds. Divide by one hundred to get one percent then multiply by five ...."

Jimmy was shaking his head.

"It's a lot. Buy you a lot of bandages."

Mum was liable to ask him to stay for his tea so I told her that his uncle was coming round that evening – which was true. In my room he told me that the den was hardly used now and his dad was thinking of pulling it down. That made me feel a little sad. He asked me if I wanted to collect my posters and a few other bits and pieces but I told him just to trash them, Mum wasn't fussed on me hanging posters in my room and there certainly wasn't room for the pool table. He hadn't seen Rip for some time and that didn't make me feel sad at all. It would be great next year (fingers and toes crossed) when we didn't even have to think about Rip and his bigotry. They could all go to hell in the High School.

*

At the start of 1980, Ronald Reagan was President, Lady Di got engaged to Prince Charles and we were all singing *The Tide is High* by Blondie.

And I passed the Eleven Plus.

I knew I wouldn't be able to sleep a wink the night before so I didn't even try. There was still the chance that I had failed. Long night. I read the rest of *Salem's Lot* and scared the shit out of myself which didn't help either. Mostly, I thought about the postman. This was his moment and, if he was of a mind, he could milk it for all it was worth. When else did postmen get the chance to flex their muscles and wield a little power? He could make me dance if he wanted to. All across the province there would be thousands of anxious eleven year old faces pressed to front door windows. I didn't even know what ours looked like but I could imagine him walking slowly up the road, enjoying the exercise and the fresh air, pausing perhaps to tie his lace or pull up his socks. And then I would see him at our gateway, shuffling the envelopes and I would squint at him because – this was the best bit – according to quite a few people (not just Pete) the passes were all in rectangular brown envelopes, the fails in square white ones. That was how my night was spent; that, and Stephen King's vampires tapping at my window.

"It's all thanks to you," I said to Ronald down the phone and I meant it. "I'd be out buying a High School uniform now if it wasn't for you."

"Rubbish."

But I could tell he was pleased.

There were a few casualties but no one of any note. Jon Park and Leo Scott would be making snowballs with the devil but Jimmy got through, and so too did the divine Stephanie. I imagined what she would look like in her crisp white blouse and pleated skirt. She might have her hair in a ponytail, like she sometimes did, and she would wear her tie loose so that you could see any little necklace that she was wearing. On a cold winter day she would toss back her scarf and snuggle into it, and her nose would be a little redder than usual but she would still smile and wiggle her fingers in a wave.

*

Bernadette McCaliskey had been attacked and almost killed. She was a well-known republican and outspoken critic of the criminalisation process. Three U.D.A gunmen smashed down her door with sledgehammers before shooting her and her husband repeatedly in front of their young children.

"Hey, Rip!"

It was Leo Scott, trying to act big.

"The U.D.A need a few shootin' lessons," he held up his little finger. "Yer woman's like this and they still couldn't put her away. Fuck me."

"You cheeky bastard!" Rip chased him around the yard but you could see he was enjoying the audience and when he caught him his revenge was lame-hearted.

"You see that," Ronald spoke softly. "A woman and a man are shot in front of their kids and they think it's a big laugh."

The I.R.A responded several days later when they shot dead Sir Norman Stronge and his son James before burning their home to the ground. Sir Norman was eighty-six and had fought at the Battle of the Somme.

"He was older than my granda!" I said, appalled. "Imagine being in the First World War and living all those years – only to get shot when you're eighty-six and watching television."

"Horrible," Ronald agreed. "But at least now you're seeing two sides."

CHAPTER THIRTY

It was early evening and we were playing tennis at the town courts. It was one of the few sports I was actually quite good at. Despite my size I was fast and had good hand eye coordination. There were six courts and we had the whole place to ourselves. Different during the summer; then you would have to book the thing in advance and make sure you were there on time otherwise someone would steal your spot. Wimbledon was to blame. I usually didn't bother playing then, there was too much noise and aggro. From outside you would constantly hear yells of "YOU CANNOT BE SERIOUS!" followed by gales of laughter like it had never been said before.

Without talking about it, we had realised that something was needed to fill the void now that the Eleven Plus had been and gone. I still liked chilling at his house and talking about the Troubles, but now we also made semi-regular visits to the swimming-pool and to here. Ronald wasn't bad at tennis and I found that if I took my foot off the pedal just slightly we could have a good competitive game.

It was seven o'clock and getting quite dark but the positioning of the street lights allowed us to play on. Best of three sets. I had won the first 6-3, and was leading this one 4-1. I was preparing an easy serve when a large piece of asphalt landed less than a metre from where I stood.

"Fuck!"

It took a moment for it to register and I think I actually looked skyward with the notion that some gigantic bird had dropped it. But then I followed the arc to the top of the wall that ran parallel to the court and stiffened at the sight of Sam.

"Alright there, Kevin? Sorry about that."

There's rubble up there – loads of it. Bricks, pebbles, jaggy little stones.

"Let's go, Ron."

Ronald did not need any coaxing. He paused to pick up a

ball and came running round the net to join me. Then we both turned towards the gates of the cage. But of course it wasn't as easy as that – real life never is. There were two other boys on the outside barring our exit. I recognised both of them from the High School fence.

"What's your hurry lads?" Sam held onto the ledge and carefully lowered himself down; he brushed the dust off his hands and smiled pleasantly at both of us. "You haven't finished your game."

My legs felt like jelly and I swear I could hear Ronald's heart thumping beside me. I looked desperately towards the far end of the court through the little square of fence where you could see the pavement. There was nobody about. Not a soul.

"My dad's collecting us, Sam – he'll be here any second."

"Oh?" he made a great show of looking bewildered. "Those your bikes over there? Funny that. You rode your bikes down and now your dad's gonna pick you up? That's a bit of a hastle is it not, putting those big bulky bikes into the boot of his car."

He was having fun and that at least was something. No real anger.

"Thought yer da was gonna kick my shit in – did he forget?"

"Let's just go, Ron."

We started to walk towards the gate. My idea was just to brush aside them or somehow dodge round them but then Sam had his hand in my hair and was yanking me back.

"Ahhh – you fuckin' bastard."

"Leave him alone – fuckin' let go of him!" Ronald brandished his racquet above his head.

"Aw, look lads – the wee fuckin' leprechaun's got some balls!"

The two boys roared.

"Go on, tough guy," the bastard still had my hair in his hand as he jutted his chin out, "make it a good yin!"

I managed to pull myself free. The pain was excruciating. I

looked down at his hand and was amazed that there wasn't some of my hair in his fist.

Ronald had lowered the tennis racquet and I could see him visibly shaking.

"Didn't think so," Sam said and he sounded disappointed. "See that lads? Wasn't even prepared to stick up for his bum chum."

More roars from the lads.

I continued to look scared – and I was – but I was also relieved. It wasn't a beating, just humiliation. I could handle that.

"You're that little cunt I've heard about, aren't you? The cocksucker who thinks he knows all about the Troubles."

"He's a Protestant, Sam."

"Shut your fuckin' mouth, Samantha."

The lads almost shat themselves at that. Samantha Fox was a famous page three girl.

Sam stepped closer to him and pulled up his shirt sleeve.

"What does it say there, cocksucker?"

"U.V.F 1690."

"What does it stand fer?"

"Ulster Volunteer Force."

"Good boy," he ruffled his hair and Ronald was wise enough not to pull away. "People like me keep an eye on people like you. You know why?"

"Why?"

"Because you're the fuckin' cancer of society."

At the mention of cancer Ronald's expression had flickered and I began to panic again. How much had Rip told him? If he made some crack about his dad I thought he might snap.

"And you know what you do with cancer, don't you?" he tore the racquet – my racquet - from his hand and produced a Stanley knife from his pocket. "You cut it out."

The boys behind me gasped with pleasure and excitement as he slowly ran the blade down the strings; the first twang was impressive, but the rest were disappointing – it would have been different in a movie.

Fuck it, Kevin. It's just an old racquet. Don't be a dick about it. At least it's not your face – it was never going to be.

He tossed the racquet aside.

"Let's go lads."

The boys stepped aside and at last we were free to go but as we collected the bikes, Sam thought of something else.

"Hold on, hold on. I'm dying for a piss," he unzipped and started to urinate over both bikes, all up the frames, hoisting himself so he could cover the seats. "Ah, that's better."

Bill and Ben the flowerpot men could hardly breathe.

And now it was danger time for me because I could feel the fury boiling up inside me. Dirty fucking beast. He was pissing over my bike – the bike Granda had bought for me. I'd have to go all the way home, get a bucket and sponge, then come all the way back here before I could touch it again.

But just then, Ronald stepped forward.

"Jaysus!" he roared with laughter and pointed down. "Look at the size of your dick –it's fuckin' tiny!" He looked to me and suddenly I found myself laughing, just on the right side of hysterical.

"Fuck me, Sam," I said. "It's like a wee dwarf dick – a wee tiny baby dick. God love you wee man!" And I laughed until my throat was hoarse.

And the joy of it was that Bill and Ben laughed too. They couldn't help it. They had already been laughing and you can't stop mid laugh to show loyalty to your pal especially if what's just been said is funny as well.

Sam put away his small penis and glowered at them. They sniffed and smirked and twisted their faces in an effort to conform and that was just enough time for me and Ronald to make good our getaway.

"Run like fuck," I said to him, surprised at the calmness of my voice.

"What about the bikes?"

"Fuck 'em."

And so we left the poor bikes to their mercy and ran away

as fast as we could – passed the bowling green and the swing set, not daring to pause or look behind, only slowing when we got to the main street and we could see cars and other people.

I sat down on the ledge of a shop window and swallowed down huge gulps of air.

"Do you think they'll wait by the bikes?"

"I don't think so. If they do, they'll get bored soon – and they might think we're bringing someone back with us."

"Bet he's slashed the tyres."

"Yeah."

We went back half an hour later, armed with wet wipes I had bought at the newsagents. No sign of them, of course, but you couldn't help jump at shadows all the way there. And he had slashed the tyres – how could he resist? Actually, although I didn't say to Ronald, I was pleased that he had. Even Stevens: we had laughed at his dick, he had slashed our tyres. He wouldn't be actively out to get us now, unless he happened upon us by chance. A new tyre was a lot for a schoolboy to fork out, two new tyres was a real kick in the wallet; but when I thought of the Stanley knife and what he might've done if he had been a member of the real U.V.F and not just a tadpole, I was quite happy with the result.

"You know, life used to be really boring before I met you," I told Ronald as we pushed the bikes through the town.

He seemed pleased at that, then he added. "But did you see the size of his thing?"

And suddenly we were both laughing again.

*

I was in his house when the news came that another hunger strike had begun in the Maze prison. It was March 1st 1981, chosen because it was the fifth anniversary of the ending of the prisoner's political status. Sinn Fein organised a march through West Belfast, but there were a lot less than the ten thousand who had marked the first strike. A statement was read out on behalf of the prisoners:

"We have asserted that we are political prisoners and

everything about our country, our interrogation, trials and prison conditions show that we are politically motivated and not motivated by selfish reasons or selfish ends. As further demonstration of our selflessness and the justice of our cause, a number of our comrades will hunger strike to the death unless the British Government abandons its criminalisation policy and meets our demands."

The first person to refuse food was a twenty-seven year old I.R.A member named Bobby Sands. It was big on the local news but nationally it was just seen as a rerun of the last hunger strike. They were all too busy chasing after Lady Di, trying to get her to smile, loving that coy look she had perfected. She was taller than Charles so the talk was that she would never be able to wear high heels, poor woman, otherwise she would be looking down on the future King of England.

"What's the point of them doing it all again?" I asked him. "Nothing's changed – Thatcher is still there."

"They won't make the same mistakes this time."

"What do you mean?"

"I mean they'll accept nothing less than all their demands."

I was confused. "But they won't get them."

He looked closely at me. "I know. And they'll go all the way."

"You mean they'll die? They'll all starve themselves to death?"

He nodded.

"That's crazy. Starving yourself for nothing."

He switched off the television so that all you could hear was the ticking of that wretched clock. "Is there any person you would be prepared to die for? Instant death – no pain."

"Christ, what a question."

"Think hard and be honest."

"I am thinking hard. Mum and Dad."

"Good. I was going to shoot your dad, but now I'll aim at you – BANG! You're dead, lying on the floor."

"Charming."

"Now think really carefully about this and again be honest: would you *starve* yourself to death for them? A long, slow, lingering death. Day after day after day after day; getting weaker and weaker – desperate for food, dreaming about it, craving it, your stomach eating itself out from the inside."

"Yeah, I still would say Mum and Dad."

"Really, Kevin? Your belly's full now – those sweets and whatever you had for lunch. But imagine what it would be like not to have had any food in your belly for fifty-three days. Can you imagine what that would feel like?"

I swallowed uncomfortably. In my mouth was the sugary sweetness of the jelly babies I had just eaten. There were still five of them in the bowl in front of me and I realised with some dismay that I would not be able to leave the house without finishing them off.

"It's hard to imagine, isn't it?"

There wasn't a lot of information about Bobby Sands and Ronald set about finding out as much as he could. I knew he was in the I.R.A and that helped me to imagine what he might look like. Wild piercing eyes; maybe a scar; definitely a tattoo somewhere – *fuck the Brits* - and he would have a black balaclava too, not in prison, but at home waiting for him to get out. He'd have his own gun, of course, a green anorak with a fur hood, and black Doc Martens – they all had those. I liked the way his name sounded – *Bobby Sands* - like a man walking barefoot on the beach, examining shells with his toes and gazing out to sea. Perhaps because I no longer had the Eleven Plus to occupy me I thought more about this strike than the last one. Not all the time, but certainly when I was eating. I thought about him when I was having my breakfast – still Rice Krispies but now also golden toast dripping with butter. Ham sandwiches at lunch; sausage beans and chips for tea; and all the biscuits, crisps and sweets in between. He was missing out on all of that. He was getting nothing to eat. Nothing.

The hunger strikers had learnt from their mistakes and this time they were going to stagger the starts so that not everyone was approaching death at the same time. The idea of this was to gain as much publicity as possible so as to pressure the Thatcher government. Francis Hughes refused food two weeks after Sands and he was followed, a week later, by Raymond McCreesh and Patsy O'Hara. There were a number of street marches and campaigns for and against the hunger strikers, a rise in tension; other than that nobody really seemed to be that bothered. Bobby Sands and his comrades were quietly starving themselves but it had all been seen and done before — and not that very long ago.

Then something happened that was to change everything.

I had never heard of Jack Maguire. He was the M.P for South Tyrone and he had died suddenly shortly after Bobby Sands pushed aside his first breakfast. His death meant that an election was necessary and someone on the H-Block committee had the idea of running Sands as a candidate. This was something that had never been done before and the papers and television jumped upon it. Would the honest, law abiding Catholics vote for a convicted terrorist? All of a sudden, the hunger strike was front page news.

We were watching the H-Block supporters demonstrating in West Belfast.

"It's ridiculous," Pete said. "A convicted murderer running for government."

Everyone was talking about it so Pete was now an expert.

"He's not a murderer," I told him. "He's inside for having a gun."

"Oh, sorry Kevin," Pete glanced at Mum and Dad and it really annoyed me to see them both smiling. "Was he playing cowboys and Indians?" he put his open hand up to his mouth and made the Indian noise, "WOW! WOW! WOW! WOW!"

"You're such a dick, Pete."

"Kevin McBride!"

"Sorry, Mum, but he doesn't know what he's talking about. He's not even interested — it's just because it's big news."

"Call me a dick? Rubber Gub! Think you know it all just

because you hang around with that freaky boy."

"Enough!" Dad glared at both of us, he even glared at Mum who had done nothing. "What the hell is happening here? Nasty name calling – and all because of that!"

I could feel my heart hammering and I knew my face would be scarlet. He had made fun of my lip in front of them both and they hadn't called him on it. I was furious. Sure, I had called him a dick, but that's because he was one.

"It's good, I suppose, that we're all taking more of an interest in what's happening around us, but if we can't be mature about it I'm going to ban watching the telly at night."

Her ridiculous statement helped lighten the atmosphere a tiny bit.

"It is a bit daft," Dad said, more to break the silence than anything. "How can you represent constituents if you're locked up inside a -" here he raised his eyebrows to me for approval "-*shitty* cell."

"Actually, Dad, his cell is not dirty anymore," I told him.

"Wha?"

"They stopped the dirty protest so the focus would be on the hunger strike."

"I know they did, *son*. I was trying to be funny, *son*."

I could feel his eyes boring into me and I felt terrible. He thought that I was being cheeky and ungrateful but I wasn't – not really, it just seemed more important to correct him than to laugh at his bad language.

"Sorry, Dad."

It was all I could risk. Anything more might well trigger his temper.

"Dad?" Pete asked. "Would you like a cup of tea?"

"No, I wouldn't."

*

It was his picture that did it for me. I must have seen it before but the grainy newspaper image had never registered. Here it was now, blown up on campaign posters all over Belfast and South Tyrone – the long haired, smiling face of Bobby Sands.

Where was the wild, balaclava wearing gangster of my imagination? Where was the I.R.A monster who would stop at nothing to achieve his selfish ends? Here was an older brother who would dig into his pocket and hand you the last of his change so that you could go to the ice-cream van. Here was a young uncle who would keep his girlfriend waiting so that he could kick a ball with you, his flared trousers flapping in the wind. Here was a handsome drummer in a local rock band who could rattle the drums like no other but would happily let you sit in his seat and have a bash. Here was a man who would never laugh at my lip.

And suddenly, the eyes of the world were focussed on our six little counties, watching and waiting. Was it possible that Bobby Sands, I.R.A prisoner, might be elected as a member of parliament? And if so, would Maggie Thatcher dare allow a fellow M.P to die? Rulers from all over the world were quick to express their opinion. Ronald Reagan said he was "deeply concerned about the tragic situation."

But then on March 30th, he had some problems of his own.

"Ronnie Reagan's been assassinated!" Pete could hardly contain himself. "Like Kennedy – come see."

It was exciting stuff but I was also annoyed with Pete. Of course, it would be the one time I hadn't been watching the telly and now you would have thought he had shot him himself.

But the news bulletin was disappointing. There was no close up of his head coming apart and he wasn't even dead. He had been shot in Washington, in the chest and in the lower right arm. They'd rushed him to the nearby hospital where he was critical but stable.

It was massive news but the details remained sketchy. The culprit was a nutcase called John W Hinckley. He had shot and wounded three other people but they weren't important enough to have names. Reagan had suffered a punctured lung and heavy internal bleeding but was responding well in hospital.

*

Ronald was so eager to speak to me on Monday that he almost tripped coming out of his auntie's battered old Renault.

"Did you hear about it?"

"Reagan?"

"What? No, no. Sands. The election!"

I glanced around automatically and put my finger to my lips. The gesture was a bit theatrical but it felt good, cool somehow, as if I was involved in something more significant than silly schoolboy capers. He managed to contain himself until we had walked around to the back playground close to the furnace.

"It's a master stroke, Kev. If he's elected that proves he's a political prisoner. Even if they don't grant them their five demands – *it proves they're all political.*"

I wasn't quite sure about that but I wasn't confident enough to argue so instead I said something I had heard either from the telly or from Granda. "But if he fails, she'll say that even his own people don't support him."

"*If* he fails," Ronald's chest swelled and you could almost feel the energy pulsating from him. "Wait'n'see. The people will come out in their droves to save him – and not just Catholics, Prods as well; decent people with minds of their own."

I found myself grinning without really knowing why. Ronald beamed at me and did that daft little jig he sometimes did. I burst out laughing. How could you be so bloody enthusiastic and excited over an election? And yet it was infectious. I could feel a strange giddiness within myself, that familiar childhood longing for time to leapfrog and gobble up the days before a birthday or a longed for treat. I wanted to know today – *now* – if Bobby Sands could do it. Could a half starved man, with his rib cage clearly visible and from his hospital bed, convince all those people to vote for him?

Mr Palmer had us painting underwater scenes for most of the morning. It was pleasant enough but not very demanding. Not that I was complaining. Painting had always been one of my favourite past times even though I wasn't that great at it. My talent could never match my imagination. I was attempting Captain Nemo in Atlantis whilst everyone else had taken the easy option of sharks, octopuses, ship-wrecks and treasure; that my

Nautilus looked more like a great grey turd than a submarine made me feel a little less superior than I deserved.

Jimmy's painting took me back to Primary one.

I had left my seat to get another brush from the back.

It was exactly the same. The lines were sharper, the detail more sophisticated, but the same painting none-the-less. For some reason I couldn't explain it made me feel tremendously sad and I wanted to reach out to him. It was as if the Primary one version of Jimmy had suddenly been transported up the stairs and through the years to the here and now.

"Remember this?" he glanced over his shoulder and there was a strange old worldliness about his smile. "Can you tell what it is now?"

"I remember. You and the pirate shipwreck."

"Well done."

I wanted to say something else. I wanted to say, *Jimmy, old pal, I've been neglecting you lately and that's not fair, I'm definitely gonna make it up to you – and soon.* I wanted to say something like that but it wasn't the right time. It would've sounded daft. Something a poof might say to his boyfriend. Instead, I set my hand on his shoulder and gave it a little squeeze. We had been very close once and I thought he might know what the squeeze meant.

Ronald plonked himself down opposite me in the canteen and whipped away my apple crumble a fraction of a second before my spoon scooped it.

"Fuck off, Douglas! Gis it back!"

He shook his head. "This is how it feels to be on hunger strike."

It was 1.20 and the canteen was all but deserted. This was actually my third apple crumble, greedy bastard, although he wasn't to know that. I was the main server in charge of my table. I had to say grace and make sure the younger kids at my table behaved themselves. That was the bad part. The best part was that I took the pudding order and collected them at the hatch. It wasn't my fault if some of the kids had left to play football by the time I got back.

"Gimmee!"

He slid it back over.

"Jaysus, you wouldn't be much use in the H- Block."

I got stuck in. I didn't feel too bad. The portions were small.

"If I was to go on hunger strike I would mentally prepare myself," I told him. "The same way Bobby Sands did. You can't just yank someone's puddin' from under their nose when they're about to eat it and their mouth's waterin.' Jesus. That's like my Ma whenever she takes a notion to clean. It's the most annoying thing ever. If she said that we were all going to clean the house next Saturday I wouldn't mind – I could prepare myself, buy rubber gloves, and get ready for it. But she doesn't do that. She jumps up during the adverts and says "This house is boggin' we have to all clean it!" and she starts plumpin' up the cushions."

"Jaysus Christ..."

"What?"

Ronald all but ran around the table so that he could sit next to me.

"You've just given me such an idea."

"What?"

His voice was an urgent whisper and he grabbed my arm so tightly that I had to pull it away. "Listen to this. The vote is on Friday. How's about you stay over at mine – stay the night I mean. I'll show you all the things I've found out about Bobby – all the newspapers and magazines Gloria got for me. And here's what we'll do: *we won't eat anything!*"

"Why?"

"To show our support. Every time our stomach's rumble we can think of him."

It was a crazy idea; the stupidest I'd ever heard.

"But I'm thinking about him anyway – without starving myself."

Ronald's eyes had that strange faraway look again. It was actually quite off-putting.

"You don't get it, Kevin. You can think of him all you like while you've got apple pie in your belly – but you can't come close to feeling what he feels."

"I don't want to."

"But imagine if you could experience even a tiny bit of what he's going through – what he's suffering..."

"By *starving* myself?"

"You don't need to starve yourself; just go without food for a time, to see what it feels like."

I pushed aside my apple pie. I had left two bites of it just to show I could but he wasn't paying attention.

"Look, Kevin, have you any idea how big this thing is? Just twenty miles away from where we're sitting a man is starving himself to death because he feels so strongly about something he is willing to die for it. Doesn't matter if you agree or disagree, you've got to respect that."

"I do respect it."

"Do you think Rip and Jackie and Sam would be willing to do the same?"

I had thought about this before and the answer was a definite no. Rip and co felt that everything belonged to them as a divine right. They would fight for it, kill for it, but never ever starve themselves for it. They might argue that they would, that their faith and loyalty was just as strong; but I didn't think it was. For one thing, they liked their food too much.

Ronald hunched forward so that we were barely inches apart.

"Kevin, the whole fucking world is watching us. In twenty years' time, you might be in America and someone will hear your accent and they'll say, "My God, you were there when the hunger strikes were happening – what was it like? How did you feel?" And you'll say, "I don't know, I was too busy watching *The Fall Guy*.""

That hurt me; it might've been true six months before – but not now.

"Come on, mate, we can do this. We can feel it. We can be a small part of this." He drew back momentarily as one of the

225

canteen ladies wiped down our table. "What do you say, Kevin McBride? You can be the eleventh man, and I'll be the twelfth."

God, he knew how to talk. I reached down and squeezed my spare tyres. I certainly wasn't going to starve to death overnight. It might even do me some, good – clean the tubes a bit, cut out all my usual garbage. One night. And what he said about the future was absolutely right as well; I could say that it had meant something to me; I could talk about what I had been feeling and what I had been thinking. *This is going to sound crazy,* I would say to some beautiful American girl who looked like Dolly Parton, *but me and my pal were so impressed by Bobby Sands that we went without food for a while just to see what it felt like.* And she would say, *Wow! Did you ever meet him? Did you know Bobby Sands?* And I would shake my head sadly and say, *no alas, but I walked the same streets as he did and I felt some of his pain.* And she would have tears in her eyes and she'd say, *God bless you Bobby Sands and God bless you Kevin McBride,* and she'd pull my head down and smother me in her cleavage.

"Is it a deal?"

We shook hands as the bell rang.

CHAPTER THIRTY-ONE

Belfast was ablaze. Protestants were outraged at the very thought of an IRA terrorist even being allowed to stand for parliament. Catholics took to the streets to show their support for the courageous freedom fighter who now had been without food for over thirty days. The violence and hostility wasn't just limited to the capital and to Derry. It began to spill out across the province so that small towns and villages, largely untouched by the Troubles, began to feel the squeeze and discomfort of mob violence. Windows smashed, tyres slashed, bins set on fire. And the divide between moderate Catholics and Protestants began to widen. Mixed communities were especially tense; you could no longer pass pleasantries with your Catholic neighbour and pretend that nothing was happening. Better just to avoid eye contact. Everyone was involved and everyone was watching each other.

And throughout it all Bobby Sands had nothing to eat.

The High School boys could not sing to save themselves. They were off-key but they were very loud and that was all that seemed to matter. It wasn't clear who had started the song but now, all along the fence, there was a row of twenty boys trying to outdo each other.

Do you want a chicken supper, Bobby Sands?
Do you want a chicken supper, Bobby Sands?
Do you want a chicken supper -
YOU DIRTY FENIAN FUCKER –
Do you want a chicken supper, Bobby Sands?
Over and over.

We stopped what we were doing to gaze up at them. It was impossible to concentrate on skipping, football, hopscotch, with such a racket going on.

Do you want a chicken supper, Bobby Sands?
"Why's no-one stopping them?" I asked Ronald.
"Don't know. Too many of them, maybe."

Do you want a chicken supper, Bobby Sands?

I looked around the playground and saw any number of different expressions: amusement, uncertainty, wonder that the big boys should all of a sudden be singing. Rip was up near the top and even from a distance you could see that he was rocking from side to side with an open mouthed expression of delighted disbelief; any second now he might break into song himself or start to conduct. The only adults I could see were the three old ladies who patrolled during lunch time. One was frozen to the spot, her face a stony mask; one was shaking her head in disgust at the bad language; the last one had a faint but discernible smile and appeared to be tapping her toe.

YOU DIRTY FENIAN FUCKER!

"Listen really closely," Ronald said. "What else can you hear?"

They were practically yelling now, faces red, a husky quality because of the effort, the smaller boys looking for approval from the older ones.

"Desperation," I decided, and I was pleased with that. "I can hear desperation."

"Me too," Ronald smiled. "And I can also hear fear."

Do you want a chicken supper, Bobby Sands?

Wednesday night, after dinner, I made Dad a cup of tea and gave him some chocolate bourbons to dunk in. I knew I had to play him a little. I had never stayed overnight before – not even at Jimmy's – and I had been sensing that he had grown wary of Ronald.

"It's not my birthday, is it?" he took a sip and pretended to choke. "Poison ...I knew this would happen someday."

I forced a giggle.

"Dad?"

"Ha! You are trying to butter me up. What is it?"

"It's something about Ronald."

I watched the smile melt off his face.

"Why don't you like him, Dad?"

"I never said I didn't like him." He sipped thoughtfully on

his tea. "Just sometimes I worry that he's been putting ideas into your head – things that you shouldn't really be worrying about."

"But, Dad, we should all be worried about the Troubles."

"There – like that! You'd never have come out with something like that before you met him."

I wasn't sure what to say. It wasn't exactly a smooth preparation for the big ask.

"You're too serious now, Kevin," he was warming up now, getting something off his chest. "You're only eleven. You're meant to be having fun but you're too busy asking questions about this and that, trying to understand things that are better left alone."

He was frustrated more than angry. He clearly didn't want to have conversations about the Troubles with his youngest son and it had been Ronald that had forced the issue. He knew that. He wasn't stupid. This strange little boy from the south who had helped me pass the Eleven Plus but had also stoked an interest in what was happening around me. Dad had lived quite happily amidst the murder and mayhem. He had never imagined having to justify himself to anyone – least of all me. That was bad enough. Worse still, I no longer laughed and complied when he said, *pull my finger.*

"If you want to see how a clock works," I said carefully, remembering something Ronald had said early on, "you need to take the back off and look at what makes it tick."

Dad nodded. He seemed to like what I had said and I was relieved. It was the way I had said it. A different way and he might have thought I was being cheeky.

"But the problem is that sometimes when you do that you can break the clock – the thing stops working because you've taken it apart. Sometimes you're better just to accept that it works at all and be happy."

He nodded to himself and dunked his biscuit into his tea.

"You're right, Dad," I told him, and part of me actually agreed with what he had said. "You're going to say no then."

"No to what?"

I allowed a pause.

"Ronald's asked me to stay over at his on Friday night."

"Overnight?" he pointed at the television; the volume was low but you could still hear the chants of the nationalist protestors in the Ardoyne in Belfast. "I don't think so, Kevin. It's unlikely there'll be trouble here – but you just never know."

"Okay, Dad – thanks anyway."

And I settled back to wait. I made sure that he knew I wasn't huffing – little smiles, a refill of his tea – nor was I kissing his arse so that he would change his mind. Neither one of those reactions would have helped, he just would have dug his heels in deeper. I had put quite a bit of thought into this.

Finally.

"What does he want you up for anyway? Is it just so that you can talk all about what's happening in the Maze?"

"We really don't talk that much about the Troubles – just a little sometimes."

"What then?"

"It's his dad's anniversary. He's been dreading it. Says he just gets so lonely."

"Oh ...right."

You are like whale shit, Kevin. It lies at the bottom of the ocean. There is nothing lower.

I could see him thinking it over; thinking that he had been a little too hard on the poor boy. And I could see him remembering his own dad and how much he still missed him and how nice it would've been to have a good friend to help fill the void. I saw all of this and the worst of it was that I didn't feel nearly as bad as I should have; in fact part of me felt quite pleased with myself.

"Let me think about it, Kev."

*

I couldn't wait for Friday to come. The only thing like it had been the time when me and Jimmy discovered an old derelict house up where the new motor way was being built. We decided that it must be haunted and for two weeks we'd abandoned the den and crossed the fields to visit it. Someone must have been murdered there; perhaps their body was hidden under the rotting floorboards. We had both lied to each other to fuel the mystery and keep the thing going. Jimmy said that he had visited the house on his own in the dark (yeah, sure) and had seen the ghost of a young girl in the upstairs window. I told him that I had found an old photograph album under some rags and there was a picture of a sad little girl that matched his description (I'd accidentally dropped the album in the swamp on the way home).

I think it was the idea of being involved in something that no one else was doing.

Nobody else in the whole of Ulster would be starving themselves in support of Bobby Sands. Even the Catholics wouldn't be doing it; they had to keep their strength up for all the protest marches.

And I had inspired it. That's what he had said – *you've given me a great idea.* The idea was his and he was doing most of the organising but if it hadn't been for me none of it would be happening at all. None of it.

We had decided that we wouldn't touch food from 8pm on Thursday until 8am on Saturday – thirty-six hours. Mum didn't always make dinner at the same time but the dishes were always cleared before 8pm. Avoiding eating breakfast would not be a problem. I could pretend to be sick or just leave the cereal and hide the toast in my lap. No lunch. No dinner. And then the long night until breakfast. That was the plan.

On Thursday evening, just before seven o'clock, I had my last meal: two beef burgers, chips, beans, two slices of bread and butter, a chocolate bourbon and a jammie dodger. There was still fifteen minutes until eight so, even though I was ready to burst, I thought it wise to slip in a couple of packets of space invader crisps as well.

I was good to go. I could feel it all digesting down below. My stomach was the engine room of the Titanic, the food was coal being shovelled into the orange furnace.

I stared up at the ceiling of my darkened room and waited for sleep to find me. I couldn't sleep on my stomach because it was too full and there was still the possibility of being sick. And I thought about Bobby Sands. What was he doing just now? How was he feeling? Almost forty days without food. Jesus Christ. What was keeping him going? How wonderful it would be to be able to talk with him now. He would be impressed and pleased at what we were doing. He would feel responsible and he would meet my eye and nod at me whilst others reached out to touch him. *I'm Kevin McBride*, I would say. *I am the eleventh man, starving myself in support of you and your comrades. I hope that old bitch gives you political status,* I would tell him. It was a fantastic feeling and it made my toes tingle. The eleventh man.

Next morning I avoided breakfast with no problem. Mum was harassed and Dad was worrying about the Belfast traffic. I felt fine, stomach still full.

"Well?"

Ronald's eyes gleamed with the thrill of it.

I wondered what he would say if I told him I had eaten breakfast.

"I feel good. Slept okay; don't feel it yet."

"Me too," he winked. "See how you're feeling at break time."

That was when I felt the first pangs. It had been fifteen hours since dinner. Usually, I would go a chocolate bar and a packet of crisps. Today I just watched others eating and found myself mildly resenting them.

By lunchtime I was hoping they would all choke on their food. I was fucking hungry by now and Ronald insisted that we take our place at the table in the canteen.

"Why for fuck's sake?"

I had the beginnings of a throbbing headache.

"It's not just about not eating, Kevin, it's about resisting the temptation when it's right under your nose," he made a big play of sniffing the air. "Do you smell that? Chicken, gravy, potatoes. Your whole body screams at you to reach out – just one bite – and you have to resist it; resist it with all your might if you truly believe in what you're fighting for."

I glared at him, hoping he would get the message; it was going to be a long night and if he thought he was going to preach at me until tomorrow morning he was wrong. Conversations and discussion were fine, but not all of this intense in your ear shit.

"Bobby Sands is in his cell," I told him. "They don't wheel him along to the prison canteen just so they can waft smells under his nose."

"What they do is worse," Ronald said. "They bring the meals to his cell and leave them there – just in case he wants to eat. Breakfast, lunch, dinner – they bring it to him, nice big portions, and let him smell it; and each time he turns his face away."

And so I watched as Ian McGloughlin stuffed himself with moist potatoes, Chloe Buchanan dribbled gravy down her chin, and Andrew Bleeks grinned as he popped his peas between his teeth. I watched them with a little smile on my face and wondered what it would feel like to jam the fork deep into their throats.

"Why aren't youse two eatin'?" Andy wanted to know.

"None of your fuckin' business." I told him and if he had held my eye for an extra second he would have got the custard over his head.

"Take it easy," Ronald said, and his tone was gentler than before and I was glad of that. "Your stomach will adjust and you won't feel as hungry after a while. It's so used to food that it's screaming at you to feed it."

It was the smell that did it. You could almost fancy that you could see colours in the air: white for the spuds, yellow for the chicken, brown for the gravy – like that stupid advert where the wee fuckers sniff their way home on the smell of the Bisto.

"Aren't *you* hungry?"

"I'm getting there but," he held his hands out apologetically to show there was no offence intended, "my appetite isn't quite as big as yours."

I reached down to feel my stomach and was amazed to find my spare tyre still in place. I didn't feel thinner or fitter at all.

Just bloody hungry. It was the longest lunch break ever. A lunch break without any lunch. I cleared the plates and then watched as one of the cooks scraped all the left-overs into a gigantic plastic bag. There was enough there to feed a small army.

I was so hungry at lunch that I didn't think I would be able to do it but when I got away from the smells it wasn't as bad. Ronald was right; it was as if the stomach tried really hard to make you eat and then got tired and went to sleep for a bit. By home time, I was feeling rough and my temples throbbed, but the hunger was now just an ache that I could almost ignore.

"Still up for it?"

"Of course."

"Good man," he handed me a little packet. "Here's something for you."

"What is it?"

"Salt tablets."

"Yum yum."

"We both need to keep our salt levels up. Don't worry, Bobby takes salt as well – it's not against the rules."

I thanked him sincerely. I had now been without food for nineteen hours – a personal record.

Ronald scurried off at the bell to arrange what needed arranging for our night together. I walked home by myself, purposefully slowly, so as not to aggravate my belly. I was just passing the TOYOTA show room when I heard footsteps hurrying after me.

"Kevin, I thought that was you."

And there she was, right by my side, like it was the most natural thing in the world. There wasn't time for any panic; no time to worry about the lip; just enough time to suck in the gut.

"Oh, hi there, Stephanie – how's you?"

And then we were walking together, no problem, just like I would walk with Jimmy or Ronald, except – oh dear God – maybe a couple of inches closer.

"You just heading home?"

And she tilted her head to one side as she said it, and the

wee freckly nose wrinkled like a bunny rabbit.

"Yeah…" come on man, you got to do better than that. "Anything nice planned for the weekend?"

That's okay, that's okay.

She gave a little shiver and I just wanted to die.

"Got to clean out the stables. They're really mucky and smelly."

Stables, by Christ? I knew she came from money – but bloody hell. Okay, Kevin, what do you know about horses? Red Rum. Black Beauty. Tick Tock.

"Horses are certainly big creatures."

Oh, my fuck.

Just say nothing, understand?

Just nod when she speaks or shake your head.

"I'm really thirsty," she said. "I'm just going to pop in here. Can I get you anything?"

"No, thanks."

Love to take you up on your kind offer, Stephanie, but I'm starving myself in support of Bobby Sands and of course, this conversation isn't even real, it's my half-starved stomach messing with my brain.

"You don't mind waiting for me?"

"No, no, it's cool."

I watched her race into the newsagents. She was wearing black leggings under her skirt and you could make out the tiny bulge of her bra buckle just beneath her shoulder blades.

Keep it together, man. She's not going down Christine Lane so you only have to keep it up until the end of the road. Then you can play it over in your head; you can commit it to memory; you can figure out what it all means and tackle it fresh tomorrow.

But isn't this fucking magic? I've even forgotten about the food thing.

She asked me to wait. Why would she say that? Why didn't she just say, *see you later?* That means something. Then I wondered if anybody had seen us together as they drove by and how we had looked. I tried to imagine. A really pretty girl with a (slightly) overweight boy with an under bite that really wasn't as bad as all that. We wouldn't look that odd. Beneath all the anxiety, I had good things to offer: I was kind, I was funny, I would be loyal and never two time a nice girl like her. I glanced up at the cloudless blue sky and remembered the aerial photographer who had been rapping doors a year before. We hadn't bought the picture, too expensive, but Dad still liked to talk about him so he could call him Biggles. Imagine he was up there now and he'd taken a photo just at the moment she had caught up with me. How fantastic would that be? We'd be able to show our kids the photo and say – there it is, captured by the Gods for all eternity, what do you think of that? There was a lovely fluttery feeling in my stomach and chest and it had nothing to do with the lack of food.

I looked down at my sneakers and pulled the tongues up just to have something to do. Then I untied the laces and retied them. She would be out soon and I had no idea what I was going to say to her but even that felt okay. *She had asked me to wait.* This was the start of something. I wasn't sure what or how to continue it; but all I had to do was complete this first transaction without messing up, then I could regroup and build upon it.

"Aw, thanks for that."

She half skipped back in line with me and her chest jiggled a little and I had to bite down a whimper. I wasn't sure I was going to be able to do it after all. It wasn't just that I had no idea what to say to her, but that I seemed to have forgotten how to form words and make them come out of my mouth. What if I accidentally spat on her? The worst thing about that was that she wouldn't turn away in disgust – oh no; she would wait for a moment and then discreetly wipe it away so as not to embarrass me. *That* was the sort of girl she was.

The perfume. Fresh green apples.

"Do you want one?"

She offered the open packet of crisps and my fingers were but an inch away before I remembered Bobby fucking Sands.

"No thanks, I don't really like Cheese and Onion."

You dick head! Look at her wee face all annoyed with herself for choosing the wrong flavour. Tell her you'll eat that dog turd if it makes her happy – that one over there, all mashed in; go on, tell her.

"Sorry, that was really ignorant. I do like Cheese and Onion, it's just," I patted my belly, "I'm trying to lose a few."

"You're not fat," she gave this little snort and I knew then that I was completely and utterly head-over-heels in love with her. Nobody in the world could have snorted like that and made it seem adorable. "Stanley Brownlie – he's fat!"

"Yeah," I said. "Poor Stan – you know, with his mum and everything."

We walked on. Together. Christine Lane was fast approaching and I knew I was going to make it. Once, twice, we were so close that our shoulders brushed together and I could taste the apples. It was summer time and we were walking hand in hand through the hay fields on the way to the beach. We might pause for an ice cream cone and lie on the sand gazing up at a clear blue sky. Afterwards, we would put on our swimming costumes – I would be thin and she would be magnificent – and we would frolic in the salty surf and then snuggle up together in front of a log fire.

"Well, I'll see you Monday." My voice was a little too high but I had made it in one piece.

She held my gaze and took a deep breath, clearly embarrassed.

"Kevin, this is really awkward," she looked around for eavesdroppers, "I really hope you don't mind me asking. It's just, you seem to be really friendly with Ronald – he's like your best friend, right?"

"Yeah..?"

"Is he going with anyone? God, I hope you don't mind me asking. Promise me you won't tell him I asked – I would die. But is he?"

And she looked at me so earnestly, searchingly; as if it was the most important thing in the whole wide world.

"You know, I'm not really sure. I'm really not that friendly with him – just a little bit," it wasn't really the answer she was wanting so I chewed my bottom lip for a moment and thought harder. "He's never mentioned anyone."

"Really?"

"Yeah."

"Aw, Kevin, thanks," she squeezed my arm. "I just didn't want to make a fool of myself. Do you think he'd be interested in me?"

"I don't know."

"Has he ever mentioned me before?"

"I don't think so. He hasn't really mentioned any girls – look, sorry but I'm going to have to fly."

"Yeah, of course," another little squeeze of gratitude and apology. "Thanks so much, Kevin – God, I was so nervous asking you. Remember," she kissed her finger, "don't tell him I asked."

"I won't."

I watched her walk away, knowing that she wouldn't look back. She was happy now, knowing that he was wasn't going with anyone. Mr Griffin's Alsatian saw me standing still and started up. It was a monster of a dog the way it crept up on you and it always made me jump even though it was fenced in. Griffin himself was a cranky old bastard. He had two grandchildren that visited him sometimes; the boy was two years older than me and his sister a year older than him. They did ballet dancing together. Like a couple only they were brother and sister. They thought they were brilliant because they won trophies; everyone else thought they were weird. The dog was chewing the fence now, snarling at me because I was daring to stand so close to its house. Any moment now, Griffin might appear and demand to know what I was doing. I wished the dog would die; then it occurred to me how easy it would be to lace a nice sausage or two with rat poison and toss them over the fence on the way to school. It would foam at the mouth and the ballet twins would think it had rabies.

I spat at the dog and hit it square between the eyes. It shook his head and looked at me in a disgusted, disbelieving way that might have made me laugh under different circumstances. Then I headed down the lane, my bag swinging by my side.

I was really hungry now.

CHAPTER THIRTY-TWO

Dad gave me a lift just after seven. I had drank so much water that I felt as if my ears, nose and eyes were about to start squirting. And already I was desperate for the toilet. My stomach was bloated; it felt cheated and pissed off and I knew it was out to get me.

Ronald opened the door to me and we both waved him away.

Then the smell hit me like a charging rhinoceros.

"What the hell are you cooking?"

He held a finger to his grin and beckoned me to follow him through to the living-room where the smell of food was so strong it felt like you almost had to push against it. On the table, moist and glistening with flavour, was food enough to feed a family of five. Pizza slices, succulent ham nestling in dripping cheese; plump sausage rolls; a bowl of steaming pasta; chicken drumsticks – and those stupid fucking wee sausages with the sticks in them.

My jaw dropped open.

"Hello, Kevin," Gloria beamed at me as she carried in some sandwiches. "Hope you've brought your appetite."

My stomach growled – actually growled like an animal – and I knew they must have heard it. It was only then that the thought occurred to me and the suddenly relief of it almost caused me to swoon. It had all been a set up. Ronald had been testing me all day to see if I would go through with it and now, satisfied that I would have, this was the reward. Yes, that had to be it. Otherwise all of this would go to waste.

He was grinning at me and I shook my head at him, allowing him his big moment.

"It looks and smells delicious," I said, and reached for a slice of pizza.

"Hold on, greedy," alarmed, Ronald leapt up and stood in front of me. "We have to wait for the others."

"The others?"

"Sure," with his back to Gloria he winked at me. "I told Gloria that Rip and Jimmy were coming. They're not staying the night – just for the meal."

"Wha?"

I was tired, hungry, and very slow on the uptake.

"That's why she's made so much."

"Ronald, don't be so silly, let Kevin tuck in before it gets cold."

And I almost did. Just to spite him. He thought he was being so clever and funny, what would he have done if I'd just reached over and wired in?

"It's fine. I'll wait." I slumped down onto the sofa and the smells jumped on top of me, licking me all over with their tongues, hugging and kissing me, desperately trying to pull me back to the table.

"I shouldn't be too long," Gloria said, reaching for her scarf. "Molly is babysitting tomorrow so she won't want a late one. Do you have everything you need?"

"The boys will be gone before you're back and I've put the mattress on my floor."

I waited until she had left before rounding on him.

"Are you fucking mental?"

"Kevin, I'm sorry," he held his hands up. "It seemed like a good idea when she offered."

I was close to throwing in the towel right then; but I didn't want him to beat me. I could do this despite him. He thought he knew it all. He thought he was in control and I was just following his lead but he was wrong in that. I could think for myself. I was the eleventh man and he was the twelfth.

"It won't go to waste. Most of it we can put in plastic boxes. It'll be cold, of course, but think about how delicious it'll be tomorrow morning."

"You should have told me you were going to do it." I was furious with him but I was also weary and you needed energy to be really mad at someone.

"Kevin, I swear to you, I only thought about it an hour ago.

I told her yesterday that we would sort ourselves out but she insisted today that she would make all that stuff."

"And you told her Jimmy and Rip were coming up."

He looked sheepish at that. "I got carried away. I thought this would be a really good test of our determination."

I shifted slightly and only then remembered my bladder. The food had taken my mind off it.

"I'm going for a piss. Get rid of it. And open a fucking window!"

Upstairs the smell was still evident but not nearly as strong. I washed my face and then had to sit suddenly on the edge of the bath as my stomach cramped. Jesus. Tiny little men hacking into me with pick axes, trying to dig their way out. Was this what it was like for Bobby Sands? Hour after hour, day after day. Would the pain grow each day or would it lessen as he got weaker? I had been on hunger strike for less than one day; he had been without food for almost six weeks.

Ronald had cleared away the food and opened one of the bay windows. The fresh breeze was lovely on my face and I made an effort to calm myself so as not to be so short with him. He was carefully setting newspaper clippings and photographs out on the table.

"This is all I have on him. Gloria got me Irish papers and journals from over the border – stuff you can't buy here. The details they leave out! He was born in Rathcoole just outside of Belfast. It was a mixed area but later on the Protestants forced them out and they moved to Twinbrook, a Catholic neighbourhood. He loved all kinds of sports when he was a kid and was an apprentice coach builder until he was forced out of his job – the Protestants threatened to break his legs if he turned up for work. The papers here never mentioned him having a job, just a layabout wanting to kill people. And listen – you'll like this – he writes poetry and short stories."

"What's that photograph?"

He handed it over to me and the image shocked me into forgetting my hunger.

"Fucking hell – that's not him surely?"

"No, no. He's from Auschwitz concentration camp; but that's the way Bobby Sands probably looks now – from this to that."

He passed over another photograph. This one I was familiar with. It was the long haired uncle from the campaign poster but here surrounded by his friends and fellow prisoners. I jumped from it to the human skeleton with the sunken eyes; back and forth, back and forth. The contrast was unbearable. To think that this was what he had been reduced to.

"My mum thinks his mum is a disgrace," I said. "She visits him and she does nothing. Imagine watching your son waste away, the same son that was growing inside of you – that's what my mum says."

"Maybe she loves him so much that she wants to do what he asked her to – even though her heart is breaking."

"My granda says the I.R.A are holding the prisoners to ransom. They say to them: if you come off the strike we're gonna shoot your parents."

"How does he know that?"

"I think he must have read it somewhere."

Ronald surveyed the table and then tapped a newspaper clipping. "The I.R.A didn't want them to strike because they said – where is it, here it is – "break the men on the inside and you'll break them on the outside."

"Maybe at the start they didn't want them on it, but it might be different now." I wasn't sure if I believed that but I wanted to show him that I didn't just accept everything he said, I could think things for myself.

"Have you heard of the novel *1984?*"

"Yes, I have. It was written by George Orwell who also wrote *Animal Farm*."

Fuck you, Douglas. I know lots of stuff.

"Peter Cushing was in it," I continued. "There's a part in it where they put a mask on his face and a rat runs down a tube towards his eyes. It was so bad the politicians in parliament said it should be banned from the telly."

"My dad told me about it," Ronald said. "Winston Smith is about to be interrogated – this is before the rats - and he wonders if he might stop his girlfriend from being tortured if he agrees to take her share as well as his own. Then, one of the thugs hits him on the elbow with a stick and the whole world explodes in white pain and he realises how stupid it was of him to even consider taking someone else's agony as well as his own; because he now knows that when you are being tortured the only thing you can wish for is for it to stop. No matter how much you love someone, you can't possibly ask for your pain to be increased."

It might have been clearer if I wasn't so ravenous.

"If he wanted to eat, he would eat - no matter what anyone said."

"So what's stopping him?"

"The only things stopping Bobby Sands from eating are his determination and his beliefs. He's prepared to die for what he believes in – a slow, nasty, incredibly painful death; and if that doesn't make you respect and admire him then there is something badly wrong with you."

I didn't like the way he was speaking to me, what Mr Palmer would have called his *tone*. I had only been telling him what Mum and Granda had said and now it felt like I had spat in Bobby Sand's face.

The hunger was gnawing at me again, enough for me to risk a suggestion. I knew he would say no; I just needed to hear him say it. When he said it I could get my head around it.

"Is it not enough that we've gone without food the whole day? Could we not have some of that nice food now to keep our strength up? We can still support him and think about him – it would just be a bit easier with something in the belly."

"You think it's easy for him?"

Just say no, Ronald, please don't preach.

"Okay. Fine. Thanks."

He showed me where I was going to sleep - a blow up mattress on the floor of his bedroom. I would have given him my bed but it looked comfy enough. There was a nice pillow and a heavy travel rug that reminded me of the time Granny and Granda had taken me home with them for a week when I'd had the measles. I might have been four. She'd snuggled me up in the back seat of their little mini and it had been the loveliest feeling in the world: the hum and gentle joggle of the engine, the smell of his tobacco, and the shock of her white curly hair. I didn't have a care in the world, apart from my dying measles, and the pair of them existed only to look after me and make me feel better. It was so long ago now and I felt the sting of tears.

"Course, poor Bobby will be covered in bed sores by now. No matter how soft his mattress, he'll not be able to get comfy."

"I suppose that's the one good thing about being overweight," I said. "Your fat protects you a bit. I'd never really thought about it before. It must be quite sore for a skinny, bony person to sit down without a cushion."

"God, I've just had a great idea," he said, but this time I was ready for him.

"I've just had one too, Ronald; there is absolutely no way I am sleeping on the floor tonight, it's gonna be hard enough going to sleep with my stomach screaming at me."

"Fair enough."

And again there was a little friction between us. I didn't know how to deal with it or even what to say. It was the not eating that was doing it. I would be okay for a while but then he would look at me in a funny way or say something that would make me want to put my hands around his throat.

"Ronald, I'm not sure I'll be able to do this for the whole night. I thought I would be able to but hitting me with those smells as soon as I came in – my mouth's been watering ever since. It's like Houdini getting punched in the stomach before he had time to brace himself."

"The whole point of this, *Kevin*, is so we can try to imagine what it must be like for him."

The way he said *Kevin* like that really annoyed me. It was exactly the way a teacher or a grown-up might say it; and he was neither.

"I think I can imagine how he is feeling, *Ronald*, I have a very vivid and colourful imagination."

And we stood there looking at each other and not speaking for what seemed like minutes but was perhaps only ten seconds. My teeth were gritted, I remember that, and he had a stubborn peeved expression that I had never seen before.

"If you want to leave that's up to you. You can phone your dad or we can wait for Gloria to leave you home – she'll be back in a while," he turned towards the open door. "I'm going down to watch the news, see what's happening with the vote."

I sat on his bed in the empty room and considered my options. It had been over twenty-four hours since my last meal and, if I stuck it out, there was another twelve to go. But this last twelve would be big test; this was like Mallory and Irvine on the last vertical climb, low on oxygen with the wind howling and the darkness creeping down. And what I had not taken into account was how snappy and short we were getting with each other. Of course, that was because of the food, but it was incredible how tiny things you had never even noticed before began to grow bigger and more obnoxious by the minute. It was a real test of friendship for sure. Would I be able to stick this out with Jimmy? The thought of it made me smile. Jimmy irritated the hell out of me even on a full stomach.

Ronald was waiting for the nine o'clock news.

"Look, forget the beds. He's got a bed anyway. I'm just trying to think how close we can get to what he's experiencing."

I slumped down on the sofa and he angled the television so that I could see it. You could still smell the cooked food, it was lingering in the corners of the room, the curtains, and the cushions. I thought about asking him to open the windows again or opening them myself – but I didn't have the energy just now to do either. If only you were allowed a piece of chewing gum or a polo mint, something to focus your taste buds on.

"Does a sugar free mint count?" It was a little joke, the best I could manage, but part of me held out some hope as well.

"Fraid so. Just water and salt – that's all."

"Jesus Christ. And he's lasted on that for all this time?"

"Yep."

"Do you think it's possible that he's being slipped food," this was one of Dad's ideas but I wanted to claim it for my own. "Maybe his parents – his mum."

"They're searched each time they visit; even if they wanted to they wouldn't get the chance."

"What about the prison officers – the screws?"

"They're all loyalists, remember? If he was taking food from them do you think they would keep quiet about it?"

That didn't need an answer. They would be straight to the press, shouting it from the roof tops. They would have pictures to prove it. Bobby's bony fingers reaching out for a fig roll.

The news, both local and national, was all about the upcoming count. People were coming out in their tens of thousands, voting stations bottle-necked, none of the apathy usually associated with local elections. They showed people from both sides being interviewed. One elderly man with glasses said the whole thing was disgusting; he had fought in the First World War and now here was an I.R.A terrorist being considered for a M.P. He wondered what his dead friends on the battlefield, his dead *Catholic* friends, would make of it. A woman in her thirties said she thought Mrs Thatcher should show some mercy and compassion to the poor men. Was she not a mother herself? She didn't have to agree to all their demands, just compromise a little and then maybe those poor boys wouldn't have to starve themselves to death. Thatcher herself insisted that there would be no discussions with terrorists – "A crime is a crime is a crime" – she said and the way her hair didn't move at all, not a strand out of place, struck me as really fitting. Even in a hurricane, her hair would look the same.

There was violence throughout the province as the tension increased. Nationalist H-Block supporters clashed with the police and army, petrol bombs arching through the air and exploding onto shields and vehicles. The police were firing back with baton charges and plastic bullets. Loyalists also took to the streets to protest and make sure their voices were not forgotten.

Gloria returned sometime after ten o'clock and asked us if we would like something for supper. When we said no, she started to make some for herself and before long the air was rich with the delicious smell of creamy, sugary porridge. I glared at Ronald and gestured the door with a jerk of my head.

"Gloria, me and Kevin's going up now. We've got all we need. Is it okay if I take the wee radio?" he had it tucked under his arm even before she came out of the kitchen.

"What do you fancy for breakfast? A nice fry? Bacon, sausages, egg, tomato?"

"We can sort ourselves out, don't worry."

He shut the door carefully and I took him by the arm before he got to the stairs.

"Did you fuckin' tell her to ask that?"

"No, no. That's the way she always gets on. She'd give you a blow by blow account of everything she did if you let her."

I changed into my pyjamas in his bathroom and drank down about a gallon of tap water. It had a strange metallic taste but I guzzled it down anyway. It flooded the empty shell of my stomach. I could hardly believe it: I had now been without food for twenty-six hours. The hunger pangs came and went; some were so savage and sudden that I had to knead my stomach, but they passed after a while, retreating into a dull ache. My energy levels felt very low, even walking up the stairs had been an effort, but that was far from the worst side effect; it was the dull, throbbing headache that concerned me. I found myself continually massaging my temples, waiting for it to develop into a sledgehammer pounder like the one I had got one Easter just before it was time to go back to school. Mum had plunged the room into darkness and I lay there with a damp cloth on my head, waiting for the elephant sized headache pills the doctor had prescribed to kick in. If that were to happen again, I might have to pull the parachute chord; I could live with hunger, just about, but not that headache.

"The water tastes the same as it always did," Ronald said. "Your taste buds are way more sensitive now – your sense of smell too."

He was twiddling with the radio, trying to get reception. It was crackling quite badly, but then he angled it a certain way and found Abba on Downtown radio station. They were belting out *Super Trooper* and I closed my eyes and imagined the blonde one with the lovely arse giving it all she had.

"I like Abba. What's your favourite song of theirs?"

The question clearly irritated him.

"I'm not really into pop music."

"Well, I am. I like *Waterloo*, it's a good one – ever heard of it?"

"No."

"Really? Don't they play pop music in the south?"

Jesus Holy Christ! I could eat the face off someone; just reach over and take a great big bite out of their cheek. It doesn't have to be the cheek – the leg, the arm, the arse – anywhere, just so long as it's a great big fuckin' bite.

"What kind of music do you listen to?"

"What, Kevin?"

"Music, you know – LA LA LA LA LA – what sort do you like? Country? Classical? Jazz? Heavy fucking Metal?" I was sweating all of a sudden. "You can't be all serious all of the time. What music do you hum along to?"

"Kevin, if you want to quit, just say so?"

"I don't want to quit! I just want to know what kind of music you tap your toe to!"

I lay back on the pillow and felt my heart beat pulsating in my temples. I knew I owed him an apology and I was going to say sorry but I was going to make him wait for it. Jimmy wouldn't have been irritated by the Abba question; he would have started singing his favourite and perhaps even got up and danced – wiggling his arse for all he was worth.

"My dad liked country music," he said at last. "Hank Williams. It's a bit cheesy but some of his stuff's good."

"Hard to imagine you in a cowboy hat," I said, but I was trying to be friendly this time. "Like J.R Ewing. He must be so glad to take his hat off at night, his neck must be aching."

"I suppose so."

"Sorry, Ronald."

"It's okay."

"I'm just so hungry. My stomach's on fire."

"Me too. It's really starting to get to me. I could really go a fruit pastille right now."

My God, the Room of the Sweets, I'd forgotten about it! Oh, what would it be like to suck on a wine gum just now? A lovely red one. The juice and the flavour of it would seep out all over the tongue, then you'd feel it passing by the tonsils on the way to the stomach. And you would chew and swallow, chew and swallow, and because the stomach was empty you would feel every tiny segment as it slid down and came to rest by the furnace.

"If we can make it to tomorrow morning you can have as many as you like," he said, clearly reading my thoughts, which wasn't especially hard. "That's the difference between us and him, Kevin. We can see the light – tomorrow morning at eight o'clock. For Bobby Sands, there is no light."

And as our stomach's snarled in unison, I pictured Bobby Sands and what he might be thinking about just now. Was he staring up at the ceiling and wondering about the vote? Ronald's papers said that he was still capable of rational thought, still talking with visitors and discussing the situation. And he had not eaten since forever. What would that feel like? Did he resent the plumpness of his guests, the smell of food on their breath, the certain knowledge that we were all tucking in even as he was hollowing out? Or was he resigned to his fate. He could eat at any time and yet he chose not to; his resolve was breath-taking.

"Ronald, if he wins tonight, do you think she'll change her mind?"

He shook his head.

"She'll let a fellow M.P die?"

"I think so, yes."

"Even if Reagan and all the Yanks put pressure on her?"

"She'll see it as a weakness."

"Do you think Bobby Sands knows that he's going to die?"

"Yes," he said without the slightest hesitation. "I think he knew from the very start."

He lowered the volume of the radio and switched off the main light so that it was just the bedside lamp. We wouldn't know the result until the early hours and I was desperate for some kind of sleep, anything to claw into the eight hours that still remained. My hot water bottle would have been a great idea, lovely and warm against the guts, and I thought about asking him if he had one. But that would mean traipsing back downstairs and having to make conversation with Gloria whilst the kettle boiled. Too much of an effort.

"We've something else in common with him."

"Yeah?"

"He sat the Eleven Plus when he was a boy."

"Yeah? Pass or fail?"

"What do you think?"

I curled myself into a little ball, dug my hands into my stomach and closed my eyes.

*

"Kevin, are you awake?"

His toe prodded my side.

"What time is it?"

"Just gone two. They're about to announce the winner."

I pulled myself into a sitting position and then had to squeeze my eyes shut as a wave of dizziness washed over me.

"You okay?"

"Yeah, I think so."

I put the water to my lips and tipped it up – but this time my stomach was having none of it and it sent it right back up at speed with some acid as interest.

"Jaysus!" He threw back the covers and reached for me as I coughed and sneezed and spluttered.

"I'm okay," I managed, for a moment it had felt like I was drowning. "Water's no good now, I need something to eat so bad."

"Shush! Shush!" he twiddled with the volume. "This is it."

We hunched over the radio, us and the rest of Ulster and the rest of the world as well. My guts were a clenched fist; my mouth the bottom of a slug.

The commentator spoke about the massive turnout - almost 90%.

A hush, as everyone in the building and in the whole of Ulster held their breaths.

Harry West, Ulster Unionist: 29, 046

Bobby Sands, Anti H-Block: 30,492

Sand's supporters erupted and for a moment I had the mad notion that the little transistor radio was going to break apart with the stress of the cheers.

"Jaysus, God!" Ronald's hands were a pyramid under his nose. "He's done it, Kev – he's actually bloody done it!"

We listened to the roars.

It had happened.

He had done it.

And we had played our part in it.

"Do you think he's happy?" I asked. "I mean – of course he's happy, but does he have enough energy to be happy?"

"He'll be smiling, Kev!" you could hear the joy in his voice. "It doesn't take much to smile. I bet he has a great big beam on his face that could light up the sky."

It was a brilliant image.

"What about his mates in prison? They don't have radios, do they? When will they find out?"

"They might have a radio smuggled in. Anyway, they'll find out soon enough – whenever they see the faces of the screws in the morning."

"Oh, yeah," I held out an imaginary tray and twisted my face into a gurn. "Here's your fuckin' breakfast, ya bastard!"

We listened to the rest of the news which was all about

the intensifying violence across the province.

"Do you fancy some fresh air?"

"God, yeah."

We took our empty stomachs outside into his front garden and I pretended that the cool air was a magic kind of cheese that you breathed in and which spread itself inside with an imaginary knife that was itself made of cheese. It was a clear sky and I could see Orion the Hunter and the Plough up above, looking as they had looked for the last million years. It was amazing to think that Bobby Sands was only twenty miles away under this same blanket of stars. Was there a window in his cell? It was a nice thought to think of him gazing up at them in his triumph.

My stomach made a strange liquid gurgle and I dropped to my knees onto the moist grass.

"Are you okay?"

"Yeah ..." I was terrified I had soiled myself, but then I realised there was nothing there to come out. Discreetly, I reached round to check. There was some sort of dampness but nothing to worry about. It was all the water.

"How's he doing it, Ronald?" I gazed out over the darkened rooftops and steeples; all quiet and peaceful, they would be waking up to the news that an I.R.A terrorist was now an M.P for local government. "I can hardly walk and I can't think straight – how can he still be here after so many days?"

"He believes in what he's fighting for – simple as that. And he's prepared to die for it."

The cool air had somehow numbed the hunger and, incredibly, some sleep seemed possible. Both of us knew that it would not last and I prepared myself to be awoken by an ice pick to the stomach. But just an hour would be something – sixty minutes closer to the end. I closed my eyes and wrapped my arms around myself. I was happy for Bobby Sands and I felt sorry for him – but Christ, was I looking forward to breakfast.

*

At first, I thought I was in the High School. I was walking along the corridor, my bare feet enjoying the coolness of the white tiled floor. But there were bars on the windows of the doors and it dawned on me that they weren't classrooms at all but little cells.

I was in the H–Blocks.

I was drawn towards the clang of cutlery and the rank stench of piss and shit ran forward to greet me. Dear Jesus. It was like falling head first into a sewer. A line from one of Palmer's poems: Gas, gas, quick boys – an ecstasy of fumbling. But then I remembered that they had ended the dirty protest and the smell evaporated in that instant. So too did the clanging. There was nothing but the whisper of my pyjama trousers and the coolness of the tiles beneath my feet.

His room was at the far end, and outside was a chair, and on the chair was a familiar face. It was the Hunt Leader from Planet of the Apes. He watched me approach with that horrible smirk of his.

"Well?" said the Hunt Leader

"Can I see him?" I asked.

"You may," said the Hunt Leader.

Bobby Sands was expecting me. He was propped up on his pillows, grey against white, and he held a hand up to me as I entered. He looked just like his picture, nothing like the concentration camp photo I had seen. There was a darkness under his eyes and his fingers were long and thin, but otherwise the hunger had not touched him. There was a handkerchief in his pyjamas pocket and the initials B.S were stitched on it in case it got lost in the wash. He patted his bedspread for me to sit down.

"Hello, Bobby."

"Hello, Kevin."

"How do you feel?"

"Happy."

"Happy?"

"Yes, and a little bit hungry."

"Oh, yeah, of course."

I looked for the window so he could see the stars but there wasn't one and that was a shame. But then I thought of something else. In dreams sometimes you could do magic.

"Would you like me to get you something, Bobby? It won't count because it's a dream," I glanced towards the door then back at him. *"Do you want a chicken supper, Bobby Sands?"*

He shook his head but smiled to show that he got the joke.

"Will you take my hand, Kevin?"

"Sure."

He held out his hand but even as I reached for it I knew what was going to happen. It changed. I saw the firm arm whither and shrink; felt his hand harden as the skin vacuumed the bone.

"Don't look at my face, Kevin!"

I squeezed my eyes shut and kept on shaking. His grip was firm.

"Think of me sometimes," his voice was starting to fade but still clear enough. *"Think about me sometimes when you're sitting at the table. Do that for me..."*

Ronald was shaking my shoulders, his hand gently clasped over my mouth.

"You'll wake Gloria!"

I rubbed my face and slowly, remembering the dizziness from before, propped myself up. The light of dawn was filtering through the curtains.

"Ronald, what a dream I've just had."

"About Bobby Sands?"

"Aye – you too?"

He shook his head and looked strangely at me. "You were calling out Bobby in your sleep. I wasn't sure if you were trying to be funny."

Trying to be funny?

"My God, I was there in his room. It was like he was expecting me. He reached out to me and I held his hand and he said, "Think about me sometimes.""

"What did he look like?"

"Just like his picture. A little bit thinner."

"A little bit thinner?" he made an ugly snorting sound that I didn't like at all. "He's been on hunger strike for almost two months."

"It was a dream. Dreams aren't always the same as real life."

"You're not wrong."

"I was about to say that his hand changed. It suddenly went all skinny and bony when I was shaking it."

"You're just adding bits in now."

"No I'm not."

He snorted again and looked incredulous. "I don't believe you."

"What the hell is your problem?"

He turned away, as if he was going to try to sleep again.

And of course I knew what his problem was, I had sensed it from the moment I had awoken. He was annoyed because I had dreamt about him and he hadn't. He knew all about the Troubles, the history of Ireland, and had found out this, that and the next thing about Bobby Sands; but he hadn't come to visit him when he was sleeping. He had ignored the teacher and shaken hands with the student. It was crazy but in that half-starved moment it made perfect sense. The whole idea of this had been to reach out and try to connect with him in some way; my little dream ticked that box quite neatly.

I lay back on my pillow, put a great big knob of butter on my knife, and began to spread it.

"It felt as if it was one of those out of body experiences, Ronald. I can remember lying here and then all of a sudden it felt like I was floating and when I turned and looked down, why there I was sleeping away – with you fast asleep beside me. Then, it all happened suddenly - I felt the coolness of the night air and I'm flying over the roof tops and everything's a blur and then I'm falling through the air and I can see the H-Blocks beneath me."

"You're right, you do have a very vivid imagination."

"Are you calling me a liar, Ronald?" my digital said it was 4.30; there was enough light for me to walk home, I didn't care. "The amazing thing is that the moment I touched his hand – I swear this is true – the hunger left me. I'm not hungry at all now."

"Really?"

"Yeah, really."

"So, you're telling me, if I go down and bring up some of that food from before you won't want any of it."

"That's what I'm telling you."

"You won't mind me eating in front of you?"

"I'd rather not watch you slobbering over cold pizza – but I won't take any, if that's what you mean. I don't want to be disrespectful to Bobby Sands."

"You're a fucking liar, Kevin."

He slapped on the main light and I was amazed to see he was close to tears.

"I'm telling the truth."

Jesus, what was happening here?

But I couldn't stop.

"I'll probably nibble at something later on today but just now I feel quite full," even as I said it my stomach meowed in utter disbelief at the lie. "It's as if meeting Bobby Sands has given me more strength and determination."

"You didn't meet Bobby Sands. You had a stupid fucking dream and now you're adding bits on," he had stopped whispering and two doors down you could hear Gloria stirring. "Why are you making all this up, Kevin? Just because I know more about it than you."

Ah, there it is; I'm your little empty saucer and you're the big clever jug of knowledge. Fuck you.

"I don't need you to tell me about Bobby Sands," I was getting dressed, pretending I had loads of energy because I wasn't hungry. "It all has to be about you, doesn't it? No one else is allowed a say."

"Where are you going?"

"Home."

"What about all the food?"

He looked miserable and confused but I didn't care.

"You can eat it. I told you I wasn't hungry."

Three knocks on the door.

"Boys, boys – is everything alright?"

I threw open the door and squeezed by Gloria who was blinking in the sudden light.

"I'm going home, Gloria."

"But it's not even five."

"Don't worry. My dad's picking me up."

I hurried down the stairs and out the door into the early morning sunlight. I was so ravenous now I felt as if I was transparent and I still had the hill to go down, half a mile of street, then Christine Lane. It felt like the start of a marathon and I wasn't sure I was going to be able to do it. It was like walking on the bottom of the ocean with heavy lead boots, pausing now and again to untangle my oxygen tubes. There was a phone box at the bottom of the hill. As a last resort I could phone Dad and get him out of bed. It would mean more lies and I wasn't sure I even had the energy for that. He would be annoyed at me for being up so early; it wasn't as bad as being up late at night but it still required some explaining. All too easy to imagine him dismissing my explanation and roaring up the hill to confront them.

Dear God, please give me strength. It wasn't even as if there was a shop open this early where I could get a Mars bar – *helps you work, rest and play* – and a can of Coke. I passed by the mouth of the graveyard and half expected to see Maggie in her coffin clothes, waving sadly at me. Nothing would surprise me now. This was awful. The hill stretched down and down. There wasn't any sign of life anywhere. Down and down and down. I was staggering now. If a car suddenly appeared and offered me a lift I would jump on board, no questions asked, no matter what Dad said. If it turned out to be a mass murderer that was too bad, as long as he gave me something to eat and I got to stop walking he could do whatever he wanted to me.

I sat down by the roadside. I had to. I was sweating and the thought occurred to me that I was going to die. Ridiculous. Nobody was going to die after one day of not eating. I knew that. But I was also certain that this was what it felt like to be dying. God, I hated him. I wasn't sure how much of that was to do with not eating; all I knew was I didn't want to be near him just now.

But I didn't hate Bobby Sands. It was just that I was too hungry and weary to think about him just now. I had been laying it on thick to annoy Douglas, but that little dream had meant something. It was a connection I would never have made on a full stomach. Bobby Sands had reached out to me, even if it was just a dream, and I had shaken his hand. And it had felt *great*. In years to come I could tell anyone that and hold my head up high. I promised myself I would think about it later and say a little prayer for him. Just now he had an advantage over me: the lucky bastard was lying in a bed.

It took me almost an hour to get home, a journey that I could cover in ten minutes on my bike. I was dead on my feet, totally and utterly wiped.

It is difficult to be subtle and discreet when you haven't eaten in almost a day and a half. The plan was to tip toe through the back door, get something to eat in the kitchen, then float upstairs and into bed. They wouldn't think to look for me in my room until much later and I could say I had come home at a reasonable hour.

Slowly, carefully, I opened the back gate, remembering that if you flung it open it made a creak that resonated throughout the whole house.

"No self-respecting burglar is going to rob our house, Dor - not with that inbuilt alarm system!"

The spare key hung in the pantry and I let myself into the kitchen, pausing only to stroke Snowy who was, thank God, the worst guard dog in town.

And now for some food.

Some food.

Food.

I hadn't quite made it to eight o'clock but that didn't bother me. All bets were off. No doubt Ronald was gorging himself right now, he'd probably got stuck in even before I had made it to the bottom of the hill. Hope he choked.

What to have?

Something quick, plain and simple. Anything would seem

like a feast.

I took three slices of bread out of the bread bin. It was going to be a double decker.

Margarine slathered on each slice.

Three slabs of cheddar cheese on the first level.

Three slices of fresh ham on the top.

A tumbler of ice cold milk, frothy bubbles at the top.

Then, for a moment, I just looked at it, sitting there on the counter top.

This is what they've done to him every day, Kevin. They've brought the food to him so that he can look at it, smell it, and contemplate it. Three times a day for the past forty days. And they must have said things to him as well when no one was listening – "Go on, Bobby, there's no shame in it. No one would blame you, she's not going to change her mind anyway. Look how scrummy it looks, Bobby. We won't tell, Bobby. Go on – just a little nibble." And each time he said no thank-you and turned away

The bread was soft and fresh.

I sliced it diagonally down the middle so that it could breathe.

Could you walk away from it now, Kevin?

If your parents were being held hostage, could you scrape that sandwich into the bin?

I picked it up, squeezed down on it, and bit into it. Savagely.

I tried to savour it, at least to half chew it before swallowing, but I couldn't stop myself from bolting it like a dog. It had vanished in less than a minute and – God help me, I licked the buttery crumbs off the plate before chasing it all down with the milk. I belched loudly – I didn't care – and then I was reaching for some more bread.

"Kevin, what the hell?"

It was Dad, in his pyjamas, in the doorway. He'd seen me licking the crumbs and his slack jawed expression was almost comical – like he had just seen Elvis buying a paper.

"What's happened, son?"

And I had no idea what I was going to say, except that I didn't want to lie to him. I'd lied enough already. But how much of the truth would be good for me? The double decker was down below now and that was something; even as I hung my head they were stoking up the furnace and shovelling it in. Pretty soon my energy levels would return and I would be able to think more clearly. But that didn't help now.

"Dad, I'm sorry."

I began to shake. It started in my shoulders and then my knees joined in.

And he came over and he hugged me, and it didn't feel awkward at all even though he'd never hugged me like that before.

"We'll sort it out, son. Whatever it is, we'll sort it out."

CHAPTER THIRTY-THREE

I told him almost everything. Not immediately, he let me sleep first, but in the early afternoon. He sat at the bottom of my bed and I gushed it all out: all about the Troubles and the discussions we'd had which had culminated in last night's fasting. Almost everything. I didn't tell him what I thought about Bobby Sands. If he'd asked me I might have told him; but he didn't ask. He was more concerned about me.

"Are you angry with me, Dad?"

"No, son. When you're concerned for someone you love it takes away any anger you have."

"Thanks."

He walked over to the window and began drumming his fingers on the sill, deciding what to do next.

"I think that boy is a little disturbed, Kevin. It's maybe something to do with all the time he's spent in adult company and his dad dying. My dad died suddenly and it was a horrible shock – but to watch your dad slowly wasting away? The old girl's good with sweets but I'm not sure she's good with kids. Both of you should be out enjoying yourself and not thinking too hard about anything. Starving yourselves?" for the first time there was a sharpness in his tone. "Did she know this was happening?"

"No, Dad. Actually, she made us a lovely big tea."

"And you just didn't eat it?"

"Right."

"And she didn't say anything?"

"No."

"She didn't think that odd?"

"Ronald told her that we were waiting for Rip and Jimmy to come up – but they were never coming up."

"So he lied to her?"

"Yes."

I knew what he was building up to and I didn't intend to put up much of an argument.

"I don't want you to go back up there, Kevin. I'd actually prefer you to have nothing whatsoever to do with him – but I know that might be hard in school."

"I'm going to ask Mr Palmer if I can sit back with Jimmy."

It had been in my head to do it. I needed to make it up to my old pal.

"That's a good idea, son. Jimmy's a sound lad."

I wondered if Ronald would phone me during the weekend and I tried to think what I should say to him. If he apologised I would say fine but I would be distant and he would quickly get the message. I wouldn't tell him that Dad said we couldn't be friends, that would make me seem like a little boy, but I would have to involve Dad if Mr Palmer refused to let me sit beside Jimmy again. He had a soft spot for Ronald, but he liked me too and I couldn't think why he would refuse now that the Eleven Plus was behind us. Ronald had helped me pass, I would never forget that; but he had clearly enjoyed his role of teacher to my student. It hadn't been any great sacrifice for him. He was a foreigner in a strange town and I had befriended him. And I had given up Jimmy and the den and all the things we did. Ronald had wanted no part of that; he mightn't have said so, but it was clear in the way he behaved and the way he treated poor Jimmy. That awkwardness I always felt when Jimmy came over to talk to us. I'd never felt that with him before. He was annoying sometimes, sure, but it was always easy to make conversation with him. When I thought back on it, Ronald had made no effort at all to include him. He wanted me all to himself and because I had been blinded by the Eleven Plus I was only seeing that now. The more I thought about that the more annoyed I became. All that business about the Troubles. It was okay so long as he was in control but as soon as someone else had something to say he started to scream liar. Cheeky bastard. You'd think he was the only one allowed to talk about him. I had lived in Ulster all of my life and Douglas had only just moved here. I had far more right to Bobby Sands than he did. It was my fucking country.

The public response to Bobby Sand's victory was as to be

expected. Nationalists took to the streets to celebrate; loyalists took to the streets to register their disgust. The headline of Dad's paper read, "Elected: The Honourable Member for Violence." On Sunday, he read to us what they were saying about the people who had voted him in. "Their attendance at Mass this morning is as corrupt as the kiss of Judas." The news was full of it: the marches, the protests, the celebrations. All eyes turned to Downing Street but there was no word of a reprieve.

On Monday morning, I again found myself second only to the cleaners as I awaited the arrival of Mr Palmer. I'd told Dad to prepare himself for a phone call at work and I had his number in my pocket but Palmer simply shrugged and said it was fine.

"Have you fallen out?"

"Yes, sir."

"Do you think you will fall back in?"

"No, sir."

"I don't do musical chairs, you know."

"Yes, sir."

When Ronald arrived just before nine, Jimmy, delighted and unquestioning, was already back in his old seat. I didn't make eye contact with him but he sat down in his old seat without a word. I think he might have shrugged or given a little nod, I couldn't be sure, but I did sense that he wasn't too upset – perhaps even a little relieved.

And it was as easy as that. Boyhood friendships worked out like that sometimes. You could be as close as brothers for months or even years and then, at a key moment, something small could come between you and it would be enough to dissolve the bond you had formed. For me and Ronald, it had been Bobby Sands and our response to his stand. I continued to admire and respect him not just for the strength of his convictions – but also for the twisted reason of wanting to get one up on Ronald. I had shaken hands with him and he hadn't. If Thatcher did show mercy then maybe someday I could shake hands with him for real. And I could send the picture to Ronald.

Strange how you can be in the same classroom and

schoolyard as someone and yet they begin to fade into the background. No attempt was made by either of us to make up; both of us clearly felt that we had been wronged. I focused all of my attention on Jimmy (who still told jokes and pulled cards from his socks) and it was a relief to be part of a dialogue that wasn't quite so intense. Ronald, after drifting for a day or two, attached himself to Ross Muir, a quirky boy from Mrs Bryson's Primary seven class. They seemed well matched.

*

Every time I sat down to a meal I would pause for a second and think of Bobby Sands. At night time, I would say a prayer for him, asking God to watch over him and take away some of the pain I knew he was feeling. It was hard to imagine; but I felt that I could imagine it a little bit more than most and that made me feel special.

Bobby Sands was now half blind and suffering from excruciating stomach and chest pains. On April 18th, he was given the last rites. He was sleeping on a sheep-skin rug on top of a water bed, to try and protect his skin. He clung on grimly but it was clear that the end was near.

And tensions in the province continued to rise. Loyalists held placards outside the H-Blocks – "Did 2,000 dead have human rights?" and offered up homemade nooses. In Belfast, 13,000 took to the streets to show their support. In London, one end of Downing Street was padlocked as police discreetly began introducing tighter security measures. The Pope called on Roman Catholics of the world to pray for their brethren (Catholic and non-Catholic) in Northern Ireland during the atmosphere of impending violence. Bernadette McAliskey likewise appealed for calm. "In the event of Bobby Sands dying we do not want a single riot, a single stoning, or a single petrol bombing. If Bobby sands can die for the five demands, we can hold our tempers."

*

It was towards the end of April, on a Friday evening, that someone set fire to the den. Dad saw the orange glow from our window and thought it was a bonfire before it dawned on him what it must be. He yelled to the rest of us and we all piled out of the house as the distant sirens began to sound.

Mrs Hood was screeching like a woman possessed. "Where's Jimmy? I can't find Jimmy?"

And only then did it occur to me.

This is real.

This is happening.

I'm about to lose someone close.

Not a neighbour; not a friend of someone's uncle; not a sister of a woman Mum works with. I was about to lose Jimmy. Dead and cremated all at the same time.

And I knew how it had happened. Not the fire but the way he had been caught. Snoozing on the sofa, that old rug keeping him warm. All on his own because I had abandoned him. Stop the clock, God, oh please stop the clock! Please, please, just one last time. Take it back. Take it back. Anything, anything – just take it back!

The den was ablaze - the heat intense, sending hot embers high up and all over the street. You could hear the wood cracking and snapping and, through the flames, glimpses of the countless hours we had spent there – the pool table collapsing into hell, the plastic darts melting and dripping off the board, Lee Major's bionics unable to save him this time.

Mum and Dad were holding Mrs Hood back from the flames.

"Are you sure he was in there?" Dad was yelling. His face was an orange mask, they all were. "For God's sake, woman – are you sure he was in there?"

It was then that I felt my bladder let go. I couldn't help myself. I hadn't even been aware that I needed the toilet. And then I had a wild and marvellous thought: imagine I was Gulliver from Gulliver's Travels! I could piss it out and the fire men could go back to bed. Yes! That's what should happen. That would make things better.

It was so hot and yet, for some insane reason, I found myself inching towards the flames.

"Kevin, stand back!" Mum screamed at me.

I looked dumbly at her. Then I heard myself say, "Mummy, if I'm good will you buy me a Tonka?"

The sirens were louder now, sore on the ears, but the flames were beyond taming.

"Look!" Pete pointed up the lane. "It's him!"

Everyone turned to look at the small boy with the Woolworth's bag and the dumbstruck expression. "What happened?" he held the bag aloft as if to explain everything. "I only popped out for some Jaffa Cakes."

Mrs Hood emitted a strange, strangled yell and began smothering him with hugs and kisses. Her relief was so vigorous and aggressive that she almost knocked him off his feet.

"Alright, Ma, let me be!"

"I saw a bunch of boys outside," Mr Richmond said. "The dogs were barking and when I looked out I saw one of them toss something through the window. At first I thought it was just a firework. It was me phoned the fire brigade."

All I could manage was a dumb nod. I had been so sure that he was toast. And here he was. I reached across, my hand shaking, and squeezed his arm. It was warm. Flesh and blood. Not his ghost then. Too many people had seen him for that. Usually only one person at a time could see a ghost. That was the rule.

"There it goes, Kev," he was awestruck as the flames danced and licked, we both were, "there it goes."

A small group of grim neighbours had gathered and Mum continued to console Mrs Hood, who was now worried about the house catching. It clearly wasn't going to; his dad had built it far away from the main house so that had there been a fire only the old girl would have gone up. An old man three doors down was shaking his head in confusion. *I don't get it,* he said, *they're not even Catholics.*

Two fire engines roared round the corner and the lead driver blared his horn at the crowd and pumped his forefinger aggressively further down, indicating that we all should shift.

"Cheeky fuckin' bastard," the old man said. "For all he

knows we could have kin in there."

There were murmurs of agreement but we all moved about twenty metres down.

"Where's your dad, Jimmy?"

He raised a Lego hand to his lips and made a drinking gesture.

His mum was weeping uncontrollably now; my mum had her hands full and then some.

We remained transfixed as the hoses fought the flames. You could hear the water sizzling and then they would focus on another spot and you could see the steam frothing and bubbling against the wood. The house was never in danger but there was no way they were going to save the den. Who would want to anyway? It was just a big daft hut and it wasn't used any more, only by Jimmy so he could stay out of his dad's way.

In less than ten minutes they had doused the last of the flames and the blackened remnants lay smouldering in the evening air. The sofa where we had watched a thousand hours of television was nothing but base and springs; the pool table unrecognisable; all that remained were Rip's old dumbbells which had survived relatively unscathed.

Mum had found tissues and she was sitting on the kerb, speaking softly to Mrs Hood. She glanced up at me and Jimmy, said something, nodded, and then beckoned both of us over.

"How do you fancy a sleepover, Jimmy? Your mum and dad have a bit of sorting to do tonight; your house is going to be a bit smoky for a while."

Jimmy was delighted and so was I. It made me feel part of the drama. This would be another bit of my story when I spoke about Bobby Sands in years to come. I would tell them that my best friend from primary school had almost been burnt alive in the Troubles and that I had given him my bed and lent him my pyjamas. It might be more impressive and dramatic if I said that we both had been in the den. Yes, that would work better.

*

"This is great, Kev," Jimmy whispered into the darkness of

my room. "Just like old times."

Actually, he'd never stayed over before but I knew what he meant. I was on the camp bed on the floor; I'd insisted that he took my bed.

"I'm glad we're friends again, Kev."

"We were never not friends, Jimmy."

"I know, but, you know what I mean."

Mum had made us both hot chocolate before bed and the taste was still in my mouth; but I could still smell the smoke. I wasn't sure if it was clinging to our discarded clothes or if it was in the wind outside.

"Kev?"

"What?"

"Can I ask you something?"

"On you go."

"What happened between you and Ronald?"

It was late and I was tired but it was a reasonable question.

"We just fell out."

"Why?"

Why indeed. How could I put into words how angry and upset I had been on the night of Bobby Sand's election? And relieved too. That was the kicker. Part of me had been so relieved that Stephanie wasn't interested in me because I would have had no idea how to deal with that. But, of course, (and this was the thing that really plagued me) he probably would have. He would dazzle her with his stories of old Ireland – even though her family bled orange – and it was far too easy to imagine them strolling (lovers never walked, they *strolled*) down the hill en route to some cosy little movie at the cinema. He had helped me pass the Eleven Plus, fair enough, but really all he was looking for was someone to listen to him talk. And who would you rather: me, or Stephanie Gillespie? Of course, that probably would never have happened; but it could have – and sometimes could haves were enough to push you over the edge.

"Are you asleep, Kev?"

"No," I could feel him patiently waiting for an answer. "Both of us weren't very good at sharing, that's all."

It didn't sound like much of a reason; but it seemed to satisfy him and it wasn't long before his breathing became more rhythmic and he was asleep.

CHAPTER THIRTY-FOUR

Early in the morning of the fifth of May, 1981, Bobby Sands MP died.

In West Belfast, women took to the streets banging dust bin lids as word of his death spread. By two o'clock, barricades were burning and Molotov Cocktails were arching their way towards police and army patrols. The police responded with plastic bullets and a few live rounds when they felt they were being overwhelmed.

I woke to the news and it felt like something incredible was happening, not just in Ulster but across the entire globe.

He's done it. He's actually done it. He's starved himself to death for what he believed in. Sixty-six days without food. Dear God almighty.

There was sorrow too; that long haired uncle would never write another poem or speak another word – but any sadness was blown away by the overwhelming feeling of awe that someone could do what he had done.

His suffering was over.

And the whole world held their breath.

Ronald Reagan's government issued a statement expressing profound regret; this was followed by a twenty-four hour boycott of British ships. Beneath the mighty New York skyscrapers that Bobby Sands would never experience, Irish bars closed for two hours in a public demonstration of mourning. In a march in Milan, over five thousand students burnt the Union Jack and shouted "Freedom for Ulster." Thousands more marched in Paris behind a huge portrait of Sands, chanting "The IRA will conquer." To the dismay of the British Embassy, the town of Le Mans announced it was naming a street after him. In Russia, Pravda described his death as "another tragic page in the grim chronicle of oppression, discrimination, terror and violence."

*

His funeral was not a small affair. Television cameramen

and photographers from all over the world recorded more than one hundred thousand people lining the route from St Luke's church to Milltown cemetery. The tricolour and gloves and a white rose were pinned to the coffin as three masked gun men fired a volley of shots in the air. Huge screens had been erected to protect nearby Protestant housing estates from the sight of an IRA martyr's funeral.

"Why don't the police arrest them?" Pete wanted to know.

"That's enough," Dad silenced him with a click of his fingers. "It's still sad. No matter who it is – it's still sad."

That week the school yard was strangely subdued. Boys still played football but it lacked the usual gusto; girls still hopped, skipped and jumped but the high pitched shrieks (if there were any) had a tinny, unconvincing quality. The High School boys had stopped singing, seeing as he had emphatically answered their question. Rip and his group were grinny and secretive; but they said nothing. What could they say? To speak about Bobby Sands in the past tense was to acknowledge what he had done. Something that no loyalist had ever done or ever would. The best they could say was that he was a coward and had committed suicide; but what kind of coward drags it out for sixty-six days? And so, beyond the *fuck him* and *hope he burns in hell,* the death of Bobby Sands was left alone.

Ronald was standing at the lower fence and he visibly stiffened when he saw me approaching.

"I'm sorry for what happened at your house. I was so fucking hungry."

He was stony faced.

"I didn't like you calling me a liar."

Still nothing. Fuck this. I turned on my heel.

"I helped you pass the Eleven Plus." His voice was low and reproachful.

"I know you did. And I thanked you – and I was friends with you when other people weren't."

"Some friend. You got what you wanted then you changed seats again."

"That's not fair, Ronald. You helped me and I helped you. You wanted someone to tell all your stories too – fair enough, they're good stories – but you don't like it when someone else stats to tell them."

"Ha!" he clapped his hands triumphantly. "I knew you were talking rubbish when you said Bobby Sands came to you that night."

"That's not what I meant. I did dream about him – but so what? Just because you didn't doesn't mean you should start calling people liars."

He could see that I was telling the truth and his face fell again.

"I only came over to say I was sorry about him dying. No one else is talking about him but I knew you would be thinking about him. That's all."

I turned away but he grabbed me by the arm and yanked me around. It was hard enough to hurt me and I clenched my fist in readiness; but when I saw his face, tears held back but only just, I knew he didn't want to fight.

"Why did he come to you, Kevin? It was my house, my idea, all the things I knew about him. Why you and not me?"

He looked so earnest that I almost felt sorry for him.

"It was just a dream, Ronald. Just a dream."

*

Primary seven was in its final throes. Mr Flynn held a special assembly and told us we were the future of modern Ulster and should hold our heads up high. When he said that, everyone looked at Jon Park (with the funny slanty neck) and there was a sympathetic hush. He told us that we should never forget our halcyon days (whatever that meant) and we were given commemorative spoons which we vowed never to use and to keep bright and shiny. There was the school prize giving and one last jumble sale which featured several of Gloria's famous sweet jars. Then there was the trip to London which I didn't enjoy at all. Incredibly, although it embarrasses me to admit it, I was homesick almost from the moment Mum and Dad waved me off on the coach, to the point where I could almost have wept myself to sleep each night. Homesickness sucks. You feel like someone has died but no one tells you who. And so, under this miserable blanket, I traipsed along to Madame Tussauds, the London Dungeon, London Zoo and that square where the pigeons eat seeds out of your hand (there was a man selling tubs of seeds for twenty pence – sad bastard. Sad *rich* bastard.)

*

On the first day of the summer holidays, Mum brought me breakfast in bed and sat on the corner as I blinked myself awake.

"Is it my birthday?"

It was a lovely Ulster Fry. Bacon, sausage, potato bread, fried egg. The works.

"Thought you deserved a treat. The end of a pretty tough year."

"Thanks."

I knew her well enough to know there was more.

"Guess who came into the pub last night?"

"Elizabeth Taylor and Richard Burton."

"Ha ha. Try again."

"Tell me."

"Gloria Douglas," she watched closely for my reaction. "She had some news."

"Oh?"

"Ronald's mum is over from America. She's come to collect him. He's going to live with her – over there."

I looked down at my fried egg to see if it could help me. It no longer looked very enticing – like a ripe boil about to spurt fourth yellow pus.

"You didn't know?"

I shook my head.

"Mum, I haven't seen him in two weeks. He was off last week and it was London the week before that."

I felt devastated and utterly confused. It was my fault he was leaving; but that was a stupid childish thing to think. No one would leave the country just because of a stupid school-boy fall out. And another part of me, a horrible nasty part, found time to be envious: he was going to make it to America before me.

He's not leaving just because of you, Kevvie; but maybe you were the straw that broke the camel's back. If a dozen camels have to transport 342 boxes, each containing 1500 straws, across 72 miles of desert; how much water must they drink if two gallons is the minimum –

"Kevin."

"What?"

"Are you okay?"

"Yeah … but I'm not really hungry." I pushed the meal aside and saw her curse herself; she was thinking that she should have told me after I'd eaten.

"Gloria thought you might want to say goodbye to him."

"Oh, God."

"I think you should. If you don't, you might regret it."

She didn't elaborate on that but she didn't have to. Once he disappeared across the Atlantic we would probably never see or hear of each other again. Did I really want that? It was a question I hadn't felt the need to ask myself because I thought he was going to the Academy with me. If I'd thought of it at all, I had imagined the iceberg between us gradually melting in the first year – a few words in the corridor, at lunch, a smile, a nod; we had been close and he *had* helped me pass that God awful test. I wasn't trying to make excuses for myself but the year had been so stressful what with the Eleven Plus, my lip, Stephanie Gillespie *and* Bobby Sands. A tough year? You're not wrong, Doreen.

Mum had more information for me. Ronald's mum wasn't staying with them but at a local hotel; that was quite telling, I thought. She was to collect Ronald at 11am and then they were off to Belfast City airport. The bulk of his stuff he was to leave, what else he needed was to be sent after him. *She won't want the history books cluttering up the place, you know that, don't you? He knows he's never going to see them again.* Ronald had asked that I be there to see him off. Gloria thought that we might arrange to write to one another.

"Ronald asked for me to be there?"

"That's what she said."

*

I cycled into his driveway at a quarter to eleven and was glad of my time keeping because the taxi was already there and the engine was running. Something had told me that his mother would not be hanging back for a second cup of tea.

I recognised her at once. She was leaning against the car, smoking a cigarette, and she watched me approach with a bemused *what now?* expression. I saw myself through her eyes: a porky little eleven year old, red in the face, jelly legs from the uphill ride.

"I'm a friend of Ronald."

"Are you?" her American accent wasn't one of the softer ones. "What can we do for you?"

Her question completely flummoxed me and I looked blankly at her as she blew smoke up to the heavens. She was tall and aloof with those same penetrating blue eyes and the thought occurred to me, childish but accurate, that he was her on the outside and his father on the inside.

"Kevin, there you are."

It was Gloria and I had never been so glad to see the old girl.

"He needs to get a move on." Ronald's mum said.

Gloria held her hands out in a pathetic, helpless gesture. She looked miserable and harassed. I'd never seen her before without her makeup (except on the Bobby Sands night which didn't count) and her hair was all over the place.

"Maybe I could hurry him up?"

Nobody responded so I took that as a yes and left them to it.

"He hasn't been himself," Gloria whispered to me at the door. "I'm hoping this isn't permanent – that he comes back to me."

Ronald turned to face me in the living room and for a moment I experienced that sensation of thinking you recognise a stranger because they share the features of someone you know.

This stranger had the same eyes, the same nose, and held his head at the same jaunty angle. But surely this was a man in early middle age? I think I might have gasped. I do remember that my hands moved slowly up to my mouth in the manner of someone who has just encountered a ghost. The skin of his face was stretched so tightly across his forehead and cheeks that you could clearly see the hollows of his mouth and the very shape of his skull. He was wearing loose fitting clothes, I remember that, clothes that hid a terrible truth beneath.

"Jesus Christ, Ronald," my voice was a husky whisper.

"Fifteen days," is what he said, and when he grinned his teeth seemed far too big for his mouth.

And then, because I hadn't responded, he said it again, louder.

"Fifteen days, Kevin."

How could Gloria have missed this?

But of course, I hadn't seen him in two weeks.

"Why?"

It was all I could think to say.

He moved nearer to me and I couldn't help but shy away. He had the appearance of being taller – no, that wasn't it, longer somehow, like a cut of plasticine that has been rolled and stretched. If you looked closely you could see the delicate crisscross of blood vessels on either side of his forehead.

I can see your brain, Ronald, I wanted to say and I had to bite down the sudden urge to laugh. If I started to laugh I wasn't sure I'd be able to stop.

What he said was this:

"I've dreamt about him, Kevin," his eyes were gleeful. "Not just once but lots of times. We talk about the Troubles – how it was, how it is, how it's going to be. We talk the way you and me used to talk."

A series of strident horn blares made him look to the door and broke the trance I had fallen into.

"This is fuckin' mad, Ronald."

"Aye, but it's a grand madness."

Gloria opened the door and this time she was crying.

"She wants you now, Ronald."

"Okay. I'll write to you both. Maybe you can come visit, Kevin. Mum says there's a really big rollercoaster park near where she lives."

It was all for Gloria's benefit.

"Can't you see what he's been doing?"

She looked forlornly at me. He had been cunning, I'll give him that.

The car horn sounded again and Ronald slid by me with feline agility.

"Wait!" I chased after him and caught him at the front door, purposefully digging my nails into his arm, trying to provoke a reaction. He twirled round and slapped me across the jaw – it wasn't that hard but the shock of it allowed him to pull free.

It was all happening so fast. The crunch of gravel underfoot; his Yankee ma stubbing out her cigarette and buckling her safety belt; the driver preparing for the off.

"Hold on!"

I rapped her window hard three times and – startled – she rolled it down. The driver scowled across and was about to say something but I got in first.

"Are you blind? Don't you see what he's trying to do? He's trying to be like Bobby Sands. He's not ill – he's starving himself!"

"He's crazy, Mum," Ronald said from the back and he made little circles at his temple. "Don't listen to him."

She rolled up the window, snapped something at the driver, and then they were off, pausing at the gate, then slowly heading for the brow of the hill.

But I had my Grifter and I was a damn sight faster going down the hill than going up. As fast as any car. I leapt on and with barely a glance at poor, miserable Gloria I chased after them.

They had forty yards on me but I was peddling like fuck and I knew that when it dipped gravity would do most of the work for me. The hill was the longest and sheerest in the whole of the county. Here went.

I stopped peddling. I couldn't keep pace. The hedgerows were a green blur.

I was gaining on them.

Ronald's oval face peered back at me and I prayed that my efforts might have some kind of impact; but the car didn't slow.

I'd be a liar if I didn't say that I enjoyed every single second of the pursuit. The wind in my face, the speedometer shaking towards fifty, and the fact that I was closing on them. Kevin McBride, on a bike, chasing after an automobile. Fuck yis all!

I honked my horn.

I don't know why – but it sounded bloody brilliant.

There was one crossroads half way down and I knew he would have to at least slow for it. I was not going to. My plan was to get in front, skid to a halt slap bang in the middle of the road and turn my bike sideways so they couldn't go round me. It was risky but the gesture might be dramatic enough to gain me an audience. If not, I had a Plan B. I was going to call her all the names of the day – cunt, bitch, whore – and see how that went down. No adult, especially a snooty horse like her, was going to let a little runt like me curse them down. She'd demand to know where I lived; she'd want to speak to my parents. *And miss her flight? Come on.* Alright, maybe not, but Plan C was perfect in its simplicity. I had my pen knife with me. It wasn't that sharp – but with enough force I was sure it could slash the tyre of a taxi cab. All this at forty-seven miles an hour. Nothing like a hill to focus the mind.

I saw the brake lights go on. This was it. I ran up alongside them, was about to overtake them – when I saw a tractor straight ahead.

"Shit!"

I slammed on the brakes and bore hard to the right, running myself aground in a ditch, the speed and momentum lifting me off the saddle and into the hedge.

"Arsehole!" the fat farmer yelled, slowing only to insult me. He did a double take and yelled back. "I'll tell the Quiz King on ya!"

My groin screamed at me and I was panting so loud a cow in the nearby field glanced over to see what was happening.

In the distance, at the bottom of the hill, I saw the tail lights of the taxi pulling onto the main road, bound for Belfast and the airport.

*

I told Mum and Dad everything. They took me up to Gloria's and she gave us the forwarding address she had been given. There was no phone number. She promised to write and I wrote six times – three to him and three to her. I wanted Mum and Dad to contact the police but of course they didn't; the RUC had more than enough to deal with without chasing a hungry boy to America. They were far too busy trying to stop Catholics and Protestants from ripping out each other's throats.

CHAPTER THIRTY-FIVE

The hunger strikers continued to die throughout the summer and violence accompanied each funeral. Eventually, encouraged by a prison chaplain, their families started to intervene when they lapsed into comas. It had finally dawned on them that Margaret Thatcher was never going to concede; she would allow as many men to die as stepped forward. Ten men had starved themselves to death. Within days, the victorious government magnanimously eased prison regulations: they were now allowed to wear their own clothes and there were limited concessions on the other demands.

It was shortly after the seventh hunger striker, Kevin Lynch, died that Mum brought me breakfast in bed again. This time she let me eat it. She came back for the dishes and launched into a story about a neighbour she had been friendly with when she was a girl. Nora Wright. She had pigtails and she liked to skip and play around lampposts (which apparently all the kids did when Mum was a girl.) Nora Wright was healthy and hearty one Thursday; on Friday she was sick; on Saturday she was very sick; and on Sunday she was dead. Meningitis. Her mother kept her watch on the mantle for years, winding it religiously every morning, marking the minutes her daughter would never see. Mum took a deep breath. Sometimes awful things like that happened. It was just a part of life. Then she told me that Ronald Douglas was dead. She told me to try not to think too much about it but when I was ready, if I wanted to talk, she would be in the kitchen. If I wanted, we could pack some sandwiches and drive up into the mountains – just her and me – and look at the beautiful views. It sounded like a lovely idea and I thought I might take her up on it. But not just now.

Just now, I fancied a walk into town. I could browse in the new book shop, buy myself a drink, and have a bit of a wander. I *could* deal with this, I *would* deal with this – but not just now; in a little while, after I had thought it all through.

Dad was in the garden doing battle with the hedge, the loop of the wire threatening to lasso the cutters. Pausing for a moment to untangle himself, the buzz died long enough for a lazy silence to descend and I lent my ear to the wind and listened intently. Mrs Templeton from next door was murdering *Bette Davis Eyes* as she washed the dishes, her wails just discernible through the double glazing. That was all – no, wait. There was something else. In the distance but carrying over the steeples, the hills and the roof tops. In the air, growing louder and nearer. Shush... shush ... listen.

The rumble of the drums and the sweet, sad music of the answering flutes.

*****

ABOUT THE AUTHOR

Keith McKibbin was born in Belfast in 1970. He grew up in Banbridge, County Down. He graduated from the University of Edinburgh with a Masters Degree in English. He now lives in Glasgow with his wife and four daughters.

BIBLIOGRAPHY

The Eleven Plus Book: Genuine Exam Questions From Yesteryear. Michael O'Mara Books Limited.

McKittrick D. & McVea D.,*Making Sense of The Troubles: A History of the Northern Ireland Conflict.* David.

BlanketMen. Richard O'Rawe.

Ten Men Dead: The Story of the 1981 Irish Hunger Strike. David Beresford.

The Troubles: Ireland's Ordeal 1966-1996 and the search for peace. Tim Pat Coogan.

Printed in Great Britain
by Amazon.co.uk, Ltd.,
Marston Gate.